LINGUISTIC PAPERS

Anders Bjerrum

LINGUISTIC PAPERS

Published on the occasion of Anders Bjerrum's
70th birthday, 12th March 1973,
by Selskab for nordisk Filologi, Copenhagen.

AKADEMISK FORLAG

Copenhagen

1973

Published with a subvention from Landsdommer V. Gieses legat.

Editors:
Niels Haastrup
Gilian Fellows Jensen
Thorkil Damsgaard Olsen

(

© Akademisk Forlag 1973
ISBN 87 500 1292 4
Printed by Zano Print, Denmark

CONTENTS

2

Items on pp. 17-86, 116-129 and 151-186 have been revised for this
volume by *Anders Bjerrum* and translated into English by *Gillian
Fellows Jensen.*

PREFACE

The present selection of linguistic papers by Professor Anders Bjerrum is published to mark the occasion of his 70th birthday on 12th
March 1973. It has been the aim of Selskab for nordisk Filologi to
make Professor Bjerrum's important and pioneering contribution to
research into the Danish language known to an international public.

Anders Bjerrum's linguistic works are concerned with the fields
of dialectology, place-name research and the history of the Danish
language. He has devoted himself particularly to the study of the
language, culture and history of North Slesvig. It was here that he was
born and spent his childhood, at a time when the province was still
under German rule, and it was here that he gained his first experience
of linguistic field-work. During the years 1928-32 he not only recorded the pronunciation of a great number of North Slesvig place-
names for use in the Danish Place-Name Commission's comprehensive
edition of *Sønderjyske Stednavne* I-V (1931-44) but also collected
and recorded folk traditions and noted down the vocabulary of a
moribund Danish dialect in South Slesvig.

Anders Bjerrum received his master's degree in 1930 and in 1931 he was appointed to a post as research assistent at the office of the Place-Name Commission (now: Institut for Navneforskning). He gave the institute devoted service for almost forty years and was its director between 1953 and 1969. Bjerrum wrote extensive portions of the manuscripts of *Sønderjyske Stednavne* and of later volumes in the Place-Name Commission's series *Danmarks Stednavne* (1944, 1948, 1950-51, 1954, 1964) and the inspiration for his important article on the language of the cadastre of King Valdemar ("Johannes Jutæ og Valdemars Jordebog" 1960) was also derived from his work for the Place-Name Commission. Together with Kristian Hald and the late Peter Jørgensen, Anders Bjerrum drew up a plan for a comprehensive study of the place-names of South Slesvig (*Sydslesvigs Stednavne*), in which were to be presented all known names of Danish German and Frisian origin. Up to the present time only a few fascicles of this work have appeared (written by Kr. Hald) but it is on the basis of his preliminary work that Bjerrum has been able to carry out his investigations into the change of language in South Slesvig (cf. below).

Within the field of dialectology Anders Bjerrum's name is linked first and foremost with the study of the language of the parish of Fjolde in South Slesvig. The local Danish dialect there was supplanted by Low German as the language of daily life in the course of the 19th century. In the 1930s it only survived as a memory from the young days of the oldest inhabitants of the parish. As one of the Dialect Commission's research-workers, Anders Bjerrum visited these old people in 1931 and 1932 and from his conversations with them he was able to codify large sections of the vocabulary of the doomed dialect. This material, together with sparser records from Fjolde made by other dialectologists, forms the foundation on which Anders Bjerrum and his wife, Marie Bjerrum, have based their great and as yet unfinished project, which includes a description of the lost dialect and the compilation of a dictionary of its vocabulary.

The most significant contribution to this project so far has been Anders Bjerrum's doctoral dissertation from 1944, *Fjoldemålets Lydsystem* (The sound system of the dialect of Fjolde). The main aim of this work, as of Ella Jensen's description of the dialect of the parish of Houlbjerg in East Jutland *(Houlbjergmålet* 1944), was to present a structural description of the system of expression that was characteristic for the dialect in question, that is the constant system of formal units of expression (phonemes) which can be assumed to lie behind the speech-sounds. These two dialect descriptions from 1944 together mark the transition to a new structuralistic phase in the history of Danish dialectology. Bjerrum's work, however, has not found imitators in the same way as has Ella Jensen's consistently carried out construction of a system of phonemes on the basis of commutation tests. Bjerrum's analysis of the doomed Fjolde dialect was made under difficult circumstances of a kind that other Danish structural-dialectologists have subsequently made great efforts to avoid. It was only on one occasion (in 1935, two years before the last reliable informant died) that he had the opportunity of observing the reaction of the dialect-speakers to linguistic minimal pairs. With this one exception, the analysis had to be based upon the existing phonetic records from Fjolde, first and foremost those made by Bjerrum himself in 1931 and 1932. Bjerrum makes no attempt to disguise the fact that this material makes a less than ideal basis for a phonematic analysis. The scholars who recorded the dialect of Fjolde were not themselves native speakers of it and they can be suspected of interpreting and recording the dialectal word-forms on the basis of the phoneme system of their own mother-tongue. It is perhaps, however, in the very solving of the problems presented by this imperfect material that Bjerrum's analysis of the sound system of the dialect of Fjolde is of greatest methodological interest. His attempts to localise and evaluate the sources of error in the material and to determine the nature and the degree of interference from the language systems of the various recorders of the dialect will continue to provide inspiration for scholars who need to be able to determine the linguistic system behind a closed corpus of dialect recordings that can no longer be supplemented. In a lecture "Über die phonematische Wertung von Mundartaufzeichnungen" (1939, printed 1940, reprinted in the present volume pp. 87-115), Bjerrum makes some general observations on the strategy to be employed in such a situation.

Structural dialectology in Denmark has taken other paths and it has attempted as far as possible to analyse the system at the stage when the dialect is actually being recorded. There is, however, a clear link between Bjerrum's analysis of the language system behind the dialect recordings from Fjolde and his structural analysis of the language systems in early Danish written texts − probably his most significant contribution to Danish linguistics in the years after 1944. An important aim of the analysis of the sound system of the Fjolde dialect is to make it possible to use existing dialect-recordings for studies in dialect-geography and the history of the language. The analyses of the early Danish texts serve a similar purpose: namely to make it possible to use the texts for the purposes of comparative linguistics by providing a precise determination of their linguistic structure. The way in which the linguistic system in a written text from an earlier period can be revealed has been excellently demonstrated by Bjerrum in two concise descriptions of the systems of expression and content in the chief manuscripts of the Old Danish provincial laws (*Grammatik over Skånske Lov* 1954 and *Grammatik over De sjællandske Love* 1967, English versions of excerpts from these grammars are printed below pp. 151-88), and in a number of detailed studies: "Verbal Number in the Jutlandic Law" (1949, reprinted below pp. 130-50), "De tryksvage vokaler i danske runeindskrifter" (1952, English version below pp. 116-29), "Høysgaards anden ortografiske prøve" (1954, English version below pp. 35-50), "Johannes Jutæ og Valdemars Jordebog" (1960), "Adjektivernes accusativendelse -æn i Jyske Lov" (1964), and "G[amme]lda[nsk] *loghtæ* og *sogthæ*" (1971).

It is emphasised in all these papers that the real object of the examination is the linguistic structure which manifests itself in the actual written texts. The aim is to rediscover the linguistic analysis which is expressed by the orthography of the texts. In the introduction to *Grammatik over Skånske Lov* Bjerrum forcefully maintains the point of view that the legitimate object of examination in a description of the language of an early written text can only be the immanent structure of the actual written text and not a different hypothetical structure of a presumed underlying spoken language. In a lecture "Sprogbeskrivelsen" (1962, printed 1965, English version below pp. 17-34), Bjerrum has discussed this point of view in relation to other points of view that have been adopted in the description of the old Danish language in the present century. The methodological stringency with which Bjerrum sticks to his point of view throughout his investigations has not gone unopposed but it has left its mark on a younger generation of historians of the language and been of considerable significance for the clarification of the conceptions employed in work on the history of the language.

Fjoldemålets Lydsystem and the analyses of the early written texts are Anders Bjerrum's contribution to the structuralist movement in linguistics known as the "Copenhagen school" which has achieved international fame because of the works of Louis Hjelmslev. Bjerrum acknowledges his indebtedness to Louis Hjelmslev and to the discussions which took place in the Copenhagen Lingvistkreds in the 1930s. He has himself made an independent and lasting contribution to the movement by his constant confrontation of the structuralistic theories with linguistic realities and by developing a structuralist descriptive technique which can be used to advantage on a linguistic text.

In his work on the dialects and on early Danish written texts, however, Anders Bjerrum is very far from being a one-sided structural linguist. Two of his text descriptions ("Utan han ær opænbarlic gen guth" 1952 and "Sproget i hyldingsbrevene fra 1387" 1969) reveal just how structural description of the language can be combined with a true philological interest in placing the text in its historical context. It is precisely the desirability of looking at, and describing, a text from as many angles as possible that has characterised the numerous seminars on early Danish texts that Bjerrum has held at the University of Copenhagen since 1953. *Studier over Blichers E Bindstouw* (1962), which is the fruit of the work of Bjerrum and his students in one such seminar, reveals the wide scope of the teaching which he based on the study of individual texts.

Bjerrum's studies on the relationship between Danish and German in Slesvig through the ages reveal views which are related to the trends which characterise modern socio-linguistics. The process by which the Danish dialect disappeared as a spoken language in Fjolde in the course of the 19th century has been described by Bjerrum in an introductory chapter in *Fjoldemålets Lydsystem* (1944), and by his studies on South Slesvig place-names ("Vort Sprogs gamle Sydgrænse" 1944 and "Den dansk-tyske sproggrænse i middelalderen" 1963, English version below pp. 75-86) he has shown that this process must be seen as merely the final phase of a change of language in South Slesvig that has been taking place for several centuries and which must have begun immediately the Danish and German populations came into contact with each other in the Middle Ages. Bjerrum is conscious of the fact that a community does not change over from one language to another at one fell swoop. In certain conversation contexts the old language is retained far longer than in others and since place-names probably reflect the language used in

8

conversations between male adults, it is the change of language in such conversation contexts whose history can be traced through place-names. Bjerrum's interest in the distribution of the two languages between the social classes and the various conversation contexts is also seen in the article "Folkesproget i Tønder gennem Tiderne" (1944, English version below pp. 51-74), a comprehensive review of the history of bilingualism in the North Slesvig town of Tønder.

In the course of the years many of Professor Bjerrum's linguistic studies have been presented in lecture form to Selskab for nordisk Filologi prior to publication (cf. the bibliography). It is, therefore, a particular pleasure for Selskab for nordisk Filologi to be able to pay tribute to Anders Bjerrum on his 70th birthday by publishing this selection of his linguistic papers.

TABULA GRATULATORIA

DAGFINN AASEN
Trondheim

GORDON ALBØGE
København

STURE ALLÉN
Göteborg

BØRGE ANDERSEN
København

HARRY ANDERSEN
København

LISE PRÆSTGAARD
ANDERSEN
København

POUL ANDERSEN
København

THORSTEN ANDERSSON
Uppsala

J. P. ASMUSSEN
København

H. BACH
Århus

G. C. BANG
København

HANS BASBØLL
København

HEINRICH BECK
Saarbrücken

CHRISTIAN
BECKER-CHRISTENSEN
København

HANS BEKKER-NIELSEN
Odense

HREINN BENEDIKTSSON
Reykjavík

JAKOB BENEDIKTSSON
Reykjavík

ALLAN BERTHELSEN
Stockholm

WERNER BETZ
München

INGER BÉVORT
København

BENT BILLE
Glamsbjerg

BOJE BJERVERSKOV
København

ELLEN BJØRNESTAD
København

ANNE MARIE OG
GUDMUND BOESEN
København

JENS BOESEN
Bellinge

INGER OG KAJ BOM
København

GERHARD BOYSEN
Odense

THOMAS BREDSDORFF
Cambridge, Mass.

TOM BROCH
København

JOHS. BRØNDUM-
NIELSEN
København

10

LAURITS BØDKER
Nivå

UNA CANGER
København

MICHAEL CHESNUTT
København

AKSEL E. CHRISTENSEN
København

BIRGIT CHRISTENSEN
København

JOHNNY CHRISTENSEN
København

VIBEKE CHRISTENSEN
Nivå

HARALD CHRISTIANSEN
Køge

KARL-HAMPUS
DAHLSTEDT
Umeå

ARNOLD DALEN
Trondheim

ELSE DALHOFF
København

HELLE DEGNBOL
Groningen

N. DJURHUUS
København

ANNE DUEKILDE
København

MOGENS DYHR
København

SV. EEGHOLM-
PEDERSEN
København

INGER EJSKÆR
København

PETRUS ENVALL
Uppsala

A. G. EPSTEIN
Århus

NIELS FERLOV
København

ELI FISCHER-
JØRGENSEN
København

LEIV FLYDAL
Oslo

BRITTA OLRIK
FREDERIKSEN
København

HANNE LOUISE OG
UWE GEIST
Jystrup

SVEND GISSEL
København

OTTO GLISMANN
København

KIRSTEN GREGERSEN
København

NIELS HAASTRUP
København

HENRIK HAGEMANN
Kolding

JAN RAGNAR
HAGLAND
Trondheim

BJÖRN HAGSTRÖM
Farsta

KRISTIAN HALD
København

BENEDICTE
TULINIUS HALLSETH
Nesttun

ERIC P. HAMP
Chicago

AAGE HANSEN
København

BENTE LIEBST HANSEN
København

CATHRINE
FABRICIUS HANSEN
Oslo

ERIK HANSEN
København

EINAR HAUGEN
Cambridge, Mass.

H. M. HEINRICHS
Berlin

JÓN HELGASON
København

KRISTINE HELTBERG
København

LARS HELTOFT
København

CAROL HENRIKSEN
Cambridge, Mass.

EBBA HJORTH
København

POUL LINDEGÅRD
HJORTH
København

DIETRICH HOFMANN
Kiel

GÖSTA HOLM
Lund

BENTE HOLMBERG
København

EVA HOLM-NIELSEN
København

RIKARD HORNBY
København

KARL HYLDGAARD-
JENSEN
København

ÓLAFUR INGÓLFSSON
Reykjavík

ANNE-BIRGITTE
JACOBSEN
København

BENT CHR. JACOBSEN
København

ALFRED JAKOBSEN
Trondheim

VALTER JANSSON
Uppsala

ANNE E. JENSEN
København

ELLA JENSEN
Humlebæk

GILLIAN FELLOWS
JENSEN
Karlslunde

HELLE JENSEN
København

OLE-JØRGEN
JOHANNESSEN
Bergen

TURE JOHANNISSON
Göteborg

CLARA JOHANSEN
København

KNUD JORDAL
Højbjerg

BENT JØRGENSEN
København

CHARLOTTE JØRGENSEN
København

NILS JÖRGENSEN
Malmö

ALLAN KARKER
Mundelstrup

STEFÁN KARLSSON
Reykjavík

IVER KJÆR
København

MARIANNE KJÆR
København

ELIZABETH KNOWLES
Witney

H. A. KOEFOED
Odense

SVEN MØLLER
KRISTENSEN
København

E. KROMAN
København

FINN KØSTER
København

A. E. ÆBELHOLT
LARSEN
København

BIRGITTE HOLT LARSEN
København

JØRGEN LARSEN
København

KAJ LARSEN
Gudhjem

KAREN RISAGER LARSEN
København

MERETE OG HENRY
VERNER LARSEN
København

MOGENS BAUMANN
LARSEN
København

PETER HARMS LARSEN
Roskilde

PAUL LIER
København

CHRISTIAN LISSE
København

GUNILLA LJUNGGREN
Lund

RAGNA LORENTZEN
København

JONNA LOUIS-JENSEN
København

INGA LUDVIGSEN
København

NIELS LUKMAN
København

IB LUMHOLT
Roskilde

JØRN LUND
København

EINAR LUNDEBY
Høn

MOGENS LØJ
København

CHRISTOPHER MAALØE
Munke-Bjergby

ELLEN OLSEN MADSEN
København

CHR. MATRAS
Tórshavn

EVA MELDGAARD
København

LENNART MOBERG
Uppsala

MERETE MUNK
København

BENT MØLLER
København

KRISTEN MØLLER
København

W. F. H. NICOLAISEN
Binghamton, N.Y.

BENT JUL NIELSEN
København

GUNHILD NIELSEN
København

KARL MARTIN NIELSEN
København

NIELS ÅGE NIELSEN
Århus

TORBEN NIELSEN
København

VIBEKE KELSTRUP
NIELSEN
København

METTE NORDENTOFT
København

MAGDA NYBERG
København

STIG ÖRJAN
OG
TOVE HOVN OHLSSON
København

OTTO KAMPP OLSEN
Løgstør

THORKIL DAMSGAARD
OLSEN
København

HELGE OMDAL
Bergen

MARIANE OVERGAARD
København

POUL PALBOM
København

ELSE PAULY
København

BIRTE HJORTH
PEDERSEN
København

INGE LISE PEDERSEN
København

KAREN MARGRETHE
PEDERSEN
København

EGIL PETTERSEN
Minde

JAN PINBORG
Blovstrød

JÓHAN HENDRIK
W. POULSEN
Kirkjuböur

PETER RASMUSSEN
Reykjavík

HANNE REGNAR
København

CLAUS REISTRUP
Tórshavn

K. RINGGAARD
Århus

JØRGEN RISCHEL
København

EVA RODE
København

BIRTE OG NIELS
ROSENKJÆR
Åbenrå

GUNNVOR RUNDHOVDE
Bergen

HANNE RUUS
København

VIBEKE SANDERSEN
København

H. SCHULTINK
Den Dolder

FRITZ SCHÖNWANDT
København

SVAVAR SIGMUNDSSON
København

PETER SKAUTRUP
Århus

INGE SKOVGAARD-
PETERSEN
København

SVEN SKYDSGAARD
København

PEDER SKYUM-NIELSEN
København

POVL SKÅRUP
Århus

SVEND SMITH
Hamborg

HENNING SPANG-
HANSEN
København

BØRGE SPANG-
THOMSEN
København

ARNE SPENTER
København

ANE MARIE SPETH
København

JOHN KJEMS
SPOORENDONK
København

PETER SPRINGBORG
Stockholm

JAMES STEWARD
København

CARL IVAR STÅHLE
Lidingö

ERIK SØNDERHOLM
København

HOLGER STEEN
SØRENSEN
København

JOHN KOUSGÅRD
SØRENSEN
Nivå

LONE TAKEUCHI
København

INGRID ELLER
THOMSEN
København

KAREN THUESEN
København

JOHN TIETZE
Køge

CLAUS TILLING
København

KNUD TOGEBY
København

OLE TOGEBY
København

EVA UHRSKOV
København

LARS VASSENDEN
Bergen

HANS VEIRUP
Århus

JØRGEN VILLADSEN
København

HANS VOGT
Oslo

LIS WEISE
København

MONIKA WESEMANN
København

CHR. WESTERGÅRD-
NIELSEN
Århus

OLE WIDDING
Regstrup

ANNE MARIE OG
PER WIESELGREN
Eslöv

NIELS ERIK WILLE
Roskilde

INGE WOHLERT
København

ULF ZACHARIASEN
Tórshavn

ELLEN ÅSTRUP
København

14

DET NORDJYSKE
LANDSBIBLIOTEK
AALBORG

THE UNIVERSITY
COLLEGE OF WALES
ABERYSTWYTH

THE UNIVERSITY
COLLEGE OF WALES
LIBRARY
ABERYSTWYTH

UNIVERSITETET
I BERGEN
NORDISK INSTITUTT

GERMANISCHES
SEMINAR DER FREIEN
UNIVERSITÄT BERLIN
NORDISCHE ABTEILUNG

INDIANA UNIVERSITY
LIBRARY
BLOOMINGTON

DURHAM UNIVERSITY
LIBRARY
DURHAM

FREDERIKSBERG
KOMMUNES
BIBLIOTEKER

GÖTEBORGS
UNIVERSITET
INSTITUTIONEN FÖR
NORDISKA SPRÅK

GÖTEBORGS
UNIVERSITETS-
BIBLIOTEK

SKANDINAVISCHES
SEMINAR DER
UNIVERSITÄT
GÖTTINGEN

STAATS- UND
UNIVERSITÄTS-
BIBLIOTHEK
HAMBURG

UNIVERSITÄT
HAMBURG
SEMINAR FÜR
ALLGEMEINE UND
VERGLEICHENDE
SPRACHWISSENSCHAFT

NORDISCHES INSTITUT
DER UNIVERSITÄT
KIEL

UNIVERSITÄTS-
BIBLIOTHEK KIEL

DANMARKS
TEKNISKE HØJSKOLE
KØBENHAVN

ANDR. FRED.
HØST & SØN
KØBENHAVN

SELSKAB FOR
NORDISK FILOLOGI
KØBENHAVN

KØBENHAVNS
UNIVERSITET
DET
ARNAMAGNÆANSKE
INSTITUT

KØBENHAVNS
UNIVERSITET
INSTITUT FOR DANSK
DIALEKTFORSKNING

KØBENHAVNS
UNIVERSITET
INSTITUT FOR
FONETIK

KØBENHAVNS
UNIVERSITET
INSTITUT FOR
LINGVISTIK

KØBENHAVNS
UNIVERSITET
INSTITUT FOR
NAVNEFORSKNING

KØBENHAVNS
UNIVERSITET
INSTITUT FOR
NORDISK FILOLOGI

KØBENHAVNS
UNIVERSITET
FILOLOGISK
LABORATORIUM

KØBENHAVNS
UNIVERSITET
LABORATORIET FOR
METRIK OG
FOREDRAGSLÆRE

UNIVERSITY COLLEGE
LONDON
THE LIBRARY

STADSBIBLIOTEKET
I LYNGBY

INSTITUT D'ÉTUDES
SCANDINAVES
NANCY

UNIVERSITY OF
NOTTINGHAM
UNIVERSITY LIBRARY

ODENSE UNIVERSITET
INSTITUT FOR
ALMEN OG ANVENDT
LINGVISTIK

15

ODENSE UNIVERSITET
NORDISK INSTITUT

ODENSE UNIVERSITETS-
BIBLIOTEK

NORSK
LEKSIKOGRAFISK
INSTITUTT
OSLO

UNIVERSITETET I OSLO
INSTITUTT FOR
NORDISK SPRÅK
OG LITTERATUR

ROSKILDE
UNIVERSITETS-
BIBLIOTEK

KUNGL. BIBLIOTEKET
STOCKHOLM

OSIANDERSCHE
BUCHHANDLUNG
TÜBINGEN

UMEÅ UNIVERSITET
AVDELNINGEN FÖR
NORDISKA SPRÅK

UMEÅ UNIVERSITETS-
BIBLIOTEK

LIBRARY OF
CONGRESS
Washington, D.C.

DIALEKT- OCH
FOLKMINNESARKIVET
UPPSALA

SEMINARIET FÖR
NORDISK ORTNAMNS-
FORSKNING
UPPSALA

UPPSALA UNIVERSITET
INSTITUTIONEN FÖR
NORDISKA SPRÅK

UPPSALA
UNIVERSITETS-
BIBLIOTEK

Descriptions of the language
in medieval texts[1]

It is the aim of my lecture to discuss philological descriptions of
Danish texts and groups of texts. Little account will be taken of
runic literature and none at all of descriptions of texts from after
c.1600. The lecture will fall into three parts. The first part will deal
with three important sources of inspiration, exemplified by three
typical works. The second part will contain brief accounts of various
works that fall outside the scope of the three groups dealt with in
part one. Finally, there will be a discussion of the kind of language
scholars have had in mind when describing texts, whether they only
reckoned with two kinds of language, dialect and standard, or with
a more sophisticated representation of the language of real life.

A.

Most of the text descriptions from the beginning of this century bear
the mark of a very strong *neo-Romantic* inspiration. I shall analyse a
typical example.

In 1909 Marius Kristensen published a paper entitled "Hvor hørte
Rydårbogens skriver hjemme?" (The origin of the scribe of the Ryd
chronicle)[2]. This paper concludes in the following way:

The conclusions to which I have come are, then, that the scribe of the Ryd Chronicle was from Djursland, most likely from Nörre Herred, that he must have been exposed to the linguistic influence of daily associates from north-west Slesvig for a considerable length of time, but that any features in his transcript that might suggest a different origin can most easily be ascribed to the influence of either conventional written forms or his exemplar. There is nothing to suggest that the scribe came from, or even spent any length of time in, the neighbourhood of Ryd. I am therefore inclined to believe that this transcript derives not from Ryd abbey but rather from its sister abbey at Løgum (p.107).

Marius Kristensen comes to the result Djursland by following much the same process as a botany teacher would use in identifying a plant: "There is, as is well-known, a very old linguistic boundary which runs down the Great Belt. To the west of this we have *o* in a number of words that have *u* to the east of the Belt". The scribe of the Ryd chronicle comes from the area to the west of the boundary because he writes *o* in words such as *-brot, bothœn.*

He comes from "a district where the distinction between masc. and fem. in the declension of certain words and forms was still a vital phenomenon" for he writes *kuningin, somarin* but *kronœn, solœn.* He must, then, belong to a district whose modern dialect distinguishes between masc. and fem. in substantives, i.e. Vendsyssel with Læsø, Djursland with Samsø, or Funen and the islands that belong to it. The ending *-inn* has undergone considerable modification in both Funen and Vendsyssel, where it appears either as *-i$_c$* or as *i,* whereas in Djursland it has survived as *-in.* Since the Ryd chronicle has the form *-in,* the scribe is most likely to have come from Djursland. This theory receives some support from the evidence of two isolated forms which have a very restricted currency in the modern dialects, namely *lawnt* "far" and *hœy[n]dœ* "hanged".

The evidence for the influence of the north-west Slesvig language is even more slender: *brollop, brullup, sextœ* and *thœn samœ aar* (common gender for neuter), perhaps also *Thorœ hœnnœ søn* (gen. case replaced by possessive pronoun).

I want to emphasise two characteristic features of this article. The first is Marius Kristensen's belief that the modern dialect boundaries have survived unchanged from the Middle Ages. Marius Kristensen was a neo-Romantic, like P.K. Thorsen and Axel Olrik. He was also a follower of Grundtvig. A great part of his life was spent as a teacher at Askov folk high school. Marius Kristensen believed literally in the "Volksgeist" and he thought that folk-speech was the most genuine expression of this spirit. For him, folk-speech was the speech of the peasants, the dialects. Marius Kristensen believed, as did the other neo-Romantics, in the peasant as the preserver of tradition. He considered that the folk-speech in each individual district had developed in the course of the 40 generations that separate us from King Gorm the Old without being influenced to any marked degree by the speech of neighbouring districts.

Marius Kristensen's belief in the antiquity of the dialects and the immobility of the dialect boundaries was strengthened by his reading of Jean Passy's book, L'origine des Ossalois, from 1904, which he reviewed in 1906[3]. Les Ossalois are the inhabitants of a mountain valley, Ossau, in the Pyrenees. According to Jean Passy, the original inhabitants of this valley, the high-Ossals, have kept their old dialect in spite of the facts that as early as the 9th century there was a migration of low-Ossals into the valley and that there has always been lively communication between the two parts of the valley. Marius Kristensen was delighted by this book. He considered — with a daring generalisation — that it had "put paid to the belief in the novelty of the dialects".

The second characteristic is the limited interest shown by Marius Kristensen in the written language and his all-consuming interest in the spoken language. This interest is, of course, bound up with the well-known Grundtvigian preference for the living word but there was also another source of inspiration for it, namely classical phonetics or the phonetics of articulation. Otto Jespersen's great Fonetik appeared between 1897 and 1899. Marius Kristensen has spoken of his own enthusiasm for phonetics: He would sometimes walk along the street with a pencil in his mouth, talking to himself so that he could observe the movements of his tongue.

These are the sources of inspiration that lay behind the great work Kort over de danske folkemål (Maps of the Danish dialects) and behind his early localisations of Old Danish MSS with the help of the dialect pronunciations and dialect boundaries that he had established, often on the basis of some few isolated written forms, as in his paper on the Ryd chronicle. The two most striking examples are the introduction to Harpestræng, which appeared in 1920[4] and in which he localised the author of the herbals to the district round Haderslev and the scribe of MS K to Djursland[5], and his paper on Karen Brahe's Folio[6], from 1928, where the ballad MS is localised to "Brande or perhaps rather Arnborg".

And Marius Kristensen had disciples.

In an article from 1906 Anders Pedersen asserted that a 14th-century MS of the Jutlandic Law, AM 19 8°, had been written in the neighbourhood of Husum by a man who spoke a mixed Danish-Frisian dialect[7]. It was reviewed with partial approval by Marius Kristensen[8] but criticised by Peter Jørgensen[9].

In his paper from 1923 Tre litterære Munke i Sorø kloster (3 literary monks from Sorø)[10], Verner Dahlerup considered that the author of Erik's Law could be localised to "north-east Zealand".

Peter Skautrup described the language in one MS of the Jutland Law, AM 286 fol., in relation to the present Jutland dialects[11]. Being familiar with medieval forms of place-names, Skautrup knew that a dialect boundary could well have shifted in the course of time. Even so, he, too, was rash: The exemplar of the first part of the MS was from Ribe, that of the second part from the district round Vonsbæk by Haderslev Fjord.

Although several of the above-mentioned works have been criticised with good reason in more recent times, it is impossible to deny that neo-Romanticism has been one of the most powerful and important sources of inspiration for the study of the Danish language. And its role is not played out yet. It has, in particular, decisively influenced Peter Skautrup.

Marius Kristensen was one of the most remarkable and sterling characters of all those who have been engaged in research into the Danish language in the present century. Not only is there a marked coherence in his scholarly production in spite of its great variety, but all his scholarly work was closely linked with his whole outlook on life and the way he behaved. He was a son of the soil and a Grundtvigian and both these facts were betrayed by his natural dignity and his impulsive artlessness.

He was always very willing to join in a discussion, even with us young men. I have often discussed the antiquity of the dialects with him but I have to confess that Marius Kristensen, unlike the scribe of the Ryd chronicle, was unreceptive to the influence of this one of his daily associates.

The second source of inspiration is *dialect geography*. As an introduction I will quote an excerpt from a paper that appeared in 1929[12], i.e. 20 years after Marius Kristensen's article.

en frugha must be assumed to be an acc. sg. (in the construction acc. +
infinitive; see, however, below), and if that is so, *en* for *ena* (cf. Maurer-Bartsch
above) would hardly occur in 13th-century Swedish (cf. e.g. Noreen ASG § 479,
Zetterberg BLB: 87 [etc. etc. a string of further references]). The older form
ena, enæ is also predominant in ODan MSS of the Scanic Law [references]. It is
a different matter, however, outside the Scanian language area. In the Zealand
Laws, for example, we have: *hun hauær en sin dottær i fælugh* VLThors: 19[28]
[etc. etc. more instances].

This is, of course, Brøndum-Nielsen's localisation of the scribal
verse from Cologne: it is located to Zealand c. 1250 and not to
Sweden.

In contrast to the older localisations that I have been talking
about, Brøndum's localisations are never based on a comparison
with the modern dialects alone but mainly on a comparison with
contemporary localised sources, in the case above the laws of Scania
and Zealand.

Why did Brøndum reject the old belief in the antiquity of the
dialects and the constancy of dialect boundaries?

Two years before, in 1927, he had published his inspiring book
Dialekter og Dialektforskning (Dialects and Dialect Research) whose
fifth chapter is a critical analysis of the various hypotheses about
the antiquity of the dialects, and whose fourth chapter deals with
the ways in which dialect phenomena extend their territory, with
examples first and foremost from the works of French and German
dialect geographers.

Language geography has made two important contributions to
language description, one negative, one positive. Its negative contribution has been to ensure that texts are no longer localised on the
basis of a comparison with modern dialects alone. Brøndum-Nielsen's
article on the Cologne verse was a model of its kind and has become
a model for imitation. The old method of localisation came to a
sudden end with Marius Kristensen's above-mentioned localisation
of Karen Brahe's Folio in 1928[13].

At this point I will name the most important of Brøndum-Nielsen's
subsequent localisations. *Mariaklagen,* ed. 1929 in collaboration with
Aage Rohmann: This is not Old Swedish from the 15th century but
Old Scanian from c. 1325, with some Jutlandic characteristics. *Siæla
Trøst*[14] : This is not Old Swedish but Old Scanian from c. 1425. The
poem on the resurrection of Christ[15] : This is not Old Swedish but
Old Scanian from c. 1325. The Scanian *Postil fra Bekkaskogh*[16] : This
is north-east Scanian from c. 1450.

No attempt has ever been made by the Swedes to resist these conquests. At this point, however, I must admit that the more stringent method of localisation introduced by Brøndum-Nielsen has not only resulted in pure gain for Denmark but also, thanks to Kristian Hald, in a single loss. Kr. Hald has proved[17] that the majority of the names on the 11th-century runic coins are Old English and not Old Danish.

The positive contribution that dialect geography has made has been to encourage examination of localised sources, so that by comparing these with younger sources, it has been possible to see how dialect boundaries have shifted.

Much work still remains to be done on this subject. The vast amount of charter material, for example, has yet to be analysed. A start has been made, however. In GG, particularly Vol. II, there are many descriptions of the shifts in dialect boundaries, e.g. the historical-geographical treatment of the weakening of stops §§ 282-286. I should like to draw particular attention to § 310 on the development of $\bar{o}gh > \ddot{o}w, \ddot{o}j$. Here it is argued, in disagreement with Marius Kristensen, that gh in the Zealand dialect develops in the same way after original au as after original ey and $\bar{o}$. In Central and South Zealand $\bar{o}gh$ normally becomes $\ddot{o}w$, in North-east Zealand and Scania $\ddot{o}j$. As early as the Middle Ages $\ddot{o}j$ begins to supplant $\ddot{o}w$. This causes the appearance of what Brøndum-Nielsen calls "Hyperscanisms", instances where an $\ddot{o}w$ that derives from ODan $\bar{o}f$ or yf is also replaced by $\ddot{o}j$, e.g. Palladius' $s\ddot{o}ynehuss$ for $s\ddot{o}fnehus$ "dormitorium".

It is, however, Skautrup who has been occupied for the greatest length of time and most energetically with problems related to the shift of dialect boundaries. In his above-mentioned M.A. thesis on the language of AM 286 fol., which was published in 1924, there is a brief discussion of the boundary between -rn > -n and -rn > -r. This boundary now runs a little to the south of Holstebro between a northern area which has $b\mathring{a}?r, ku?or$ etc. for Stand.Dan. $barn, korn$ and a southern area with $b\mathring{a}?n, ku?on$ etc. With the aid of old place-name forms, Skautrup was able to demonstrate that this boundary earlier ran further to the south.

It is this kind of examination that lies behind Skautrup's plan for a large-scale treatment of "Hardiske kilder" and "Hardiske Mål" (sources from, and the dialect of, Hardsyssel).

Another interesting dialect-geographical examination is found in Peter Skautrup's book on the Danish of Jacob Madsen[18] in a digression[19] on the svarabhakti vowel *u* before *gh* (*-balugh (balg)*, *-bierugh (bjerg)*). In medieval documents *u* is found as a svarabhakti vowel in a large area of East Jutland from south of Vejle to the middle of Himmerland. *o* is now only found in north Djursland but *u* is found in Jacob Madsen 1586 so the *u* area must then also have included Århus.

Of other dialect-geographical surveys I might just mention that Harry Andersen and I have reached agreement[20] that in runic inscriptions from the period around 1200 are to be found some slight indications of vowel balance in two of the most outlying parts of the Danish language area, namely North Jutland and Scania. Further, my examination of the language of Johannes Jutæ[21] contains dialect-geographical perspectives, since it is asserted there that a number of phenomena, e.g. a-mutated vowels in *both, hol* etc. were characteristic of both Zealand and Jutland in the 13th century, while a century later they are generally speaking confined to Jutland (and Funen).

What I said earlier about the neo-Romantic inspiration also applies to language geography: it continues to be a source of inspiration. One source of inspiration does not simply replace another. On the contrary, the various sources of inspiration interact and make the state of affairs more and more complicated.

The third source of inspiration is the *structural concept*. Paul Diderichsen concludes his paper Probleme der altdänischen Orthographie[22] (1938) with some "methodische Programmsätze für eine sachgemässe Geschichte der dänischen Sprache im Mittelalter". I quote the first item of his programme:

> Die Grundlage einer adän. Sprachgeschichte muss von einer Reihe von Einzelbeschreibungen möglichst verschiedener Handschriften gebildet werden; in jedem einzelnen Fall müssen auf Grund einer mit Umsicht interpretierten einfachen Statistik die orthographische Norm des Schreibers und die innerhalb derselben gestatteten Variationen festgestellt werden, wonach die normfremden Elemente teils als der Vorlage entstammende Archaismen, teils als "phonetische" Zeugen der Umgangssprache des Schreibers (bzw. als reine Zufälligkeiten) zu bestimmen sind (p. 162).

It is not until this has been done that these descriptions can be compared.

We have now reached the period of the methodological programmes, when concepts such as norm and variation played a decisive role in language description.

24

In the period around 1930 the discipline of structural linguistics began to make itself felt in Denmark. Hjelmslev's Principes de grammaire générale appeared in 1929[23], Viggo Brøndal's Morfologi og Syntax in 1932[24]. Their inspiration had been Ferdinand de Saussure's stimulating book Cours de linguistique générale from 1916.

Many of us experienced all this as an emancipation and an inspiration. An impression of our situation at that time can be gained by reading Karl Jaberg and Jacob Jud's book Der Sprachatlas als Forschungsinstrument (1928). This gives a staggering impression of how complex, inconsistent and chaotic the mass of linguistic material appeared to a consistent linguistic geographer. Jaberg compares linguistic geography to the impressionist school in painting and this comparison is apposite in two ways. Firstly, linguistic geographers, like impressionist painters, were interested in complexity and variety. Secondly, they did not actually describe the language or the dialect but reproduced for us the impression that the words of the language had made upon a single recorder on one particular occasion.

Some of us had collected together a fair amount of material of this kind and were faced with the task of bringing order to chaos and of extracting an objective result from all this subjective information. The structural concept came as a revelation to us. We saw the possibility of drawing up an abstract system of invariants and treating the motley variations as representatives of these invariants.

In my view the essential feature of the new linguistics is the structural concept itself, that is in Saussure's words, the distinction between la langue and la parole. There are other important distinctions in the new linguistics, fine and useful distinctions, for example the one which is most clearly brought out in Diderichsen's article, Saussure's differentiation between synchronism and diachronism. It was perhaps this that caused the greatest hubbub but it is not the most significant feature.

The works inspired by the structural concept have been discussed by Karl Martin Nielsen[25]. Here I shall content myself with making a few supplementary comments.

Diderichsen's works were inspired by the Prague phonologists and by Viggo Brøndal. Therefore, they place the texts in relation to the spoken language. My works were inspired by Hjelmslev and I abstain from advancing theories about the spoken language and describe the written language and only that. Then again, Diderichsen, in Sætningsbygningen i Skaanske Lov (Sentence structure in the Scanic Law)[26],

was inspired by Brøndal's Morfologi og Syntax from 1932 and by
Aage Hansen's Sætningen og dens led i moderne dansk (The sentence
and its members in Modern Danish) from 1933. Diderichsen's aim is
to present a sentence analysis in which each individual sentence ·
member is characterised in two ways: firstly by its logical relationship to the other sentence members, i.e. as subject, object, adverbial
member etc.), and secondly topographically, by its position at the
beginning, middle or end of the sentence). The first description, the
relational one, belongs to la langue, the second description to la
parole. In this Diderichsen differs from Brøndal, who considers that
morphology alone belongs to la langue and the whole of syntax to
la parole. The first part of Diderichsen's paper is very brief. It is
the second part that is most detailed and most interesting, i.e. the
discussion of which members can stand at the beginning, middle and
end of the sentence, often with comprehensive statistical surveys.

B.

I will turn now to some important philological text descriptions that
do not fall naturally into one of the three types of study that have
been treated above. They can be divided into two groups, one containing works designed to cast light on the history of the language,
often with the particular aim of dating a text, and one containing
works which are primarily concerned with the history of culture or
literary history.

The first group includes, among other items, the numerous discussions of runic inscriptions. The monographs on individual inscriptions
by the old runologists, particularly Sophus Bugge and Ludvig Wimmer, had laid the foundations for a highly-developed genre within
the discipline of philology[27]. One of the supreme achievements was
Wimmer's great work De danske runemindesmærker (The Danish
runic monuments) I-IV (1893-1908). A supplement to this work is
Danmarks runeindskrifter (Denmark's runic inscriptions) by Lis Jacobsen and Erik Moltke with Anders Bæksted and Karl Martin Nielsen (1941-42). This is particularly valuable because of the photo-
graphic technique developed by Moltke and the numerous biblio-
graphical references which precede the treatment of each individual
inscription. Of particular interest for the study of language description is Karl Martin Nielsen's treatment of the morphology in cols.
747-766 of the text volume. Mention should also be made here of
a long and important article by the same author, Til runedanskens
ortografi (On the orthography of runic Danish)[28].

Apart from the above-mentioned works it is Harry Andersen who has been particularly concerned with the runic inscriptions from a linguistic point of view. From among his many important contributions to runology should be mentioned: Runeindskriften paa Guldhornet fra Gallehus (The runic inscription on the golden horn from Gallehus)[29] and his two articles on the Glavendrup stone[30]. Besides these there are his numerous articles on historical phonetics that have been discussed elsewhere by Karl Martin Nielsen[31].

From among the many examinations of the language of MSS I will just mention the very important one by Kr. Hald on King Knud's deed of gift[32], Brøndum-Nielsen's treatment of the MSS of the Scanic Law[33], and the same author's many studies on Danish historical phonetics in APhS, particularly the classic one on vowel harmony and vowel quantity in MS B 74[34]. I should also mention Svend Aakjær's introduction from 1943 to his edition of King Valdemar's cadastre[35] and Erik Kroman's book about this cadastre[36], in which a shrewd attempt is made to date the individual sections. In addition, Kroman's article on Danish palæography[37], in which some important datings are presented in laconic style, e.g. of B74, which is not from the first half of the 14th-century but contemporary with the municipal law of Tønder from 1243, of AM 4 4° of the Jutlandic Law, which is not from c. 1350 but contemporary with the Flensborg MS from c. 1300, and of the Zealand manual of medicine AM 187 8°, which was dated by its editor Såby in 1886 (ed. p. III) to the second half of the 14th century but is in fact from the first half of the 15th century, written by a monk of St Clara's Abbey in Roskilde.

Finally, I must name the short MS descriptions with datings in the standard works of reference: the edition of the Laws, GG I and Skautrup's History of the Danish language.

To the second group, the one concerned with cultural and literary history, belong among other items, Brøndum-Nielsen's M.A. lecture from 1910: De danske folkevisers betydning i sproglig henseende (The linguistic significance of the Danish ballads)[38].

The title of this lecture is inapposite, for it is first and foremost a linguistic dating of the ballad genre to c. 1200. The same subject is dealt with by Agnes Agerschou in Oprindelige Træk i dansk Folkevisesprog (Original features in the language of the Danish ballads)[39].

The influence of the language of Swedish charters on that of the Danish ones is the subject of an important paper by Peter Skautrup[40].

Brøndum-Nielsen's Sproglig forfatterbestemmelse (Determination of author on the basis of language) from 1914 contains, among other identifications, that of Hans Michelsen's two co-translators of Christian II's New Testament, Christiern Vinter and Henrik Smith. The bible translations from the period of the Reformation are also treated by Lis Jacobsen in Grundlaget for Christian den Tredjes Bibel (The basis for Christian III's Bible)[41], by Skautrup in his History of the language[42], and by Bertil Molde in Källorna till Christian III:s bibel 1550 (The sources for Christian III's Bible 1550) (Lund 1949).

In his Om Rimkrønikens Sprogform og Tilblivelse (On the language and origin of the rhymed chronicle)[43], Brøndum-Nielsen demonstrates that the poem has several authors. Brøndum-Nielsen's Om middelalderlig Nedskrivning efter Diktat (On medieval copying from dictation)[44] deals with linguistic problems in the oldest Danish bible translation. This paper was criticised by Diderichsen[45]. Brøndum-Nielsen's two most recent descriptions, Om Christi Opstandelse (On the resurrection of Christ) and Fra Skaanes Senmiddelalder (From the late Middle Ages in Scania) also have a primarily cultural-historical aim. The last-named work is perhaps the best of all Brøndum's text descriptions. In it his linguistic-historic method and his intuition — his Fingerspitzengefühl for texts — unite in an extremely fertile but probably also dangerous combination.

C.

What kind of language did the scholars have in mind when writing their descriptions?

I will make a brief preliminary foray into the 19th century. Lyngby and Wimmer claimed that there was no difference between the written language and the spoken language at the time of the compilation of the medieval Laws. The language normally used for written sources in the Middle Ages was Latin. When a man did write in Danish, he wrote exactly as he spoke Lyngby and Wimmer assume, then, that there was only *one* kind of language.

Objections to this view were raised by Molbech, Jessen, Såby and Oluf Nielsen. Jessen and Såby asserted that the written language soon became archaic as compared with the spoken language. Molbech and Oluf Nielsen asserted that the written language in Jutland and in Scania was mainly the language of Zealand, although the native dialect of the scribe occasionally betrayed itself.

It is Oluf Nielsen who uses his arguments to best effect. First in a review of Lyngby's Udsagnsordenes Böjning (The conjugation of verbs)[46] but in greatest detail in the fine introduction to *Gamle jydske Tingsvidner* (Old Jutlandic court reports) (1882). Here he compares the language in the medieval municipal law of Flensborg with that of the Jutlandic Law. The result is that the language of the Flensborg Law contains more dialect characteristics than that of the Jutlandic Law but that even the scribe of the Flensborg Law "has attempted to write otherwise than his own pronunciation would lead him to do naturally". – "In Scania and Jutland people tried to write the language of Zealand, in Scania by making their language more modern, in Jutland by giving it forms more archaic than the ones they spoke. It is therefore necessary to assume that there was a conscious attempt to create a common written language or a standard language at an early period" (p. XXXI). It is assumed, then, that there are *two and only two kinds of language:* a common written language and the spoken dialects. These two kinds of language are both found mixed up in the surviving texts and it is the philologist's task to differentiate them correctly: *"the texts which have been written by Jutlanders must be treated with great caution from the point of view of the history of the language, for the scribes have tried to write a language other than their own and this has resulted in many impossible forms"* (in the conclusion p. XLII).

This conception of the early common Danish written language was accepted enthusiastically by the neo-Romantics P.K. Thorsen and Marius Kristensen. Marius Kristensen was, indeed, unwilling to concede that this written language derived from the spoken language of Zealand but would acknowledge its antiquity and its significance[47]. Upon this admission are based his attempts to localise a MS with the aid of some few dialectal forms.

P.K. Thorsen expressed his opinion very clearly in an article *Skriftsprog* (Written language) in Salomonsens Konversationsleksikon, 1st ed. (1905):

> The language which was written in the Middle Ages and the century of the Reformation was understood by everyone but spoken by none. Everyone at that time spoke dialect. These dialects can sometimes be traced in written works, either when some word or other which rarely occurs in the written language slips in or when serious breaches of the rules of language are committed. It was not until the middle of the 17th century that the cultivated spoken language began to appear (p. 153).

Thus the possibility of the existence of a third kind of language is dismissed.

This was the generally accepted view at the turn of the century. In Verner Dahlerup's Det danske Sprogs Historie (History of the Danish language) (1896), it is stated that the Zealand dialect formed the basis of the written language in Christian III's Bible, with the qualifying remark "perhaps with *kancellisprog* (the language of government offices) as an intermediate link".

It is against this background that Lis Jacobsen wrote her thesis Studier til det danske Rigssprogs Historie (Studies on the history of Standard Danish) (1910), which has been fully discussed by Karl Martin Nielsen[48]. He also deals with Paul Diderichsen's Fragmenter af gammeldanske Haandskrifter (Fragments of ODan MSS) (1931-37) and Diderichsen's corrective to Lis Jacobsen's much too heavy-handed division of the language of the late Middle Ages into on the one hand a conservative *kancellisprog* and on the other a literary language that was closer to the spoken language and showed more traces of the influence of the dialects.

The realisation of the fact that the language in the MSS of the Laws is essentially a written language has been of significance for our interpretation of its syntax, vocabulary and style. The old Romantic interpretation had been that the laws were exceedingly old, handed down orally from generation to generation, recited at the assemblies by the law-speaker, and eventually copied down more or less word for word from such recitations. In opposition to this view, Stig Iuul and Erik Kromann argued in Danmarks gamle Love paa Nutidsdansk (The old laws of Denmark in modern Danish)[49] that the provincial laws are not the direct result of the copying down of a recitation of the laws at an assembly. They refer in this context to the long sentences which are characteristic of the Zealand Laws in particular.

In his long article on the language of the Jutlandic Law[50] and also in Det danske sprogs historie[51], Peter Skautrup attempted to salvage as much as possible of the Romantic conception. He described the syntax of the laws as being typical of the spoken language and asserted that the compilers retained archaic words out of respect for the old oral formulations and not simply as the result of an archaising tendency. In Sætningsbygningen i Skaanske Lov, Diderichsen treats the law-style as *kunstprosa* (artistic prose). In spite of the fact that the Scanic Law does not contain a single provable latinism that is incompatible with old Scandinavian usage, Diderichsen says in his conclusion (p. 168) that it is "natural to explain this stylistic superiority by assuming that the compiler was familiar with Medieval Latin and thus had a sure instinct for the texture of the prose". In Syntaktiska och stilistiska studier i fornnordiskt lagspråk (Syntactic and stylistic studies on the language of the old Scandinavian laws)[52], C.I. Ståhle describes the style of the laws as one of transition between an old oral style and a new literary one.

The hypothesis that there was a third kind of language in the Middle Ages, namely a standard spoken language, was first put forward by Brøndum-Nielsen in an article in the daily newspaper Politiken 18-4-1925. His theory was based on an examination of the dialogue in Peder Thøgersen's school play De mundo et paupere from 1607. In this play some Jutland dialect forms are employed by characters from the lower classes but not by higher-ranking people.

In 1928 Brøndum-Nielsen asserted in GG I § 7 that the written language must have influenced certain categories of spoken language as early as the Middle Ages, e.g. the language of preaching and reading aloud. He makes a similar assertion about the language of preaching in his article on Siæla Trøst and in Fra Skaanes Senmiddelalder.

While Brøndum-Nielsen's hypothesis that a superior spoken language showing the influence of the written language was to be found as early as the 16th century has hardly met with general acceptance, everyone, I think, would agree with his assumption that a literal pronunciation was employed in the language of preaching. Thus Paul Diderichsen in Fragmenter af gammeldanske Haandskrifter (1931-37) p. LXI. The idea is, in fact, very obvious because the art of silent reading has only recently become general.

The existence of a fourth kind of language, namely regional written languages, was postulated as early as 1866-67 by Edwin Jessen in Småting om dansk (Brief notes on Danish)[53]. He considered that the provincial laws were "composed in a kind of written language, although not a standard written language but what could be called "an assembly language", based upon the spoken language of the jurisdiction". In GG I § 5 II Brøndum-Nielsen, presumably independently of Jessen, refers to the legal language of the areas subject to the three landsting as a "kind of provincial standard language, in which a tendency towards a common linguistic norm for the whole kingdom has made itself felt".

This theory of differences in regional written languages has received support from two recent studies: Poul Andersen's edition of Jens Peerszøn's *En merckelig grundfest disputatz* from 1531 (1952), in which "characteristic features of a peculiar Jutlandic orthography" are pointed out, and particularly from an important survey by Karl Martin Nielsen (1956), *Tre jyske bønnebøger* (Three Jutland prayer-books)[54]. In these three prayer-books, which derive from the period around 1500, Karl Martin Nielsen has traced a number of Jutland dialect characteristics, e.g. *i* for old *æ* in *brinne, hinne; o* for *a* in *wone, fogher; anten* for *enten, kam* preterite for *kom*. These characteristics are found in each of the three prayer-books and they appear with great consistency there. In other respects, however, the language of the prayer-books agrees with the Zealand written language and in this, too, the three books are uniform and consistent. Almost all of the consistently sustained Jutlandic features reflect dialect developments that are common to the whole of Northern Jutland, while other features that reflect dialect developments from more restricted geographic areas are absent. From this fact Karl Martin Nielsen draws the important conclusion:

> The Jutland characteristics cannot, therefore, be assumed to betray the dialect (spoken language) of the scribes; both their frequency of occurrence and the fact that the three texts agree on their use show that the Jutland characteristics belong to the orthographical norm of the scribes, the orthography which they had been trained to use.

It is natural to conclude that this orthography had been taught in the cathedral and abbey schools. Karl Martin Nielsen's survey emphasises very strongly how important it is to undertake an examination of the language in the letter books and cadastres of the various cathedrals and abbeys.

I shall conclude by attempting to give a general characterisation of the development of linguistic research as reflected in the descriptions of texts.

The method employed has become more rigorous but also more elastic. More stringent demands are made of both the formulation of the problem and the operations employed in its solution. Theories are phrased more carefully, sharper distinctions are drawn and the reasoning employed is clearer than before. At the same time a great variety of problems has been drawn into the sphere of interest of philologists and new techniques, including very complicated statisti-

32

cal calculations, are constantly being employed in an attempt to solve new kinds of problems. The generally accepted view of the state of the language in the Middle Ages has become more and more complicated, developing from the straightforward picture of the dialect-speaking scribe who vainly attempts to write Standard Danish to the picture of the scribe, competent in both dialect and standard Danish, who employs a regional standard language but is also familiar with a higher norm. Similarly, our picture of the changes and variation in the language has received more nuances under the influence of the dialect geographers and others.

We are abandoning an easily comprehensible, almost monumental simplicity and moving towards a complexity that is difficult even for the specialist to master and which tends to make our researches inaccessible to the layman. It is easy to be envious of Marius Kristensen, who was able to speak to the people man to man about all these difficult conceptions.

This development has been inevitable. It has been necessary for us to improve our methods and to refine our terminology. We must accustom ourselves to being subjected to the same rigorous demands for the production of evidence as are natural scientists. This means, however, that we shall inevitably find ourselves ensconced within a horrible ivory tower.

NOTES

1 Based on a lecture given at a meeting of Selskab for Nordisk Filologi on the 27th September 1962.
2 In Festskrift til Ludv. F.A. Wimmer, Nordisk tidsskrift for filologi, 3. rk. 17 (1909) 98-107.
3 In DSt (1906) 150-52.
4 Harpestræng. Gamle danske urtebøger, stenbøger og kogebøger (1908-20).
5 This localisation was criticised by Brøndum-Nielsen in APhS 4 (1929-30) 186-90.
6 In DSt (1928) 133-44.
7 En grænsedialekt, in ANF 23 (1906) 53-89.
8 In DSt (1907) 127 ff.
9 In APhS 12 (1937-38) 25-32.
10 In Sorø. Klostret, Skolen, Akademiet gennem Tiderne. Skr. af gl. Soranere 1. 1: 132-45, 1. 2: 658-59 (1923-24).
11 In ANF 41 (1924) 1-56 – an M.A. thesis from 1921.
12 In APhS 4 (1929) 65-71.
13 In Folkemål og sproghistorie (1933) 184-201, Marius Kristensen presented a better argument for his localisation of Harpestræng K.
14 Om Fragmenterne af den gammeldanske Siæla Trøst, in APhS 9 (1934) 187-92.

33

15 Et gammeldansk Digt om Christi Opstandelse efter Fragment Stockh. *A 115 (c. 1325), in Det kgl. Da. Vidensk. Selsk. Hist.-filol. Medd. 35, 1 (1955).

16 In Fra Skaanes Senmiddelalder, Festskrift udg. af Københavns Universitet (March 1959) 3-151.

17 Om Personnavnene i de danske Møntindskrifter, in Studier Tilegnede Verner Dahlerup (1934) 182-87.

18 Jacob Madsens dansk, in Jacobi Matthię Arhusiensis (Jacob Madsen Aarhus) De literis libri duo herausgeg. und erläutert. v. Chr. Møller u. P. Skautrup m. einer dän. Übers. nebst einer Abhandl. üb. Text u. Quellen v. Franz Blatt 2, Acta Jutl. 3, 1 (1931) 67-98.

19 Pp. 74-81 with a map which is also reproduced in Skautrup's history of the Danish language, Vol. II (1947) 190.

20 Harry Andersen, Om tryksvage vokaler i runedansk, in APhS 24 (1957) 46-54; Anders Bjerrum below pp. 116-29.

21 Johannes Jutæ og Valdemars Jordebog, in Ti afhandlinger, Navnestudier 2 (1960) 163-214.

22 In APhS 12 (1938) 116-69.

23 Det kgl. da. Vidensk. Selsk. Hist.-filol. Medd. 16, 1 (1928 on title page).

24 Morfologi og Syntax. Nye Bidrag til Sprogets Theori, Festskrift udg. af Københavns Universitet (November 1932).

25 In Sproghistorien, in Det danske sprogs udforskning i det 20. århundrede (1965) 26-51.

26 In APhS 15 (1941) 1-252.

27 A survey of these works can be found in DR. Text (1942) cols. 1059 f. and 1092 f.

28 In ANF 75 (1960) 1-78.

29 In Sønderjydsk Maanedsskrift 14 (1938) 131-38.

30 In APhS 20 (1949) 311-33 and 25 (1962 for 1960) 1-30.

31 In Sproghistorien (cf. n. 25 above) 40 ff.

32 Knud den Helliges Gavebrev. Et Bidrag til det danske Sprogs ældste Historie, in APhS 21 (1952) 105-42.

33 In ANF 34 (1917) 105-37.

34 In APhS 2 (1927) 173-83.

35 Kong Valdemars Jordebog, ed. by Svend Aakjær, Udg. af Samf. t. udgiv. af gl. nord. litt. Vols. 1-3 (1926-45).

36 Kong Valdemars Jordebog. Et Haandskrifts Historie (1936), a revised version in German translation appeared in APhS 11 (1936) 1-81.

37 Dansk Palæografi, in Palæografi. A. Danmark og Sverige, Nordisk Kultur 28A (1943) 36-81.

38 Printed 1911 in Nord. tidskr. f. vet., konst & industri, utg. av Letterstedtska fören. (1910) 587-602.

39 In Sprog og Kultur 12 (1943) 65-74.

40 In Studier tillägnade Axel Kock, Arkiv. Tilläggsbd. t. bd. 40. Ny följd (1929) 342-49.

41 In Nord. tidsskr. f. filologi 4 rk. 2 (1914) 151-63.

42 Vol. II (1947) 210 ff.

43 In Festskrift udg. af Københavns Universitet (September 1930) 3-97, with a supplement in APhS 17 (1944) 129-44.

44 In Studier tilegnede Verner Dahlerup (1934) 63-66.

45 In APhS 13 (1939) 77.

34

46 In Slesvigske Provindsialefterretninger Ny Rk. Bd. IV (1863) 232.
47 In Samlende kræfter i sprogudviklingen (Unifying forces in the development of the language), Sprog og Oldtidsf. 41 (1899).
48 In Sproghistorien (cf. n. 25 above) 28 ff.
49 Vol. I (1945) p. VII n. 3; cf. also Vol. III (1948) p. II.
50 Sproget i Jyske Lov, in Med Lov skal Land bygges, Udg. af Juristforbundet (1941) 200-50.
51 Vol. I (1944) 208 ff.
52 Acta Univ. Stockh.: Stockholm Studies in Scand. philology, New ser. 2. (1958).
53 In Aarbøger for nordisk Oldkyndighed (1867) 371-84, particularly 377.
54 In Festskrift til Peter Skautrup (1956) 223-37.

Jens Pedersen Høysgaard's second orthographical specimen[1]

I shall begin with a short account of Høysgaard himself and the reason for the appearance of his orthographical specimens. There will follow a critical analysis of the second orthographical specimen and to conclude I shall give an assessment of the significance for linguistic scholarship of the new ideas that are contained in it.

The information which Høysgaard's works provide about his own spoken language, however, falls almost exclusively outside the scope of this lecture and it will be sufficient here to refer to Axel Koch in ANF III, Brøndum-Nielsen in DSt 1918, Marius Kristensen in Studier tillägnade Axel Koch (1929) 32-36, Henrik Bertelsen in his great book Jens Pedersen Høysgaard og hans Forfatterskab (1926) 188-257, and Peter Skautrup in Det danske Sprogs Historie III (1953) 14 ff.

1.

When Jens Pedersen Høysgaard's two first publications, the orthographical specimens, appeared in 1743, he was 44 years old. He had earlier acquired the lowest academic degree, the baccalaureus degree, and on the strength of that obtained the post which he held for the rest of his life, that of third beadle at the University of Copenhagen. Four years later, in 1747, appeared his first full-length book, *Accentuered og Raisonnered Grammatica* (Accentuated and Reasoned Grammar), and five years later again, in 1752, his second book, *Forsøg til en Fuldstændig Dansk Syntax* (An essay towards a complete Danish syntax), and many years later, in 1769 when he was 70 years old, came *Første Anhang til den Accentuerede Grammatika* (First Supplement to the Accentuated Grammar). A second supplement never appeared. Høysgaard died in 1773.

Høysgaard wrote about the motivation for the appearance of the two first papers in the Supplement to his accentuated grammar[2] :

"The orthographical specimens appeared at the beginning of 1743. The motivation for writing them came from outside and I as little thought then about them as I do now about this that they would have any particular practical value. My only two reasons for writing them were firstly to act as a second in a dual and to parry some blows that had been blindly aimed by a journalist at another orthographist, and secondly to act as a peace-maker and try to make those headstrong parties to the recent *Orthographical War* understand that they had been quarrelling over a small nuisance that neither of them was in a position to remedy except by means which I well knew, and had in fact said, that few if any would be willing to employ".

The phases in the orthographical war have been described in detail by Henrik Bertelsen.[3] Here it will be sufficient to note that in 1741 Niels von Hauen published "Et lidet orthographisk Lexicon" of "the spelling and signification of homonyms and how they are commonly pronounced" and thus became embroiled in a violent battle with Thomas Clitau, who published a fat and extremely boring book attacking him.

In the first orthographical specim   , which was published under the pseudonym "en Dansk *Patriot*" (a Danish patriot), Høysgaard came to von Hauen's defence in a very subtle way. Among the topics dealt with in the orthographical specimen was one of the most vexed points of disagreement in Danish orthography, namely the indication of vowel-quantity in words of one syllable such as brød and smør. Henrik Gerner, who was unwilling to double vowels, doubled consonants to indicate that a preceding vowel was short, writing brød and smørr, and von Hauen did the same. Peder Syv, on the other hand, doubled the long vowel in words of one syllable, thus avoiding the necessity for doubling consonants. He wrote, then, brøød, and smør.

Høysgaard's finding was as follows: There ought to be "some indication of the length of a syllable" (this condition disqualifies Clitau's proposal: Brød and Smør); but two consonants were too many,
since no more than one was heard, and two vowels were also too
many, since only one was heard: "in this way, however, we become
involved in a vicious circle; it is, therefore, necessary for us to find
some better method so that we write neither too many letters nor
too few". The method that Høysgaard had in mind was not, however,
revealed until the appearance of the second orthographical specimen.

2

The Danish patriot's second orthographical specimen, a small pamph-
let of 26 octavo pages, is of much higher scholarly standard than the
first. It contains new ideas and daring proposals that the author only
puts foreward hesitantly "with a sideways glance and his hat in front
of his eyes", as he says. Part of the time he is speaking openly and
with enthusiasm, part of the time he is concealing his true purpose
behind artifice and clowning.

Bertelsen has earlier described the artfulness which characterises
the introduction[4]. We shall proceed directly to the first of the book's
two main sections. These deal respectively with the accents and with
the vowels and their correct employment.

A. The Danish accents are:

1. *Acutus* or sharp-tone, which can be indicated by a small stroke
above the vowel slanting from right down to left, as in the words
Lóft, Fád, Mád etc. and in the final syllable of the French word *aimé*.
Most Danes, however, pronounce this word incorrectly as *aimè* and
are censured for so doing by their language-teachers.

2. *Gravis* or thrusting-tone, which can be indicated by a stroke
slanting from left down to right, as in Sèng, Knìv etc.

3. *Circumflexus* or twisted-tone, which is a combination of the
two first accents, as in Bôrd, Stôl etc. and

4. *Apostrophicus* (sive *Compensativus*) or drawling-accent, which
can be indicated by an *Apostrophe,* as in Kjo'l, Fa'r, Mo'r etc. in the
Copenhagen pronunciation, for some Jutlanders pronounce these
words *per Circumflexus* (i.e. as Kjôl, Fâr, Môr).

There follow some convenient examples for practising the accents,
e.g.

et Húl paa strømper, en Hùld Ven, en Hûl skjelm and et Dyrs Hu'le.

Finally, there are some remarks on the relationship between the tone or accent of a syllable and its tone-fall. By tone-fall is meant what we would call stress. "In the word Forstànd the first syllable has *Acute* accent without tone-fall and the second syllable *Grave* accent with tone-fall". We would say that the first syllable is un-stressed and has no glottal stop and the second syllable is strongly stressed and has a glottal stop on the consonant. There then follows an important law which has subsequently been discovered by other scholars: in connected speech many one-syllabled words become un-stressed and change their tone to *Acute*.

In order to understand Høysgaard's presentation of the accents, it is necessary to realise that his terminology cannot be translated di-rectly into the terminology that is current today. There is a rough correspondance between Høysgaard's

syllable with acute accent and what we would call a syllable without a glottal stop which contains a short vowel, possibly followed by a consonant,

syllable with grave accent and syllable with a short vowel plus a voiced consonant with glottal stop,

syllable with circumflex accent and syllable with a long vowel with glottal stop, possibly followed by a consonant, and

syllable with apostrophic accent and syllable with a long vowel without glottal stop.

The correspondences are not, however, exact for three reasons:

1. Høysgaard's accents have each been analysed into two elements, namely vowel length or shortness plus glottal stop or lack of glottal stop.

2. Høysgaard's accents represent characteristics of the syllables, while we tend to consider length as a characteristic of the vowel or consonant.

3. Høysgaard's accentuation and our descriptions diverge on a significant point:

In words such as sò, snè, sè, where we would speak of a long vowel in final position with glottal stop, he does not use a circumflex accent (as in Bòrd, Stòl) but a grave accent (as in Sèng, Knìv). We have already had one instance of this, namely the incorrect pronun-ciation *aimè*; and in the sections of his paper in which he employs accents, Høysgaard has snè and màa with grave accent. A couple of pages further on, where Høysgaard is giving instructions as to how children can be taught the correct use of accents, he uses vowels for practising all four accents:

á, å´, ǽ . . .   à, å` , æ̀ . . .
â, å^, æ̂ . . .   a', å', æ' . . .

We can well understand that Høysgaard could use vowels to illustrate accents no. 1, no. 3, and no. 4 but he also illustrates the grave accent by means of a vowel without a following consonant. How was it possible for him, then, to make a distinction between grave and circumflex in an isolated vowel?

Høysgaard himself answers this question in his description of the accents in the accentuated grammar. Here he says of the grave accent that it is "almost as though it stops the breath" and of the circumflex accent that it "first stops the breath and then immediately and unnoticeably speeds it up again". This is why he says in the second orthographical specimen that circumflexus is a compound of the two first accents, namely gravis and acutus.

He has thus practised the grave accent by saying [a˙] and circumflexus by saying [aˑᵃ] or something like that.

This characteristic that a long vowel with glottal stop and following consonant has a weak repetition of the vowel sound after the glottal stop, while a long vowel in final position with glottal stop does not have such a weak vowel sound after the glottal stop is due to the fact that Høysgaard came from Århus: this feature can still be heard in the dialects of East Jutland, cf. Marius Kristensen in Studier tillägnade Axel Kock 32-36, and Ella Jensen in Houlbjerg-målet (1944) 25 f.

We have now gone through Høysgaard's account of the actual theory of accents. It occupies only 2 1/2 pages. It is followed by a circumstantial refutation of two hypothetical objections, which occupies 2 1/2 pages, and a detailed account of the practical advantages offered by the use of the written tones, which occupies 10 pages. From among the 8 advantages I would single out for mention:

Advantage 1: There would be an end to disagreement between orthographists on several points and a standardised orthography would then become feasible.

Advantage 2: Jutlanders and others would, with a very little instruction, be in a position to learn the chief characteristics of the spoken language current in Zealand so that dialect differences among the most cultivated and intelligent people would be greatly diminished.

Advantage 4: Written tone would also always indicate which

words were to be read with thrust and stress, if it were omitted above neighbouring words which were to be pronounced with little or no tone-fall. In this way it would be possible to avoid *amphibolie*. By amphibolie Høysgaard means "ambiguity in construction or expression" as opposed to æquivatio "ambiguity in one word"[5]; by tone-fall he means strong stress in general, by "thrust and stress", elsewhere called "emphasis and stress", he means a strong stress which serves to emphasise a word.

Advantage 5: Numerous *dreje*-ord (turning words) could be distinguished by written tones. Turning words or æqui-voca are words that are spelt in the same way, such as nòdder, pl. of en nød (nut), and nòdder, pl. of en nødde (cudgel).

Advantage 8: Children, simple people and foreigners would have less difficulty in learning to read aloud correctly.

To the numbered advantages is added an unnumbered one: Once a language had been put into a grammar and a dictionary, both accentuated, the tendency for innovation would be counteracted.

Then the section about the accents concludes with a list of over 200 pairs of words which are spelt alike but pronounced differently.

Some early drafts for this list survive and most of the material has been printed in the sixth volume of Danske Grammatikere. They reveal with certainty that the list was compiled from von Hauen's dictionary and supplemented with the help of the Danish word-list in the Latin dictionary of the period, Nucleus latinitatis, 3rd ed. (1733). This can be seen from the alphabetical order of the words in the various lists, from their spellings and from the translations into Latin of some of the words. It is possible to refer to these dictionaries when there is any doubt as to which word Høysgaard had in mind.

On the other hand, the fact that Høysgaard's drafts are younger than von Hauen's book must not be taken as evidence in support of Bertelsen's assertion that Høysgaard's interest in the Danish sound-system was first aroused by von Hauen's book. We know the way in which two of Høysgaard's disciples, Rask and Lyngby, experimented for many years before they finally arrived at a provisional understanding of the Danish sound-system that enabled them to devise a consistent notation, whereas in Høysgaard's surviving papers his notation is fully worked out. Before it would have been possible for him to have achieved so much, he must have scrapped a great deal of paper that is now lost.

B. On the vowels and their correct use.

We have 10 vowels, namely a, aa, æ, e, i, ৪, ø, u, y. The new vowel ৪ is the clear ö in főr "formerly", tőr "dry", which is different from the thick ø in főr "stout", mør "tender". In the same way e is clear, like æ, in dèn, dét, rét, but thick in én, ét, fét. o is pronounced with its correct thick sound in fórt, hós, knópper, but clear like aa in kórt, lós, kópper. And i, u and y retain their correct sound in words such as tit, kuld, nyt, but are pronounced as e, o, ø,in words such as list, bukke, nytte.

aa ought to be written in the Swedish way as å or even better as an open o, ɔ, since aa opens the mouth more than o.

We can accept Høysgaard's vowel system and there is no difficulty for us in understanding it. It is followed, however, by a section which is rather more difficult. The dreadful confusion that reigns in the employment of the vowel symbols "can perhaps in part be blamed on the Germans, who did not understand the Danish language and yet, in the time of insanity (he must mean the Catholic period), had the task of teaching us, or rather our ancestors, to read and write Danish. The difficulty would not have been so great, though great enough, if the clear sound (i.e. the open one) of the vowels' pronounciation had only occurred preceding so-called half-sounding consonants in the same syllable. I have been experimenting, however, to see whether our vowels in the current orthography could be subjected to binding rules of pronunciation and I have found that it would be ten times as complicated a business as for French".

The half-sounding consonants are also called semi-vowels, in contradistinction to the silent consonants or mutæ. This classification of the consonants derives from the Classical grammarians and it was misunderstood even in Antiquity to mean that among the semi-vowels were numbered not only l, m, n, r, but also the other consonants whose names begin with a vowel, i.e. f, s, x, while mutæ are those consonants whose names end with a vowel, e.g. p, t, k, b, d, g. Jacob Madsen Aarhus, in his work De litteris from 1586, gives a detailed and extremely clear criticism of this classification. Høysgaard says that it is the result of "an error committed by the oldest grammarians" but none the less he takes it into account both here, in the accentuated grammar §§ 12 and 15 and in the Supplement to the accentuated grammar § 2003. This latter paragraph reveals that Høysgaard, when he had first looked for the reason for the "fluctuating use and pronunciation of the vowels", came to "this reasonable conclusion that our old orthographers must have made up for themselves a law such as this" and then there follows a law which is almost identical with the one that had been tried and found wanting in the second orthographical specimen.

If we compare these paragraphs, the meaning becomes quite clear: Our earliest orthographers — the men who created the written Danish language — were Germans; they were accustomed to the incorrect classification of the consonants; they attempted to implement an orthographical law based on this classification but the attempt was unsuccessful and confusion arose as to the use of the vowel symbols because the orthographers were not themselves sufficiently conversant with the Danish language.

Next follows Høysgaard's proposal for a radical change in the orthography. The principle is that each vowel symbol should always indicate the same vowel sound and each vowel sound always be indicated by the same vowel symbol. He recommends this bold suggestion for favourable consideration and discussion by experts. The request for an authoritative treatment of the matter is emphasised in a subsequent subtle treatment of one of the issues in the orthographical war, the use of initial capitals. This matter does not interest him particularly but it gives him an opportunity for praising the tolerance of which he is now himself in need.

And then Høysgaard withdraws with a sideways bow: "The kind reader must content himself for the time being with this strange specimen and by showing his approval encourage the appearance of additional ones.

3.

In order to be able to make a correct evaluation of the main thesis in Høysgaard's paper, it is important to recognise two fundamental traits in his works.

Firstly, in spite of the fact that Høysgaard's books include several excellent observations on the function of the organs of speech, his reason for studying the sounds is his interest in the role they play in language and not in the way in which they are produced. He is, as Otto Jespersen has said so rightly, a philologist and not a phonetician.

As far as the study of accents is concerned, Høysgaard's achievement is first and foremost that he was the first to recognise the four accents as essential elements in Danish syllables. In the supplement to the accentuated grammar, Høysgaard says that "the uncertain and changeable elements in the sound of the words ought not be confused with the certain and constant ones". This distinction between the changeable and the constant is significant. It reappears in the Syntax in Høysgaard's teaching on the meaning of words.

According to the Supplement, the certain and constant elements in the sound of the words include firstly "letters" and secondly what Høysgaard calls "Ordforskiellende Aandepasninger" (word-differentiating breath features). These latter include what Høysgaard in the second orthographical specimen refers to as accents and tone-falls.

The uncertain and changeable elements include what the supplement calls tones, i.e. modulations that express states of mind. "What is most significant", he continues in the Supplement, is that it is not tones that distinguish one word from another but "Qvantiteter og Aandelave", i.e. tone-falls and accents.

If we leave the Supplement and return to the second orthographical specimen, it becomes quite clear that Høysgaard had already realised that this word-differentiating function was an essential feature of the accents; one way in which this is revealed is his long list of "turning-words".

This realisation is the essential difference between Høysgaard and his predecessors. In their works – both those of the prosodists, notably Søren Povelsen Gotlender, and those of the grammarians, notably Gerner and Syv, can be found many scattered and chance references to various phenomena that they call either quantities or tones. Gerner, for example, had noted that the adjective viis "støn-ner" (groans), whereas viss does not. He drew no conclusion from this observation, however. Syv and von Hauen employ length marks above the vowels but without really knowing what they are doing. Høysgaard's achievement is not first and foremost that he noted the phonetic pecularities but that out of the jumble of quantities and tones that had been noted by his predecessors he seized on exactly those four accents that are constant and word-differentiating elements in the language. In the second orthographical specimen he contents himself with demonstrating the accents, giving them names, and providing some suitable examples to be used in practising them. In the accentuated grammar he describes the accents and places them in a system, a system which is then further developed in the Supplement.

The case with the vowel theory is rather similar. Høysgaard's predecessors, notably Henrik Gerner, had made important observations about the vowels, too. In Orthographica Danica caput 15, for example, Gerner says that most of the vowels have two pronunciations, one when they are short and followed by two consonants, and another when they are long and sometimes also when they are short.

Høysgaard's achievement, then, is not the fact that he increased the number of vowels from 9 to 10. It is that he discovered that the open pronunciation of a vowel corresponds to the closed pronunciation of the next following vowel in a series arranged according to the degree of opening, i.e. that we have, for example, the same vowel sound in list as in et and the same in búkke as in knopper. No one before Høysgaard had made this discovery and the next to recognise it after Høysgaard was Rask. The fact is that it is more difficult to see that there is only one vowel where two had been expected than it is to discover vowel nuances that had not previously been noticed.

It was not Høysgaard's wish to discover as many vowel nuances as possible but to construct exactly the series of vowel symbols that was both necessary and sufficient for an adequate notation of the Danish language. And the number of symbols required is 10, neither more nor less.

The second requirement before an evaluation of Høysgaard's contribution to scholarship is possible is a recognition that the interest of Høysgaard and his contemporaries in philology was born of a practical need, namely the need for a standardised orthography.

It has been asserted that Høysgaard was not in fact very interested in orthography and that, in true scholarly fashion, he was not really concerned with serving any useful purpose. In support of this view of Høysgaard, which was inspired by the ideals of a later period, quotations have often been made from his last work, the Supplement to the accentuated grammar. One of these is the following splendid passage: "It is a matter of fact that a people can derive many advantages from its language without being particularly well acquainted with it; yet it should not be left to connoisseurs alone to know it well; let it be called a matter for connoisseurs, however! for it is quite as good a matter as so many others". It is completely to misunderstand the tendency in Høysgaard's last work to read more into this last outburst than the self-defence of a disappointed man. Another statement that has been quoted is his comment that when he was writing his two orthographical specimens, he was not particularly concerned with the practical use to which they could be put. This simply means, however, that he had been doubtful from the very beginning as to whether his proposals would ever be followed and not that he was indifferent to their fate.

If he had really been indifferent, he would hardly have devoted half of the second orthographical specimen to the practical advantages that his reform proposals would result in and only a quarter of it to the actual scientific discoveries (the last quarter of the work is mere light entertainment).

It would also be incomprehensible why Høysgaard should have chosen as the sub-title for his second orthographical specimen the quotation from Sallust, Concordia res parvæ crescunt, "it is by concord that small states grow" (res stands for res publicæ); the continuation runs: discordia maximæ dilabuntur, "by discord that the greatest fall to decay". Concordia here does not only refer to concord between the two fighting-cocks, von Hauen and Clitau. The word has a much wider reference: agreement between all orthographers as to the most rational orthography and a resulting standardised written language. In the treatise reference is also made to the fact that a rational orthography would promote uniformity in the spoken language throughout the whole country.

Høysgaard has expressed this wide aim elegantly and precisely in the conclusion to his treatment of the vowels: "It would be my wish for the children and young people of my fatherland that they should have a smooth and easy way to learn what they ought to learn, and for the Danish language the honour of being called more accurate and more easy than any other".

The patriotic and practical endeavour was entirely in the spirit of the eighteenth century.

But how was this linguistic uniformity that everyone agreed was desirable to be achieved?

First it would be necessary to have a fixed spoken-norm. On this matter Høysgaard is in entire agreement with Peder Syv: The best Danish is spoken in the towns of Zealand by the wisest and most learned people, when they are speaking carefully and in public.

Next it would be necessary to have a written language that corresponded exactly with this spoken language. With the exception of Gerner (and Clitau), everyone was agreed on the principle: People ought to write as they speak. This principle had been taken over from the 16th-century European grammarians, notably Scaliger the Elder, and these in turn had adopted it from the Classical grammarians.

Høysgaard, however, differs from his predecessors on two points. For the first in that he understood more clearly than they did what was really meant by saying that a written language corresponds exactly to a spoken language.

He distinguishes between symbol and sound more clearly and with greater consistency than his predecessors. This is revealed by a passage in the section on the vowels, where he argues against the hypothetical objection that some of the ten vowels are diphthongs. The question of diphthongs was of absorbing interest for all the contemporary grammarians, partly because the letter æ was at that time called ae and because the sound that corresponded to the symbol was considered by many people, including Gerner and Clitau, to be a compound. Høysgaard, however, wrote, "*I* say no; for b, in so far as it is a character, is not a consonant but indicates a consonant, similarly the 10 characters in question are in fact neither vowels nor consonants but only symbols, each of which signifies no more than one vowel or one single sound, and hence would not signify a diphthong, even if the symbol itself were threefold". I do not think that this distinction has ever been stated more precisely, either before or since.

Taking this distinction as his starting point, Høysgaard draws an important and audacious conclusion in the same section of his work: "It cannot be said, therefore, that a language has been altered just because the form of the letters has been changed, as long as rules have been given for pronouncing these letters in such a way that the language seems, and is, quite unchanged to the ears of those who hear it". Exactly the same thought is expressed in a footnote to the discussion of Advantage 1: If the expression "the genius of the language" were to be correctly explained, then it would be necessary to compose a whole sermon on the text: Usable words are like current coins. N.B. Latin could be written with Danish characters and still retain its *genius*". No sermon on this text is to be found anywhere in Høysgaard's works and it is, of course, impossible for us to reconstruct it. It is possible, however, to establish the link between the text and its interpretation. The text is a proverb which is found in Peder Syv's great collection[6] and also, as mentioned there, in Syv's Betenkninger om det Cimbriske Sprog (Reflections on the Cimbrian language) § 57; it has doubtless been translated from Latin; in the introduction to P.A. Heiberg's Sproggranskning[7] (Linguistic researches) it is recorded as "an old proverb" in the form verba valent usu ut nummi, "words, like coins, receive their value by agreement". The coin, then, has no intrinsic value but is an agreed symbol for a value. Whereas Peder Syv and P.A. Heiberg in their employment of the proverb emphasise the fact that one and the same coin under changing conventions can represent now a greater and now a lesser value, in the same way that a word by convention can receive a different stylistic value, Høysgaard is obviously emphasising the other aspect of the proverb: namely that two different coins can by convention represent the same value, in the same way as two different letters can represent the same sound. The word genius in Høysgaard's works, as in Heiberg's, has the meaning "nature, specific character".

Secondly, Høysgaard differs from his predecessors in that he realised that the discrepancy between written Danish and spoken Danish was much greater than had previously been suspected: 1. the spoken language contains more elements than there are symbols in the written language; among these additional elements are numbered the four accents; 2. there is no reasonable correspondence between the vowels of the spoken language and the vowel symbols of the written one.

In this new situation, Høysgaard could make his choice between three possibilities: 1. He could abandon the old maxim about the relationship between speech and writing and acknowledge that the written language and the spoken language can well be two different languages. This possibility, however, was foreign to Høysgaard's way of thinking. 2. He could develop the idea with which Henrik Gerner had toyed and claim that there ought to be complete agreement between speech and writing, that the written language is a language in its own right, that it is the most dignified language, and that we ought, therefore, to speak as we write. This conception, too, was rejected by Høysgaard. 3. He could stick to the standpoint held by Peder Syv and most other people that writing ought to represent the best spoken language and as a consequence of this advocate a radical reform of the orthography. (Besides the three above mentioned possibilities, there was an unlimited number of inconsequent viewpoints such as: It is correct that we ought to write as we speak but why object to a reasonable number of discrepancies? An idea such as this would be most foreign of all to Høysgaard's way of thinking.)

Høysgaard chose the third possibility, in spite of the fact that from the very beginning he had doubts as to the practicability of his reform proposals. "Usage and abusage are mighty fellows, especially when they grow old", he says in the accentuated grammar. The nucleus of his practical proposal was the orthographical dictionary, under the influence of which he hoped that the new orthography would gradually come to be used in literature. He stuck to his plan for this dictionary throughout his life, in spite of the fact that no one took any notice of his proposals.

When Høysgaard was almost 70 years old, Jacob Baden's Anweisung zur Dänischen Sprache appeared, with a glossary in which no account was taken of Høysgaard's proposals. It was his disappointment over this that led Høysgaard to publish his last work, the Supplement to the accentuated grammar, in which he deals with the disposition of words in an orthographical word-index. In this he maintains his standpoint with great obstinacy and not without many spiteful remarks at Baden's expense. This one, for example: "There are only a few men who understand the uses to which the science of accents can be put. It is a touchstone which can quickly expose some false metals".

I am perhaps being too brutal in using this quotation to mark the transition to the last section of my lecture in which I intend to discuss Høysgaard in relation to his immediate successors.

Høysgaard's contemporaries and immediate successors — Jacob Baden, Bloch, Dichmann, Nyrup and others — almost all express great admiration for Høysgaard but only a few of them take any account of his writings. Some of them are not even really familiar with his views on the various problems but, in spite of this, they praise him. They bring to mind Holberg's "halvstuderede røver" (smatterer); not because he was a smatterer but because he had the following words to say about the text of a sermon:

Jeg tekstens ord har glemt, dog det vil intet sige:
det kan jeg sværge, at den haver ei sin lige.

(I have forgotten the words of the text, but no matter: I can swear that there is no other like it.)

The first man really to understand Høysgaard was Rasmus Rask.

That he did understand him was due above all to the fact that his mind worked in the same way as Høysgaard's. This was betrayed at an early age by an overwhelming desire to understand the mechanism of language and to make new and improved orthographies. And we might add that Lyngby was bitten by the same craze. He too created one new orthography after another in his student days.

These three men form a group, not only because of the way their minds worked but also because there is an historical connection between them. Rask became acquainted with the accentuated grammar while he was still quite a young student. He refers to it in a letter in 1811 and in this same letter we find the first rough draft of the book which was to appear in 1826 under the title, Forsøg til en videnskabelig dansk Retskrivningslære (An essay towards a Danish orthography on scientific principles). This book does not only contain Høysgaard's theory of accents but, with the exception of the historical sections, it is written entirely in Høysgaard's spirit. As a young student, Lyngby became acquainted with both Rask's orthography and Høysgaard's accentuated grammar and from these works he received a crucial incentive. Not only did he adopt Høysgaard's theory of accents but he also compiled his excellent phonetic system for the Jutland dialect in Høysgaard's spirit.

The third beadle of the university has had his disciples then. He bequeathed his accent system to his two kindred spirits in later generations and, by setting them an example, he gave them the courage to follow their inclinations and the inspiration to make new discoveries.

Of the three men, Rask was the greatest and the most all-embracing but it was perhaps Høysgaard who had the most original genius; he it was who was the first of the three, the giver of the impulse.

In the second orthographical specimen we can see how he nervously and hesitantly came forward with his new discoveries and the radical reform proposals that resulted from these. We can see how he tried to protect himself by hiding behind a show of clowning. And we can see how, when he is presenting his actual discoveries and describing the practical advantages of the reform proposals, he lets himself be carried away by his anxiety to present his arguments in a clear and convincing manner and by his simple joy in communicating to others his own understanding of the genius of the Danish language.

50

NOTES

1 A lecture given at the University of Copenhagen on the 13th November 1952.
2 Danske Grammatikere, ed. Henrik Bertelsen, V 512.
3. Jens Pedersen Høysgaard 65 ff.
4 Jens Pedersen Høysgaard 70 ff.
5 "Register og Forklaringer" to Syntaxens kunstord, in Danske Grammatikere V 452 ff
6 Aldmindelige Danske Ordsproge og korte Lærdomme (1682) no. 7103: Oord og penge skulle være gængse.
7 In Udvalgte Skrifter 547.

The language of the people
of Tønder through the ages

I.

The small town of Tønder in west Slesvig is named for the first time c. 1130, when it is referred to as a port on the Vidå, and its first church, which has now disappeared, would seem to have been built about this time. In the middle of the 13th century the town was enlarged and re-aligned on the model of Lübeck and at the same time the municipal law of Lübeck, which had been taken over unchanged, was confirmed to the town by Duke Abel[1].

In the medieval period the town was known by the Danish name Litle Tunder, in distinction from Mykæltunder (1288), the large village to the west which is now known as Møgeltønder. This fact suggests that the first inhabitants of Tønder came from this Danish-speaking village, in the same way as the first inhabitants of the town of Haderslev in east Slesvig came from the neighbouring village which is now known as Gammel-Haderslev. Most scholars have assumed, therefore, that the language spoken in Tønder must have been Danish from the very beginning[2]. Tønder, however, is situated only about 10 km to the north of the northern frontier of the territory of the North Frisians and a few scholars, therefore, consider that the original language of Tønder must have been Frisian[3]. Finally, one scholar considered that the first inhabitants of the town must have spoken both Danish and Low German, assuming that the expansion of the town and the confirmation of the law of Lübeck must have taken place in connection with German colonisation[4].

It is impossible to prove the correctness of any one of these three hypotheses. The only evidence available is that provided by personal names and place-names and this will only allow us to make some reasonably well-founded conjectures.

It is not to be expected that the *personal names* borne by the inhabitants of Tønder will be able to give us much information about their everyday language. Personal names are among the least stable elements in any language. They are very frequently borrowed from one language into another. It is impossible, therefore, to determine the language spoken by a man or by his parents on the basis of his personal name alone. Most present-day Danes, for example, bear names of foreign origin.

Further, only very few personal names from Tønder survive from the early part of the medieval period. From the time before 1450 there are only 24 names[5]. Nine of them must be left out of account, as being doubtful, either because they can equally well be Low German or Frisian as Danish (Petrus Fisker, Jo.[6] Blek, Petrus Bron, Johannes Smyd) or because forename and surname point in different directions (Boyk Niclesson has a LG forename and a Danish surname, Boo Lythyk has a Danish forename and a LG surname, Nis, Eryk and Johannes Culige would seem to have a LG surname but their forenames are more likely to be Danish than LG. Of the remaining 15 names, 2 are certainly LG, namely Hennik Foghelkin (i.e. "little bird") and Johannes Scroder (i.e. "tailor"), one probably Frisian, namely Gunno Friis, and one either LG or Frisian, namely Feddir Sutor. Of the remaining 11 names, the following 9 are certainly Danish: Tuky Niclesson, Tochy Wughensson, Petrus Olyfson, Lasse Jensson, Petrus Ivarssen, Bo[7] Sutor (the by-name has been translated into Latin; it means "shoemaker"), Boetius Baker, Nicholaus Humblehave, Jo. Niclesson. There remain 2 names. Oluf Nanenson has a Danish forename and a patronymic surname formed in Danish fashion from the name Nanne, which was originally Frisian but had already become quite common in Denmark. Finally, Bege Nichelsson has an originally LG forename (Beke) in a Danish form (with g for

k) and a Danish surname. It is, of course, impossible to reach any definite conclusions on the basis of these names alone. We cannot be certain that Johannes Scroder's mother-tongue was LG and Toke Vognssøn's Danish. Besides, the names that have survived are too few and scattered. It is only possible to say that these 2-3 LG names, 1-2 Frisian ones and 11 Danish ones can most easily be explained if it is assumed that the nomenclature in Tønder in the first part of the medieval period was predominantly Danish. The names do, however, make it possible to assert that the hypothesis about a colonisation from Lübeck is not very likely.

The *place-names*, in this case particularly street names and field-names, can give us more information. Unlike the personal names, these names must have had a meaning at the time of their formation. They were the result not of chance selection but of deliberate construction. They are rooted in the ordinary vocabulary of the language and only gradually became fossilised as conventional appellations. It is, therefore, safe to say that the language from whose vocabulary they are formed must have been the mother tongue of the inhabitants at the time of the creation of the names.

The name Tønder itself gives us no definite information. It did not begin as the name of the town but as that of the neighbouring village now known as Møgeltønder. In the old sources the town is referred to as Litlætunder. This name contains the ODan adj. litæl "little", while Mykæltunder contains ODan mykæl "great". This does not in itself, however, enable us to say that the inhabitants of the town were Danish-speaking at the time of its foundation. The philologist P.K. Thorsen has made one of those true remarks which, once spoken, seem so obvious: The name of a settlement is not created by its own inhabitants but by the neighbours. It will therefore be necessary for us to turn our attention to such names as can be assumed to have been given by the inhabitants themselves, i.e. street names and field-names.

There are, however, problems connected with the study of these names. The cadastres and accounts containing the early forms of the names were all written in LG, while their modern pronunciation has been recorded from the present-day Danish-speaking inhabitants. In the majority of cases the difference between the German written forms and the Danish pronunciations is so great that translation must have taken place, either from Danish to German in the written sources or from German to Danish in the spoken forms. A tax-list from

1721 contains the forms Hinter den Ställen and Mühlenweg, while the present pronunciation is [ɛ bax ɛ ˈsdɔl:] and [ɛ ˈmoel: ˌvaɪ]. How can it be determined whether such names were originally Danish or German?

We have evidence from other parts of Slesvig that street and field-names could be wholly or partly translated. It has been shown, however, that translation of this kind only takes place when certain conditions are fulfilled. The second element of a name is only translated if its meaning is well known and if it can be translated by a word having the same meaning. More or less the same is true of the first elements. A few examples will be quoted from the town of Haderslev, where it is obvious that the translations have been made from Danish into German: The Danish word *naf* is not translated, presumably because the scribes did not know what it meant; the Danish words *toft* and *kær* are not translated either, obviously because there is no exact equivalent to these words in German. This is why a form such as Goskier can be found in a German source from 1564. On the other hand, first elements such as Sønder- "south", Nørre- "north", Øster- "east", Vester- "west", Høj- "high", Law- "low", Præst- "priest", Slot- "castle", and second elements such as -bro "bridge", -gade "street", -mark "field" are all translated into German. A place which appears as Sønderbro in a Danish source from 1635 is referred to as Süder Brücke in a High German source from 1745; i slotte gade in a Danish source from 1517 becomes in der Slotstrate in a LG source from the same year, and both in der Schloßgaßen and in der Schloßstraßen in a High German source from 1679.

If we now turn to the old street names in Tønder, we shall soon see that they all belong to the type that is translatable: e.g. LG sources have the following names, 1543 by der Lutken bruggen, 1607 Suderbrugge, Suderport, Westerbrugge, and 1670 Wester-Straeße and Oester-Straeß[8]. Names such as these can tell us nothing about the language spoken in Tønder. They can have been given by a Danish-speaking population but for proof of this it is necessary to look elsewhere.

We are more fortunately placed with respect to the field-names. Attention will be confined here to those names which are recorded before 1600 and no account will be taken of the lands which were annexed to the town at the end of the Middle Ages or later. Danish names for these lands may derive from the period before their annexation and hence have been given by the farmers from neighbouring villages. This leaves us with 29 names. 10 of these have to be left out of account, either because their etymologies are doubtful or because they can equally well be Danish or LG. They are cited here in the 16th-century LG scribal form[9] : Abelwatt, Bremeßholm, Kniep, Langschiffte, Lusborch, Madenschift, Ockholm, Schmedefenne [ɛ 'smaɪ : fɛn], Swinholm, Swinwatt. Words such as fenne "fen", holm "island", made "meadow", skifte (Schift) "section of a field", and vad (Watt) "ford" are found in both Danish and LG. In addition there are 6 names of the translatable type: Hogefeld, Osterwisch, Niefeld (also written Niemark), de 6 Sweed, de 7 Sweed, de 9 Sweed. These names may well be translations of the familiar Danish field-names of transparent meaning: Højmark, Østereng, Nymark. Sexskår, Syvskår, Niskår, but they are not necessarily so. The first two names have not been recorded with Danish pronunciations but the other four names are pronounced [ɛ 'nymarɣ̊ə], [saissɣ̊a], [ɛ 'syusɣ̊a] and ['niːsɣ̊a].

The remaining 13 names cannot be translations. 11 of them are Danish. 5 of them have second elements which can only be Danish, while the first elements could be either Danish or German: Aschesodd (second el. Dan od "point", first el. perhaps the ODan pers.n. Asgut, which was quite common in Slesvig in the Middle Ages), Bartelskjer (second el. Dan kær "marsh, water meadow", first el. the pers.n. Bertel in LG form), Langeng (second el. Dan eng "meadow"), Prestertoft [ɛ 'pʀɛːsdtaut] (second el. Dan toft "building plot, croft", Stakstoft (second el. Dan toft, first el. uncertain). 5 names have first els. which can only be Danish, while their second els. (fenne, hem "enclosure, meadow", holm) can be Danish, LG or Frisian: Exholm (the Dan gen. of the tree name eg "oak"; an originally German *Ekholm would have been translated as Egholm not Egsholm), Jegge Holm (the tree name eg in a form which appears in numerous field-names in Slesvig), Horßfennen (the Dan animal name hors "horse" or "mare"), Owßhem (the animal name okse "ox" in the common Dan dialect pronunciation), Spangholm (first el. the Dan subst. spang "plank across a stream"). In one name both first and second els. may be Danish, namely Stupkarr ['sdoˀbkəɹ] (first el. the Dan subst. stub "stump"; great tree stumps have been found here; second el. Dan kær with LG pronunciation). Of the two remaining names, one has a Danish second el. and a LG first el., des hilligen Crutzes Toft, and in the other name both els. are LG, des hilligen Crutzes Wisch [klɛuɔs'visg̊]; (the LG subst. Krüz means "cross" but is also used of the card suit "clubs", which is called [klɛuɔ] in Tønder Danish; the Danish pronunciation thus represents an incorrect translation from LG. Both des hilligen Crutzes Toft and des hilligen Crutzes Wisch were ecclesiastical property and the rents for them were paid to the church of St Nicholas. It can be assumed that before the Reformation the lands belonged to the altar of the Holy Cross in this church. These two names are peculiar in that their first element denotes an ecclesiastical concept, the Holy Cross. In that part of Slesvig where German was the language of the church after the Reformation, it is only the most common ecclesiastical concepts that have Danish names, e.g. kirke "church", præst "priest", degn "parish clerk"; the remaining terms are German, e.g. Abendmal, Gebot, Segen, Vaterunser, Heiliggeist. These terms were used even by Danish-speaking people. Tønder is situated in the part of Slesvig where such German ecclesiastical terms were current. It would be impossible, therefore, for a man from Tønder to express in Danish what had been written in German by the keeper of the church accounts, namely that the meadow and the toft belonged, or had previously belonged, to the altar of the Holy Cross. These names, then, would have to be German, or partly German, even if the daily language of the people were Danish. On the other hand, it is not possible to explain the existence of the 11 names which are certainly Danish, if it is assumed that the townspeople were German-speaking.

Ludwig Andresen, who does not deny that the majority of the field-names are Danish, nevertheless attempts to provide such an explanation: some of the field-names are older than the town of Tønder itself and must thus have been given by Danes from the surrounding villages. It is not very likely, however, that the field--names are as old as that. On the contrary, several of the names clearly reflect the bond between the lands in question and the inhabitants of Tønder. We know that the townspeople had arable land in Langager and Tværager, that they had pasture land in Maderne and that they gathered in hay from Sexskår, Syvskår and Niskår (skår means "the breadth of the stroke of the scythe"), and that their pigs were let loose in Svinvad and Svinholm (to where the driving of pigs was prohibited in 1569); it would be unreasonable to deny that the names borne by these places derive from the use to which they were put. Even though the inhabitants of the town kept their cows in the Horsfenner in 1542, we can rest assured that at an earlier date they must have put their cows out to grass in Owshem and their horses in Horsfenner. Finally, Stakstoft and Præstetoft, which are situated near to the town, must have been excluded from the open--field system and they, too, must have been given their names by. the townspeople.

The examination of the oldest field-names in Tønder, which were recorded in the period between 1533 and 1594, leads to the following likely conclusions: 1. The names were given by Danish-speaking people. 2. These people lived in Tønder. It is therefore probable that the mother-tongue of the men of Tønder was Danish at the time when these names were created.

II.

Danish was, however, only the spoken language in Tønder. In the early part of the medieval period the only written language was Latin and when the dominance of Latin was finally broken about 1400, its place was taken by LG. In the 16th century the Latin municipal law was translated into LG. Right up into the 17th century the Court Records continued to be written in LG, as did all accounts, contracts etc. The first documents in Danish from Tønder are from the period after the conclusion of the 1848-51 war. The question now is whether the predominance of LG in written sources means that the inhabitants of Tønder could speak and understand LG in the period between c. 1400 and c. 1670.

Many scholars have been inclined to answer this question in the negative[10]. Claus Eskildsen wrote about the language of Tønder as follows: "The citizens came together once a year to hear the laws read out in German. Most of them probably understood about as much of this as their forefathers had done of a Latin Mass"[11].

This opinion is untenable, however. In more recent years a good deal of weighty evidence has been presented, notably by the two local historians Ludw. Andresen and Th. Achelis, in support of the theory that the ability to understand and speak LG was very wide-spread in the towns of north Slesvig in the 16th and 17th centuries[12].

Firstly, the inhabitants of Tønder attempted to resist the replacement of LG by High German as the language of the church. The priest Richard Bennichius began to preach in High German about 1630 but the mayor and council requested him to employ "die Sechsische Sprache" (i.e. LG), which would be more easily understood by "these simple parishioners", in order that the congregation "could understand and profit from the preaching of the divine word". The priest bowed to their request and it was not until 1652, that is at a comparatively late date, that LG was replaced by High German as the language of the church. The mere fact that the parishioners could understand LG better than High German is not in itself a sufficient guarantee that their knowledge of LG was particularly sound. It shows, however, that the men of Tønder in the 17th century understood the services in LG better than their forefathers had understood the services in Latin.

Secondly, three of the field-names are LG. The two oldest of these, des hilligen Crutzes Toft and des hilligen Crutzes Wisch, have been discussed above. The German first element in these names could be explained by the ecclesiastical connotation. This explanation does not, however, apply to the third and youngest name, Bleekswisch, which is pronounced ['blɛxviʃ], showing that the LG el. has not been translated. It is the name of one of the town's bleaching-places and is first recorded in 1693. Two older bleaching-places have Danish names (Synnerbleeg and Jøsterbleeg). Ludwig Andresen refers to many other field-names in his attempt to demonstrate that "the German section of the population" played as large a part in name--giving as did the Danish one. All these other names, however, can equally well be Danish as German. The vast majority of the field--names, then, old ones and young ones alike, are Danish. The three German names, however, are irrefutable evidence that the inhabitants of Tønder were familiar with LG.

Thirdly, the transition from LG to High German as the language employed in such registers and documents as were designed for, or written by, the ordinary citizens, e.g. guild enrolments, letters, bills, took place at a very late date. The mayor and council had composed a petition to the Duke in quite reasonable High German as early as 1587 but the accounts of the town continued to be kept in LG until 1672. The Town Court Records changed to High German in 1612 but the evidence of witnesses is sometimes recorded in LG as late as the 1670s. This suggests that some of the townspeople spoke LG and not Danish when they gave evidence before the Court.

Th. Achelis has drawn attention to a similar state of affairs in Haderslev[13], where the language in the Court Reports alternates between Danish and German. Here, too, the evidence of witnesses is sometimes recorded in LG in reports that are otherwise written in High German. Sometimes the questions that were put to the witnesses are also recorded in LG. That witnesses took the oath in German is revealed by the fact that in 1718 Kirsten Hansdatter from Århus was given express permission to take the oath in Danish "weilen sie der Teutschen nicht kündig".

It is therefore necessary to accept that the inhabitants of the towns of north Slesvig were to a great extent able not only to understand LG but also to speak it. This is even more true of Tønder than of Haderslev, Åbenrå and Sønderborg.

It is not strange that the people of Tønder should have gone in for LG. In this period they saw LG as the language of religion and culture. As a language of religion, Danish only played a very minor role in the form of the Danish sermons preached at Matins. These sermons were probably held first and foremost for the benefit of the parishioners of the rural parish. It would presumably only be the very poorest inhabitants of the town itself who would attend the Danish services. An account survives from a rather later period[14] of how the Danish services in Flensborg and the other towns in north Slesvig were held "for the sake of the many Danes, most of whom are to be found in the servant class" (by "Danes" is meant people from the kingdom of Denmark). Even at the Danish services in Tønder, hymns continued to be sung in German until Christmas 1732, when Hans Adolf Brorson published his first collection of hymns. – The majority of the townspeople, however, and in particular those of the highest standing, must have attended the German services, at which the sermon, too, was preached in LG. The result must have been that very few of the men of Tønder would be likely to express any thoughts about religion in Danish. For them the language of the Bible and the Prayer Book was LG. This was the only language which was thought to be sufficiently sublime and dignified for religion. – A contributory cause to the adoption of LG as the language of literary culture may have been the fact that the Duke of Gottorp occasionally resided at Tønder Castle. The most important reason, however, was the pre-eminent position enjoyed by the LG centres of culture. Of the 81 men from Tønder who had had a university education (mainly in theology) up to 1627, more than half had studied in Rostock and none in Copenhagen.

A knowledge of LG was also, however, a practical necessity for the people of Tønder. We have already seen how the language of the administration and the courts was LG. The same was true to a great extent of the language of trade. Practically all the commercial links of Tønder were with LG or Dutch towns. It was not only the students who travelled south. Young men seeking training in trade and commerce would always go south and never north. It is understandable, therefore, that when the town's grammar school was joined by an elementary school, the teaching there, too, had to be in German, even though the children were Danish-speaking. It was desirable for the children to learn German at as early an age as possible. The first elementary school of which we have any record did admittedly use Danish in teaching. In 1614 the town council granted permission to Johann Ketelsen to teach writing and arithmetic to as many as 10 boys through the medium of Danish, on condition that the boys did not give offence in the church or elsewhere. This experiment was a failure, however, and in 1616 a German school was opened, where the subjects taught were the reading and writing of German, and arithmetic. This school was a success.

It has earlier been thought that there had been a great deal of immigration from the south to the towns in the north of Slesvig. More recent studies, however, have shown that on the contrary this immigration was very limited[15]. The only reason for LG's obtaining such a predominant position is the fact that not only cultural development but also worldly progress must have seemed to be available only to those who mastered this language.

The question now is whether the familiarity of the townspeople with the LG language meant that they used it to a great extent as their normal spoken language in this period. Ludw. Andresen, who is very well informed about life in the frontier town, asserts in his book about Tønder (p. 258) that the townspeople must have been bilingual as early as the 16th century (or even earlier): "Everyone, including the common man, was obliged to be bilingual, both on work-days and particularly on holy days". Even though there is a certain amount of exaggeration in this claim, there can be no doubt that Andresen is right in principle: For the fifty years preceding and the fifty years following 1600, the period when the influence of the LG language on the towns of Slesvig was at its zenith, a very considerable proportion of the people of Tønder must have been bilingual. The question is, however, whether LG was only the language of culture and trade, or whether it had also come into use as a normal language of daily life among the native inhabitants of the town. Ludwig Andresen would seem to think that the latter was the case.

"LG was definitely spoken beside the Danish dialect and, what is more, LG was the more commonly used of the two languages"[16].

The most satisfactory attempt to prove that LG was in common use in the towns of north Slesvig at that time has been made by Th. Achelis[17]. The court reports occasionally contain some words in LG even in cases which are otherwise reported entirely in High German. Normally these LG words are a rendering of the threats or abusive words uttered by the accused, as when Sunnicke Petersen from Haderslev in 1611 threw Christian Brink out of the pew which they shared with the words: Stah buten edder ich schlae dy up de Schnuten (Stop outside or I'll hit you on the snout). There is one instance of an insult which may be Danish: Kanaille und Keltring Pack (rabble and pack of scoundrels). On a few occasions an exchange of words is reported with High German and LG alternating with one another; in 1635 Nis Eriksen from Haderslev took the liberty of saying to his fellow townsman Jes Ravn: Ich bin so gut alß du bist (High German. I am quite as good as you are), while Jes Ravn retorted: Neen du bist ein horen sön (LG. No, you are a son of a whore). Th. Achelis continues: "It is exactly this alternation of LG and High German which seems to me to prove that the report is a word for word rendering of what was said and not a translation from Danish".

It is not inconceivable that in the course of the 16th century LG was beginning to come into use as the daily language of the people of Tønder but we can know nothing definite about this. If that were the case, the LG spoken language would probably only gradually have been replaced by High German – in Flensborg LG is still the most common spoken language. Information about the following period, however, is so meagre that we do not know with certainty how long LG continued to be spoken in Tønder. Most topographers only talk about German and Danish and they do not generally distinguish between High German and LG. Besides, many of them are not reliable observers of linguistic matters.

On the other hand we do know for certain that the majority of the townspeople could both understand and speak LG. There remains a third question: Was LG ever spoken in the home in Tønder? In other words: Was a genuine change of language beginning to take place at this period, with the most wealthy merchants of the town starting to bring up their children in LG in order to equip them as well as possible for the future and give them the best possible educational opportunities?

This question is more important than the two preceding ones. The decisive phase in the centuries-long process which is known as a change of language sets in when the most educated section of the population begins to bring up its children in the foreign language. The inhabitants of those parts of central Slesvig where a change of language is at present in process emphasise that this phase is the decisive one when they make a distinction between people who have been "brought up German" and those who have been "brought up Danish". Both groups may well be bilingual, for they can have taught themselves the second language. Generally, however, their knowledge of the acquired language will be more or less imperfect, often in spite of years of practice. The reason must be that childhood is the age at which the ability to learn a language is greatest. This is why the language of the home is of such significance.

We are fortunate in having some very reliable information about the language of a patrician family from Tønder in the 16th century. It derives from one of the most renowned sons of Tønder, namely Jacob Fabricius, born 1560, died 1640 as superintendent (bishop) in Slesvig. His father, the merchant and surveyor Jacob Schmidt, was born in Tønder as the son of one of the most respected merchants in the town. His mother was also born in Tønder. She was the daughter of Alderman Jannick Heichsen and his wife Marine, daughter of the mayor, Olde Ditmer. Jacob Fabricius's childhood home, was, then, one of the most distinguished in the town.

When Jacob was five years old, his father was appointed County Clerk and customs officer in Rendsburg in Holsten. In his MS auto-biography[18] Jacob Fabricius relates how his mother travelled to his father in Rendsburg to deliver some household equipment and the boy Jacob, whom the father wanted to have with him. When it was time for her to leave her son to travel back to Tønder to fetch the other children and the rest of the furniture, she had to send the boy away on a fool's errand in order to get him to stop with his father. "Mother's carriage was brought to my late father's door; they spoke to me with fair words and assured me that I should be going home with her and sent me to Elsebe's house (where mother had been lodging) to fetch something that mother was supposed to have forgotten there. It was without doubt a put-up job ("ein vnterbawetes werck"). I did not know a word of German ("kein wort teutsch"). I stood there and gravely asked for the object for which I had been sent. They pretended not to understand me. In the meantime, mother drove out of the gates, leaving me behind watching miserably and weeping as she disappeared from sight". Four years later, in 1569, his father died and in 1571 his mother returned to Tønder with the boy, who was now 11 years old. Here new language difficulties arose: "When I arrived in Rendsburg, I had been unable to speak a word of German with the exception of prayers and hymns. Now that I had come back to Tønder, I could not speak a single word of Danish and I have never been able to learn Danish properly again, with the result that they called me German Jacob ("also das sie mich nenneten den deutschen Jacob") and later at school my countrymen thought it amusing to ask me to speak Danish, for I made a dreadful mess of it until anno 1581-82, when I had to practise preaching in Danish, since I was expecting to be called to preach Danish sermons, as in fact happened in 1586. (In 1586 Jacob Fabricius was appointed deacon and Danish preacher in Tønder).

From these vivid recollections we learn two important facts about the language of Tønder. 1. In 1565 the five-year-old son of an old patrician Tønder family could not speak German but had learnt some German prayers and hymns. 2. In 1571 an eleven-year-old boy who could not speak Danish properly was given the nickname German Jacob by the boys of Tønder. From these we may conclude that the normal language of the home, even in high-ranking families, was Danish at that time[19].

It would seem, then, that the state of affairs with regard to language in Tønder about the year 1600 was as follows: The written language, the language of the church, the courts and the administration, the language of cultural and commercial intercourse was LG. The only exception was the morning service in Danish. Most adults were able to understand and speak LG; the normal language of adult conversation was Danish and perhaps also LG; the home language of the native inhabitants of Tønder, rich and poor alike, was Danish. It is only by assuming this kind of bilingualism that the various fragments of information that have been discussed up to now can be combined to form a whole. It will be seen that the townspeople retained LG as the language of the church, that they spoke Low German when giving evidence in court, that they wrote their bills in LG, that Jacob Fabricius's father in Rendsburg was able to teach the boy LG so that he could come into contact with his new surroundings, that the 5-year-old boy only spoke Danish and had not learnt any German with the exception of prayers and hymns, and that the schoolboy who could not speak Danish was given the nickname German Jacob.

III.

This bilingualism is in itself a lesser danger to the mother-tongue than many people are inclined to believe. "Our own language that we have spoken from childhood, that I'll never forget," said an old woman in Tønder to Marius Kristensen, when he was studying the Danish dialect there in 1931. It is the mother-tongue that teaches the child to think; however well we manage to learn a foreign language, we can never quite avoid finding ourselves in a situation where we need to express a thought for which only our mother-tongue has a word. The language of culture can be more flexible and richer and superior to the mother-tongue in many respects but whenever the conversation turns to the simple things of life in the house and at work, it often lacks the accuracy of the mother-tongue. Parents will always find it most natural to speak their mother-tongue to their children. That is why the Danish mother-tongue of the people of Tønder survived, while Latin was replaced as the written language by LG and this in turn by High German.

It has often been asserted by the Germans that the position of the Danish language was improved when High German supplanted LG as the written language. It is difficult to say whether or not this was the case in Tønder, for our information about the succeeding period is very poor. The general impression is, however, that there was no particular change in the following century.

It is tempting to see the fact that in 1729 better conditions were obtained for the Danish-speaking parishioners as evidence of the progress of the Danish language. In that year Hans Adolf Brorson was appointed Danish third priest and at Christmas 1732 his first collection of Danish hymns was published. These were the first Danish hymns to be sung in Tønder church and Brorson's book was the first Danish book to be printed in Tønder.

Our information about the following century derives almost exclusively from foreign observers and does not perhaps give a completely reliable impression of the opinion of the inhabitants themselves. In 1752 the German geographer A.F. Büsching wrote[20] that in Flensborg and Tønder people spoke "a mixed language of Danish and German" but in Haderslev, Åbenrå and Sønderborg "pur Dänisch". By "mixed language" he may perhaps have meant — in agreement with contemporary theories about special "mixed languages" — a Slesvig dialect (Sønderjysk) containing many German loan-words, by "pur Dänisch" perhaps a Slesvig dialect containing fewer loan-words. Martin Richard Flor, assistant priest in Tønder, had little respect for the Danish dialect. In 1758 he writes: "It is no longer the custom as it was earlier to speak Frisian but instead German and to an even greater extent Danish. Most of the inhabitants speak both languages but their Danish is, according to the judgment and taste of experts, only inferior and rather corrupt ("nach der Kenner Urtheil und Geschmack nur schlect und ziemlich verdorben")[21].

The impression gained from reading these more or less reliable accounts, however, is that German can only have played an insignificant role as a spoken language in Tønder in the course of the 18th century. This impression is confirmed by the only native of Tønder whose opinion we know, namely Balthasar Petersen, the founder of the Training College, who describes Tønder succinctly as "this Danish place"[22].

During the first half of the 19th century this situation seems to have continued more or less unchanged. In 1814 the report submitted by the mayor and council to the Government[23] states that the language of polite society is High German but the language of the people is "ein korrumpiertes Dänisch, ein Gemisch aus dem Dänischen, Deutschen und zum Teil aus dem Friesischen". In 1835 Dean Ahlmann states[23] that a quite considerable section of the population only knows Danish. In the same year a teacher from Meldorf applied for permission to establish a Training College in Holsten. Among his reasons he includes the fact that many of the students from Holsten at the college in Tønder were obliged to make use of interpreters in order to be able to communicate with their landladies[23]. In 1840 H.N.A. Jensen, who knew a great deal about the history and topography of Slesvig, stated that the Danish language was dominant in daily life, in spite of the fact that the teaching at school was in German[24].

In 1851 it was decided that German should be the language of the church, the courts and the administration in Tønder, while Danish should be used for teaching in schools. This arrangement was met with a great deal of displeasure by the majority of the townspeople, who particularly desired to keep High German as the language of teaching. In the Assembly of the Estates a merchant called Green from Tønder stated the reasons for this wish: "It was correct that the language of daily life was in part Danish but apart from this German was very necessary for the forwarding of the material and spiritual interests of the town. As far as trade was concerned, Tønder was linked most closely to the South — the education of the people was based on the German language and German was the language of the educated people — cultural and material relationships were German and the German language was therefore unavoidably necessary for them and it was the sincerest wish of the parents that their children should be educated in German[25].

Green had no interest in emphasising unduly the Danish of Tønder. His expression "in part Danish" must, therefore, be reckoned as the weakest one he could use. At that time Danish was the mother-tongue of the vast majority of the people of Tønder. The philologist K.J. Lyngby, who admittedly only spent a few days in Tønder but who was a keen observer, wrote in 1857: "After I had arrived in Tønder, I walked through the streets and felt depressed at seeing the houses with their gables to the street in German fashion. It turned out, however, that Danish was spoken at the Inn where I was staying. And little by little it was revealed to me that the town was completely Danish in language, although it attempted to look German on the surface. Theatre posters were in German because otherwise "the Germans" would not attend the performances"[26].

This information also reveals, however, that the majority of the townspeople were not well-disposed towards the Danish written language and remained faithful to German. They reacted strongly against the unwise decree of 1851, which was based on a fatal underestimation of the preference of the bilingual population for High German, the language of culture. From the year 1861 we have a reliable statement from an unbiassed native of Tønder, namely C.E. Carstens, who was assistent priest at the time. In his book Die Stadt Tondern we read p. 60: "In daily life it is the Danish language which is dominant, in a peculiar dialect much mixed with German words" and p. 62: "In some homes German is also spoken, in several with the children at least". This last sentence contains the very significant piece of information that some Danish-speaking parents were beginning to bring up their children in German; that is to say that a start had been made on a change of language even before 1864, while the language of teaching was still Danish. The reason must be partly a feeling of contempt for the Danish dialect, and partly the fact that the townspeople, who were well-disposed to Slesvig-Holsten, were resentful and defiant of the Danish policy with respect to language.

That the Prussian government did not wait long after 1864 before repeating the error of the Danish government but with the opposite intention and on a far larger scale had little effect in Tønder because this time the attack was directed at a language of culture which meant very little to the townspeople. On the contrary, the majority of the population rejoiced when German once again became the language of the schools in 1864. In the following decades the position of German was gradually strengthened.

According to the Prussian census of 1889, out of 416 burgher families, 181 spoke High German, 13 Danish and 222 both languages[27]. H.V. Clausen has criticised these figures, particularly the distribution between the bilingual families and the Danish-speaking ones, and pointed out that it is unfortunate that the census only includes the burghers, that is the wealthiest half of the population[28]. That High German was winning ground in leaps and bounds, however, is incontrovertible. Adler says, "Whereas the young people spoke Danish on the streets before 1864, now they can almost only be heard speaking German. . . . Incidentally, most burgher families in Tønder master both languages. LG, on the other hand, is seldom heard. In very many of the families in which the parents speak Danish together and when talking to third parties, High German is spoken with the children — only in rare cases LG. Adler's words agree only too well with H.V. Clausen's observation: "While the boys on the streets in Åbenrå, Haderslev, Sønderborg, Gråsten etc. speak Danish, the boys of Tønder speak German. And the case with the girls is even worse". However cautiously we judge Adler's information, we cannot deny that a change of language was in progress: Many Danish-speaking parents were bringing their children up in German.

The result of the next language census from 1905 cannot be directly compared with the result of that from 1889, partly because in 1905 the statistics included the whole population of the town and partly because it is now individuals who are counted and not families as in 1889. This is one of the reasons why it is difficult to judge whether there had been a significant deterioration in the course of the 16 years. According to the 1905 figures, almost three quarters of the 4,244 inhabitants of Tønder spoke German (2,954) and over a quarter Danish (1,117), while 116 spoke "another language" (105 of these Frisian) and only 57 "German and another language"[29]. It is not easy, however, to get people to give correct answers to linguistic-statistical surveys while a conflict between the two nationalities in question is in progress. The vast majority of the people of Tønder were pro-German and some of them may, for that reason, have been tempted to keep quiet about the fact that they spoke Danish at home. It is at any rate obvious that the number of bilingual speakers must have been much greater than 57. More significant than these total figures are, however, the figures which confine themselves to the languages spoken by children. August Sach gives the following information about the language spoken by children in the municipal schools in 1906: 308 spoke only German, 76 both German and Danish, 154 only Danish[30]. These figures make a more reliable impression than those of Adler but even in this case the number of bilingual speakers must have been greater than stated.

In spite of the imperfections of the German language statistics, however, there can be no doubt that the Danish mother-tongue of the people of Tønder was now in serious danger for the first time in the history of the town.

A change of language is a slow process, however, and it is not brought to completion within a mere half century. The Prussian administration could encourage the change of language but it was not in a position to oust the Danish language from Tønder.

There are no language statistics from the period after the reunion of North Slesvig with Denmark in 1920. There is every indication, however, that the retreat of the Danish language had not only been stopped but also replaced by a marked advance. According to information from a very knowledgeable man, Danish now predominates over German among schoolchildren. The pupils in the Danish school, almost all of whom come from Danish-speaking homes, all speak Danish in the playground. The pupils in the German burgher school, almost all of whom come from German-speaking homes, all speak High German in the playground. Bilingualism is very common, particularly among the pupils of the German school. When Danish and German schoolchildren play together, which often happens, the language generally spoken is Danish. In 1943 there were 346 pupils in the Danish school and 200 in the German one. In 1921 the corresponding figures were 235 and 386.

The Danish dialect in Tønder is now under greater threat from standard spoken Danish than from High German. While the children from homes which speak standard Danish in Haderslev and Åbenrå learn the Slesvig dialect from their playmates, the situation in Tønder is rather the opposite, where the pupils of the Danish school almost all speak standard Danish in the playground. In the future the struggle will be more and more between standard Danish and High German, while the old dialect of Tønder will gradually be supplanted.

Attention can be drawn to two reasons in particular for the development that has taken place since the Reunion: 1. A Danish municipal school has been established beside the German burgher school. 2. Danish-speaking civil servants have replaced German ones.

It would be premature to believe that High German is now in the process of disappearing from the town of Tønder. Tønder is situated on the linguistic battle-field where Danish and German are still engaged in combat. That is the reason why bilingualism has been the most obvious linguistic characteristic of the town for centuries and is likely to continue so in the future. It is not, indeed, the aim of the Danish educational policy to drive out the German language. With the Reunion, compulsion was replaced by liberty and this has been fortunate for North Slesvig, not least for Tønder.

IV.

In conclusion we shall look a little more closely at the Danish dialect in Tønder, "det gammeldaws Tynneringer" as it is called by the townspeople, the language which, in spite of the scorn to which it has been subjected, has shown itself to be vital enough to survive for seven centuries, while the languages of culture have replaced each other in turn: Latin, Low German, High German, standard Danish.

We have already met some tentative descriptions of the Danish dialect of Tønder as "a mixed language with Danish and German elements" and as a "rather corrupt" language.

These attempts at characterisation already betray the marks of propaganda and amateurism. The conception of a "mixed language", which played such a large role in the agitation about Slesvig-Holsten, has been outmoded since the time of Rasmus Rask. Eiler Hagerup and K.J. Lyngby proved conclusively that the Slesvig dialects are Danish and this fact is no longer questioned by any serious scholar. There is, therefore, no reason for treating this particular question in any more detail. It will be sufficient to demonstrate briefly that the two elements which are essential for determining the origin of a dialect are both Danish in the dialect of Tønder. Firstly, all the inflexional endings. For example, the 3rd pers. sg. pres. of verbs ends in -er and not in -et or -t (Stand.Dan. "han finder", German "er findet", Tønder dialect "han finner"). Even German loan-words are given Danish endings (e.g. *de gefåller vos int* (German "es gefällt uns nicht" with the ending -t), *han vunnerer sæ* ("er wundert sich" with -t), *begge Pumpe: di · -sager* ("beide Pumpen versagen" with -en). The word Jungen· ! . been borrowed in the German pl. form. It had already not one but two pl. endings, namely first the adjectival pl. ending -en and on top of this the LG substantival pl. ending -s; the word could not be adopted into the Tønder dialect without receiving yet another pl. ending, however, the Danish -er: *I Jungenser, I skul ha Pryggel* ("You lads deserve a whipping"). Secondly, all the most essential words in the dialect are Danish, i.e. the words which are not normally borrowed from one language into another. Some Tønder examples are: *far* "father", *mor* "mother", *søster* "sister", *bror* "brother", *dætter* "daughter", *søn* "son", *van* "water", *eel* "fire", *træ* "tree, wood", *hoj* "head", *yh* "eye", *ør* "ear"; *gammel* "old", *ung* "young", *stor* "big", *lille* "little", *uun* "bad", *goj* "good"; *se* "see", *hør* "hear", *få* "get", *gå* "go, walk", *gør* "do, make", *ha* "have", *være* "be", *å* "and", *int* "not"; *jen, tu, tre* "one, two, three"; *æ* "I", *do* "thou", *han* "he", *hun* "she", *vi* "we", *I* "you", *di* "they"; *a* "of", *etter* "after", *fra* "from", *i* "in", *mæ* "with", *te* "to", *ve* "at, by".

The second allegation, namely that Tønder Danish was corrupt, must, although it is not clear exactly what is meant, be grounded in the belief that the dialects are derived from the standard language and hence can be considered as a kind of corrupt standard. This theory, too, is outmoded. K.J. Lyngby has demonstrated that the dialects must be juxtaposed with the standard language and not subordinated to it in regard to originality and that all the Danish dialects, on an equal footing with standard Danish, derive from Old Danish.

Tønder Danish is closely related to the other West Slesvig dialects.

Unlike East Slesvig it has the glottal stop in words such as *hus*
"house" and *gård* "farm". It has å or u in the pret. forms of certain
verbs where East Slesvig has a, e.g. in *æ vår* ("I was", ESlesvig *æ va*),
æ bun ("I tied", NESlesvig *æ band*). The pret. of certain verbs of the
weak conjugation ends in -et and not as in ESlesvig in -er; Stand.Dan
jeg snakkede "I talked" is in Tønder *æ snakket* and not *æ snakker*
Adjectives are not normally declined in gender, e.g. *æ van æ kool*
(Stand. *vandet er koldt* "the water is cold"). Only a few adjectives
such as *god* "good", *hård* "hard", *kold* "cold" have neuter forms in
certain positions, particularly after *det er* "it is": *De er int godt å
kom i dæn sin klæwwer* "it's not good to get into his clover" of a
hot-tempered and masterful person).

Within WSlesvig the Tønder dialect agrees in certain features with
the northern part, e.g. in that only a few verbs show mutation in the
pres. tense, namely *gå* "go", *få* "get", *slå* "hit", *stå* "stand", which
give *æ gær, æ fær, æ slær, æ stær* with *æ,* but e.g. *æ har* with *a.* In
other respects the dialect belongs to the southern part, e.g. in having
f and an unvoiced open g-sound (like High German ch) for ODan p
and k, e.g. in *æ sliffer* (Stand. *jeg sliber* "I grind"), *æ løffer* (Stand.
jeg løber "I run"), *et æfel* (Stand. *et æble* "an apple"), *æ skricher*
(Stand. *jeg skriger* "I scream"), *løchel* (Stand. *en nøgle* "a key"). The
northern boundary for this feature passes just north of Tønder.
Finally, Tønder belongs to a small WSlesvig area bounded by Tønder,
Højer, Rømø and Mjolden, where ODan dd becomes r, while to the
north it becomes j and to the south and east jt. In Tønder, then, "a
pike" (Stand. *en gedde*) is called *en gjerr,* and "I was born" (Stand.
jeg er født) is *æ æ förr.*

The Tønder dialect differs from the surrounding dialects on some
few minor points:

1. The people of Tønder, in common with those of Haderslev,
Åbenrå, Sønderborg and a few other places in ESlesvig, pronounce
r with the back of the tongue in contrast to most other Slesvigers,
who pronounce r with the front of the tongue.

2. In Tønder ej and aj are now pronounced identically, just as in
most of the towns of ESlesvig. *et sted* "a place" and *en stad* "a town"
are thus pronounced alike [sdaɪ].

3. In Tønder, as in the towns of ESlesvig, n and nd are pronounced
alike, whereas the two n-sounds are distinguished in the surrounding
dialects. Here they poke fun at the men of Tønder for saying *en
span van* for *en spand vand* "a bucket of water". In the same way l

and ld have coalesced so that *ulv* "wolf" and *uld* "wool" are pronounced alike in Tønder. This is the reason why the townspeople write Uldgade for Ulvgade and keep to the wrong spelling with an almost admirable loyalty.

The first of the above mentioned characteristics cannot be due to German influence. The two others can be the result of German influence but are not necessarily so. The following characteristics, however, can only be due to German influence.

4. There are many more LG and particularly High German loan-words in the Tønder dialect than in the Danish dialects of the surrounding areas. The LG loan-words are generally common to Tønder and central Slesvig; this is the case with words such as *kleenigkeit* "trifle", *urdeel* "to judge", *oppenhol* "stay, sojourn", and with the numerals that make up the most striking group of LG loan-words, namely the tens from 50 to 90: *føftig, søstig, søventig, tachentig, negentig*. These numerals are the most obvious reminder of the fact that the language of trade was once LG. From among the High German loan-words there is a group which belongs to ecclesiastical affairs, e.g. *almosen* "alms", *gebet* "prayer", *gebot* "commandment", *geduld* "patience", *forgi* "forgive", *Erløser* "Redeemer". There are many other loan-words, however, e.g. *behaupt* "assert", *fürchterlich* "frightful", *gesetz* "law", *gescheit* "clever", *gewöhnlich* "customary", *harmlos* "innocent", *smoksager* "jewellery", *wüst* "desolate, deserted", *überhaupt* "on the whole". At the time of the Reunion the language of Tønder was probably just as rich in High German loan-words as English is in French loan-words. Even by 1943, however, many of these words had been replaced by the corresponding Stand.Dan words. A train is now called *tåg*, whereas earlier it was *sog*. Earlier it was possible to hear a sentence such as: *Har I hør, te æ Sog er ræn a æ Geleise omm ve æ Anlåg?* (Have you heard that the train (der Zug) has run off the lines (die Geleise) over by the park (die Anlage). Now it would be *tåg* and *skinner* at least. On the other hand, the following sentence can never have been correct, even by the standards of Tønder Danish. It deserves to be quoted, however, because it illustrates the detached moderation of many Tønder people in matters of national politics: *Æ finner et sørgle, ven tu Minnesker å den sam Bildungsstufe aus politischen Gründen int kan forkeer* (I find it deplorable when two people of the same standard of education are unable to associate with each other (verkehren) for political reasons).

It is possible that the majority of the words in the Tønder dialect are of German origin but this is not the same as saying that the most essential part of the vocabulary is German. On the contrary, the essential words, the most common ones, are almost all Danish. When there is talk of complicated and specialised concepts such as Schmucksachen, behaupten and Bildungsstufe, the man of Tønder can be driven to thinking in the language of culture with which he is most familiar, but when the talk is of simple, everyday things, he thinks in Danish. He does not distinguish between the prepositions *an* and *bei* but only uses *ved*, and he is familiar with the distinction between *nævne* "name" and *kalde* "call", both of which are *nennen* for the German.

In a few instances, the Tønder dialect, in common with other Slesvig dialects, has retained an old word that has long since been lost from the written language. I shall conclude by citing a single example.

K.J. Lyngby relates in one of his letters how he discovered the ON verb *æpa* "to shout" in living use in Slesvig. It happened in a barber's shop in Tønder. Lyngby, upon whom, as we have heard, the town had at first made an impression of being German, and who had a feeling that barbers in particular were likely to be German, was not very happy at the thought of going in and addressing the barber in Danish. It might offend him and it can be an uncomfortable business to incur the enmity of one's barber. At last, however, he summoned up his courage and went in. The barber was out but his wife or daughter answered Lyngby's enquiry with the words: *Æ vel se, æ kan øf ham op, han gik jawn herfra* (I will see. I can call him. He's just gone out).

These simple and straightforward sentences are the first to have been recorded in genuine Tønder Danish. They are more typical of the dialect than the complicated sentence about the two people of the same standard of education and the language in them is pure Danish because they are expressing normal everyday concepts.

NOTES

1   Cf. Tønder gennem Tiderne, ed. M. Mackeprang (1943) 34.
2   E.g. Aug. Sach, Das Herzogtum Schleswig in seiner ethnographischen und nationalen Entwickelung III (1907) 308.
3   C.E. Carstens, Die Stadt Tondern (1861), Caspar Danckwert, Newe Landesbeschreibung (1652) 60, 85, Martin Richard Flor, MS in the Royal Library, Copenhagen, Thott 1797 4° (1758) §6, Erik Pontoppidan, Danske Atlas VII (1781) 276.
4   Ludwig Andresen, Geschichte der Stadt Tondern (1939) 4-15; and the same author in Zeitschrift (1936) 462.

5   Almost half of these are found in an undated entry on the first page of the municipal law. This can probably be dated to before 1450, while the forms taken by the names show that it must have been written after c. 1350. Ludwig Andresen's dating to c. 1300 (Bürger- und Einwohnerbuch der Stadt Tondern (1939) 158) cannot be correct.

6   Abbreviation for Johannes.

7   Bo is an originally Scand name that was not borrowed into North Frisian until the close of the Middle Ages.

8   Cf. DS V 1-7.

9   DS V 8-14; Ludwig Andresen's review in Zeitschrift (1936) 456-76; Ludwig Andresen op.cit. 105-08.

10 E.g. Marius Kristensen in Sproget gennem Tiderne (Sønderjyllands Historie I 77-78).

11 Schleswigs Boden und Volkstum (1938) 54.

12 Andresen in, e.g. Deutsches Archiv für Landes- und Volksforschung I (1937) 80; Achelis in his review of Sønderjyllands Historie I in Göttingische gelehrte Anzeigen (1933) 27-37.

13 In Göttingische gelehrte Anzeigen (1933) 30 f.

14 J.Fr. Hansen, Staatsbeschreibung des Herzogthums Schleswig (1758) 8.

15 Ludwig Andresen, Bürger- und Einwohnerbuch der Stadt Tondern (1939), Johan Hvidtfeldt, "Tønders Befolkning gennem Tiderne", in Tønder gennem Tiderne (1943) 399-439.

16 Geschichte der Stadt Tondern 256.

17 Göttingische gelehrte Anzeigen (1933) 30.

18 Royal Library Copenhagen, MS Thott 1928b 4°.

19 Ludw. Andresen, who is clearly unwilling to draw this conclusion, has tried pp. 179-80 to explain away Jacob Fabricius's account, in part by giving an incorrect summary of it (e.g. the nickname German Jacob is not mentioned).

20 In Kurzgefassete Staatsbeschreibung der Herzogthümer Holstein und Schleswig 104.

21 MS Thott 1797 4° in the Royal Library Copenhagen § 6. Hans de Hofman's remarks on the linguistic conditions in Tønder in Erik Pontoppidan's Danske Atlas VII (1781) 276 are essentially a reproduction of those of Flor.

22 In the charter from 1786: "Es kann auch an diesem dänischen Orte nicht mangeln, sich durch Besuchung der Frühpredigten in der dänischen Sprache zu üben; folglich können auch die, welche in der Marsch unter uns erzogen sind, und doch an einem dänischen Orte ihre Beförderung suchen, sich auch dazu bequem bereiten". (H. Eckert, Gründung und Entwickelung des Königl. evang. Schullehrer-Seminars in Tondern (1888) 8.

23 According to Aug. Sach, Das Herzogthum Schleswig III 314.

24 In Versuch einer kirchlichen Statistik des Herzogthums Schleswig 365.

25 Tidende for Forhandlingerne ved den syvende Provindsialstænderforsamling for Hertugdømmet Slesvig 1853 og 1854, cols. 650-51.

26 DSt (1939) 51-52.

27 J.G.C. Adler, "Die Volkssprache in dem Herzogthum Schleswig seit 1864", in Zeitschrift XXI (1891) 54-56.

28 In Sønderjydske Aarbøger (1933) 99.

29 G. Adler, "Die Volkssprache in dem vormaligen Herzogthum Schleswig auf Grund der Sprachenzählung vom 1. Dezember 1905", in Zeitschrift XLV 67.

30 Das Herzogthum Schleswig III (1907) 118.

The Danish-German linguistic frontier in the Middle Ages

About the year 1800 the southern boundary of the Danish dialects ran from Husum to Slesvig, leaving both towns to the south of the frontier, and then east of Slesvig and up the Sli to the Baltic. Since 1800 there has been a change of language in the area between this boundary and the present Danish-German frontier so that the inhabitants of almost the whole of this area now speak either Low German or High German. This change of language was, and is still, felt by most Danes as a distressful defeat and in the period up to 1864 enthusiastic efforts were made to ascertain its causes and try to remove them.

The nationalist historian C.F. Allen, in his great work The history of the Danish language in Slesvig I-II (1857-58), asserted that the chief cause was the unwise Danish policy which permitted German to be used as the language of preaching and teaching. It was about the year 1800 that elementary schools began to be opened in South Slesvig.

In the 1890s the historian Peter Lauridsen discussed the linguistic situation in detail in some articles in the periodical Sønderjydske Aarbøger. One of the facts he demonstrated was that to the south of the frontier with which we are concerned there was a fairly wide belt of land whose inhabitants had earlier been Danish-speaking but where the change of language had taken place before 1800. With the aid of information gleaned from place-names, it was possible for me to reconstruct a more accurate southern boundary for this belt in an article published in Sønderjydske Aarbøger in 1944. The belt comprised the parishes of Svavsted, Mildsted and Ostenfeld, the northern part of the parish of Hollingsted, the greater part of the parish of Michaelis, the town of Slesvig, the parish of Haddeby and the whole of the Svans peninsula. Lauridsen tried to find out the reason for the early date of the change of language in this belt and the result to which he came confirmed by and large the correctness of C.F. Allen's nationalistic theory, namely that a change of language is an abnormal phenomenon whose cause can easily be demonstrated. Lauridsen's theory is that the change of language in the belt in question was the result of immigration from the south. He based this theory on the evidence of personal names culled from tax lists and cadastres from the time of the Reformation, making the assumption that nationality can be inferred from personal names. He even went so far as to determine an individual's country of origin on the basis of his name alone and considered that the inhabitants of a village had changed their language at the point in time when the number of immigrants had topped a certain figure.

These conclusions are untenable. Lauridsen overlooked the very obvious fact that Danish-speaking men may well have adopted the nomenclature of their German neighbours. That such borrowing of names did in fact take place is indicated by the personal names in use in parishes to the north of the belt in which the change of language had taken place before 1800. In a 16th-century tax list from the village of Tolk in South Angel, there are entries for two farmers by the names of Marten Peters and Peter Schomaker. Their forenames can be either Danish or German but their surnames are German.

To the south of the belt in question lay the area known as "the land between the Sli and the Ejder". Peter Lauridsen considered that this area had remained uninhabited until about 1200, at which time it was populated by immigrant Saxons from the south. In the article referred to above I have shown that this colonisation began at a much earlier date. King Valdemar's cadastre suggests that the colonisation must have been as good as complete by the time of the compilation of the cadastre in 1231, for it names 420 farms in the area between the Sli and the Ejder[1]. These 420 farms are sufficient to make up 42 10-farm villages. There are now just over 50 villages in this area.

The works of Reinhold Trautmann[2] have made it possible for us to compare the German colonisation of South Slesvig with the great German expansion into Slav areas in the period after c. 1100. This expansion was characterised not only by the foundation of towns such as Lübeck and Rostock and the formation of great manorial estates but also by the establishment of numerous villages in between the already existing Slav ones. It seems to be characteristic for these German villages that they lie on higher ground than the Slav ones, presumably because they were established after the clearing of woodland rather than after the draining of marshland.

The German colonisation of South Slesvig presents a rather similar picture: the town of Eckernförde, whose name is German, came into existence as early as the end of the 12th century, and in Dänischwold and Svans there is evidence for German manorial estates in the 14th and 15th centuries. In addition, a large number of villages were established there.

The analogy with German colonisation in the Slav regions would be even more obvious if it could be shown that the German colonists in the belt in question established their villages in between already existing Danish ones.

There are in fact a number of villages with German names in this belt, particularly in its western part; from the two parishes of Mildsted and Svavsted can be named: Rödemis; Lehmsick, Fresendelf, Süderhöft, Hude, Wisch, and perhaps Ramstedt. The question is whether these villages were founded by German colonists. If they were, it would be possible to go part of the way towards accepting Lauridsen's theory that the change of language in this area was a result of German immigration. The alternative explanation is that the villages with German names are the result of secondary colonisation from the old Danish villages, after the change of language had taken place.

It is the aim of the present paper to discuss the origin of the German-named villages on the basis of the large number of fieldnames that survive from the two parishes.

Attention must first be drawn to two characteristic features of the villages with German names. Firstly, the majority of them are very small and this in itself suggests that they are probably young.

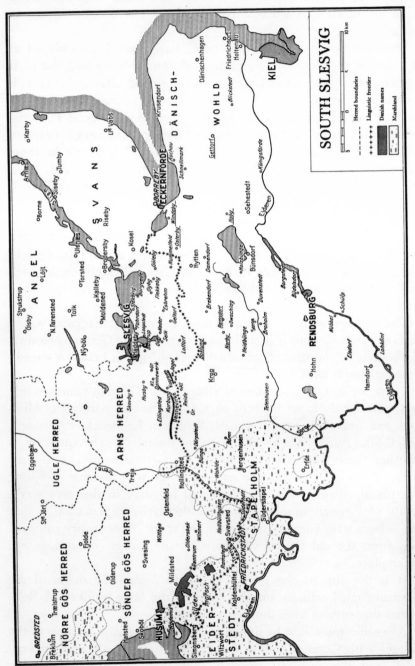

Fig. 1. Map of the frontier area.

Secondly, they all lie on the edge of the moraine, close to the extensive marshland areas that are found in the two parishes. This fact
might suggest that the establishment of the villages was connected
with the intensification of the exploitation of the marshes that took ·
place towards the end of the Middle Ages. These two characteristic
features are perhaps more consistent with internal colonisation than
with German colonisation, for it was the Frisians and not the Germans who were superior to the Danes in marshland farming.

There are two well-defined areas in the parish of Mildsted, the
moraine, known as the geest, and the marshland. In the early Middle
Ages the marshland covered only a part of the sound between
Eiderstedt and the mainland. The sound, which became increasingly
narrow in the course of the Middle Ages as a result of diking on both
banks, is referred to in the register of the Chapter of Slesvig from
1352 as *Myld* and in Knytlinga saga as *Mild*. This name is probably
derived from the adj. mild, perhaps in the sense "generous", i.e. "rich
in fish". Since this adj. is found in all the Germanic languages, it
can tell us nothing as to whether the name was originally Danish,
Frisian or German.

The parish of Mildsted has taken its name from this sound. In a
papal bull dated 6/4 1304 (surviving in a transcript in a papal letter-
-book) the name is written *Myldesect* and *Myldeseet,* in the register
of the Chapter of Slesvig 1352 as *Mildeset,* in a papal bull of 30/3
1398 (transcript in papal letter-book) as *Myltzeth,* and in later
sources always with the second el. as *-stede* or some similar spelling.
The second el. must originally have been -sæt (or -sætæ), which is
also found as a second el. in other place-names in Slesvig (Sønderjylland)[3] and as a simplex name in the village name Sæd near Tønder,
14/4 1237 (transcript in the book of Løgum) *Sethe*[4] , but also in the
village name Seet in the purely German part of South Slesvig, the
cadastre of the Bishop of Slesvig 1436 *Zete*. The element must derive
from the root in the verb to sit, which is common to all the Germanic languages, and it cannot therefore reveal anything about the
nationality of the people who first gave Mildsted its name.

If we want to know what language was spoken by the inhabitants
of Mildsted in the Middle Ages, it is necessary to examine its field-
-names.

No really old name material survives from Mildsted *geest*. The
oldest source is a document from 9-15/9 1490, which survives in an

18th-century transcript. The second oldest source is from 1512. Most of the names are German, several can be either Danish or German and there are close on 20 names which can only be Danish. Among the certain Danish names can be mentioned: *Gammelland* (the adj. gammel "old" is peculiar to the Scand languages); *Medelvang*, 1490 *Medelwang, Medelwangh* (from ODan mæthal "middle-" and the ODan subst. *wang* "field", both els. which are common in Danish place-names); *Handerslund*, pronounced [halə'ɹ'ʃlund̦], 1490 *Handerß Lund* (the first el. must be the gen. of a pers.n., whose original form is uncertain, the second el. is the typically Scand subst. lund "grove". The Danish names which can be localised are indicated on the map fig. 2 by shading.

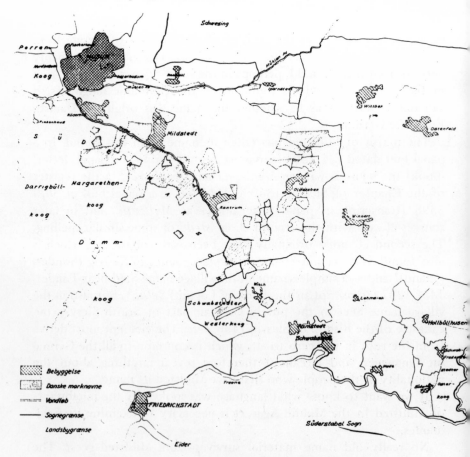

Fig. 2. Sketch map of the parishes of Mildsted and Svavsted.

A great many names survive from Mildsted *marshland,* The oldest source is the register of the Chapter of Slesvig from 1352, the next oldest the cadastre of the Bishop of Slesvig from 1436, and the third oldest an original document from 24/4 1461. Most of the names are German, many can be either Danish or German, e.g. 1486 *holm wische* (the subst. holm is found in both Danish and LG, *wisch* is the regular LG word for meadow but there are certain instances of the translation of the common Danish el. eng to wisch in LG sources); and there are a few names which can only be Danish. Among these can be named: *Bol,* 1490 *up dem Bohle,* 1512 *vp de bole* (the ODan subst. bōl n. used as a unit of land; the possibility cannot be excluded, however, that the word may have been adopted as a technical term into the Low German of Slesvig); *Gaardemose,* pronounced ['xuɬ,mɔ:s], 1585 *vp Gordemase,* 1648 *gardemaes* (the ODan subst. garth m. "fence" and the ODan subst. mosi m. "marsh, swamp"); *Mose,* pronounced [mɔ:s]; 1352 *Mosæ,* 1436 *Mose,* 1461 *vppe de Mose* (ODan mosi); *Odde,* 1593 *in der Odde* (the typically Scand subst. oddi, a derivative of oddr m., which corresponds to Old Saxon ord). The Danish names which can be localised are indicated on the map fig. 2 by shading.

The names in the marshland have a characteristic geographical distribution. German names are found throughout the area and so are the uncertain instances. The Danish names, however, all lie in a broad belt running along the boundary with the geest, i.e. in that part of the marshland which was most likely to have been exploited earliest and consequently to be the first part to be given names.

This geographical distribution suggests that the Danish names in Mildsted marshland are older than the German ones, and hence that the inhabitants of Mildsted must have spoken Danish before they spoke Low German.

At this point it is necessary to define precisely what is meant by the phrase "spoke Danish". Recent studies on the change of language immediately to the south of the present national frontier[5] have shown that it is not possible to obtain a clear picture of the progress of the change of language by speaking vaguely of "the spoken language" in a parish or village but only by distinguishing between various speech situations, e.g. the conversation of men, the conversation of children in the school playground, the conversation between husband and wife, the conversation of parents with their children. The Danish dialect survives longest as the language of conversation between man and wife and it disappears earliest as the language of conversation between men. The time-lag between these two phases in the change of language can be very great, as much as a century or more.

Field-names provide us with information about the language employed by men talking together and only about this. Even if it is possible to date the change-over from Danish to LG field-names then, this is not the same as determining the date of the completion of the process of change of language. It only marks the first phase of this process.

Besides Mildsted itself there are two other villages in the parish of Mildsted which lie on the edge of the geest and have extensive territory in the marshland. These are Rantrum and Rödemis.

Rantrum appears as *Ranthem* 19/9 1381 (transcript from c. 1500), *Rantem* 31/7 1406 (authenticated transcript from 1443), *Rantem* in the Bishop of Slesvig's cadastre of 1436. It is not until about 1500 that spellings with -tr- occur: *Rantrum*. The name is probably identical in origin with North Jutlandic Ranum, Swedish Rannum and Norwegian Randum. In that case the first el. is the ODan subst. rand f. "hill-crest", here used of the edge of the geest, and the second el. the subst. hēm, cognate with Old English hām[6]. That the first el. came to be written with -t must be the result of Low German hardening of a final consonant[7], which also takes place in the first el. of place-names. Compare, for example, the LG field-name *Sant-horst* in the parish of Svavsted, which is recorded in the cadastre of the Bishop of Slesvig 1436 (MLG subst. sant "sand").

The majority of the field-names in Rantrum geest and marshland are either German or of uncertain origin but a few are definitely Danish, e.g. *Broacker*, pronounced [ˈbʀoːaɡ̊əʀ] (the first el. is the ODan subst. brō "bridge", which is not found in German).

The name *Rödemis* appears for the first time in a document from 31/7 1406 (authenticated transcript from 1443) in the form *Rode-misse*. The first el. must be the MLG subst. rode "clearing" and the second el. MLG misse, musse "swamp"[8].

An attempt will now be made to answer the question which was put above p. 77 as to whether Rödemis is a result of German colonisation or of secondary colonisation from Mildsted.

The second possibility can only be taken into account if the village can be considered to have arisen after the inhabitants of

Mildsted had substituted German for Danish as the language of conversation between male adults.

The earliest source for LG field-names in Mildsted is the cadastre of the Bishop of Slesvig from 1436. As undoubtedly LG names can be considered among others: *Brokemeyde* (from the MLG subst. brôk n. "low-lying scrub, undergrowth" and mede, meide "meadow for hay", a derivative of the verb meien "to mow, to reap"); *Hunneham* (the second el. is the MLG subst. ham m. "piece of marshland surrounded with a ditch, the first el. is doubtful, perhaps the animal name hunt "dog"); *Poggenborch* (the first el. is the gen. pl. of the MLG animal name pogge f. and m. "frog", the second el. is MLG borch f. "castle", used ironically). In later sources more and more new German names appear, e.g. 1489 *in palholte* (the MLG subst. pål m. "pole, stake" and holt n. "small wood"), and 1511 *Sunte Margreten Kog* (from the saint's name Margaret in the LG gen. form and the MLG subst. kôch m. "marshland with dikes").

Südermarsch was diked in in the course of the 15th century[9] and the newly reclaimed land there received LG names. It seems, then, that German had replaced Danish as the language of the adult males before the reclamation of land began. It is impossible to ascertain how early this took place because there are no sources of evidence which are old enough. It is most likely, however, to have taken place in the 14th century.

There is, therefore, no reason why the village of Rödemis should not have been established by German-speaking men from Mildsted.

There is a slender piece of evidence which supports the theory of secondary colonisation from Mildsted rather than German colonisation. This is the survival of a single Danish field-name in Rödemis geest, namely *Lund,* 1664 *von dem Lunde,* 1675 *uff de lundt.* It is indicated by shading on the map fig. 2.

It would be natural for the farmers of Rödemis to preserve a Danish field-name if they came originally from the village of Mildsted, whose farmers, as we have seen, continued to use the old field-names even after the change of language had taken place. On the other hand, it is difficult to see why German colonists should make use of a Danish place-name.

It must be emphasised, however, that the evidence is very slight, since there is only this one isolated Danish name.

This slender piece of evidence, however, receives reinforcement from the parish of Svavsted.

The parish name itself is Danish. It is written 4/2 1326 *swauestath*, 28/3 1329 *Swavestath*. The first el. must be the gen. of the masc. pers. n. *Swāvi*, which is otherwise only evidenced on coins[10]. The second el. is the common ODan place-name el. *statha*.

Some few Danish field-names are found in the parish, particularly in the territory of Svavsted itself. The most important are the following: *Vangeholm*, 1436 *Wangeholm; Fruvang*, pronounced [fə'vaŋ], 1663 *Fruwang*, 1703 *frowang* (the first el. is perhaps the subst. frø n.); *Bol*, 1580 *vp dem Lutken boel*, 1593 *in minem Boele* (as has been mentioned above p. 81 under Mildsted, this word may have been borrowed into MLG; it should be pointed out here, however, that the unit known as bol in Danish bears the LG designation staven in Svavsted); *Boesbol*, 1559 *in boeß bole*, 1684 *Boesbol; Mose*, 1561 *de Mase*, 1559 *de mose tho Swauestede; Toft*, 1744 *die Tofft*. The Danish names which can be localised, Bol, Fruwang and Mose, have been indicated on the map fig. 2 by shading.

The name of one of the other hamlets in the parish, *Ramstedt*, 26/3 1378 *Ramstede*, may perhaps be Danish, and that of yet another hamlet, *Hollbüllhusen*, 7/5 1435 *Holbelinghusen*, probably is Danish.

The other five hamlets, all of which are small and lie at the edge of the geest, have German names and are recorded for the first time in the cadastre of the Bishop of Slesvig in 1436: *Lehmsiek*, 1436 *dem Lemzike* (MLG lêm m. "clay" and sîk m. "hollow); *Fresendelf*, 1436 *Vresendelue* (gen. sg. or pl. of the folk-name MLG vrêse "Frisian" and the MLG subst. delf m. "ditch"); *Hude*, 1436 *Hude* (the MLG subst. hude, hode f. "place where something is guarded"); *Wisch*, 1436 *Wisch, Wysch* (the MLG subst. wisch f. "meadow"); *Süderhöft*, 1436 Suderhouede (second el. the MLG subst. hovede n. "farm".

The question remains as to whether these hamlets, in the same way as Rödemis, can be the result of secondary colonisation from Svavsted after the adult males of that village had adopted German as their everyday language. An attempt will be made to answer this question by examining the earliest instances of field-names which are certainly German. For these names, too, the oldest source is the cadastre of the Bishop of Slesvig from 1436 but here we find many more certainly German field-names than in Mildsted, e.g. the following: *vppme Hamme; Rozenlant; Hogherod* (the MLG adj. hôch "high" and subst. rot "clearing"); *Würde* (pl. of MLG wurt "building plot, croft"); *Santhorst* (the second el. is MLG horst f. "shrub"); *Coppele* (the MLG subst. koppel f. "fenced enclosure"); *Lintlo,* silva (the second el is the MLG subst. lô n. "wood"; *Molencamp* (the gen. of MLG mole f. "mill" and the MLG subst. kamp "field"); *Eykenuenne* (the gen. of the MLG tree name êke f. "oak" and the MLG subst. venne f. "low-lying pasture surrounded with a ditch").

Since there are also fewer Danish field-names here than in Mildsted, it is reasonable to assume that the change of language took place earlier in Svavsted than in Mildsted, perhaps in the course of the thirteenth century.

As in the discussion of Mildsted above, the question must be asked as to whether any Danish field-names survive in the small German hamlets in the parish of Svavsted. The answer is in the affirmative. In the territory of *Süderhöft* is found *Āvending,* 1665 *owending,* 1744 *O Wennings Land* (the ODan subst. āwænding "headland"; the corresponding MLG word is anewende, anewendinge). In the territory of *Wisch* are found *Bol, Fruwang* and *Mose.* Only these last three names can be localised. They are indicated on the map fig. 2 by shading.

These four Danish names were probably given by the inhabitants of Svavsted at a period when the adult males still used Danish as their everyday language and before the small hamlets on the edge of the geest had been established. As was the case with Lund in Rödemis, it seems reasonable to treat these Danish names as evidence that the small hamlets were founded by men moving out from Svavsted itself rather than by German colonists. The four Danish field-names in the parish of Svavsted provide rather better support for this theory than does the single name in the parish of Mildsted.

The survey has revealed that the adult males in the oldest villages in the parishes of Svavsted and Mildsted used Danish as their everyday language in the Early Middle Ages and that Danish was replaced by Low German in the fourteenth century or perhaps even earlier. Evidence has also been produced to suggest that the younger villages at the edge of the geest arose as the result of secondary colonisation from the old villages and not of colonisation from the south.

This means, however, that it is still very doubtful whether Peter Lauridsen is correct in claiming that the change of language in South Slesvig before 1800 was due to German immigration, while the change of language after 1800 was the result of the unwise policy of permitting the use of the German language in church and school.

86

It would be more satisfactory to seek an explanation for the change of language that would be valid for the whole of South Slesvig, and in my opinion, this explanation is to be found in the great social prestige that was enjoyed by the Low German language even as early as the Middle Ages, not least because of the practical skill of the Germans.

NOTES:

1   "Dominus rex habet inter Slæ et Eydær cccc houæ et xx". Valdemars Jordebog ed. Svend Aakjær I 10[16].
2   Die elb- und ostseeslavischen Ortsnamen I-II, 1948-49 (Abhandl. der deutschen Akademie der Wissensch. zu Berlin, philos.-hist. Klasse 1947 nos. 4 and 7), Die slavischen Ortsnamen Mecklenburgs und Holsteins, 2. verbesserte Auflage, 1950 (Abhandl. der Sächs. Akademie der Wissensch. zu Leipzig, philos.-hist. Klasse vol. 45 no. 3).
3   Cf. DS III 544 s.n. Højst.
4   Cf. DS III 504f.
5   Cf. particularly Paul Selk, Die sprachlichen Verhältnisse im deutsch-dänischen Sprachgebiet südlich der Grenze, 1937; Christian Stentz, Det danske Sprogs Stilling i Mellemslesvig 1946, Sønderjydske Aarbøger (1947) 153-91.
6   Cf. Kr. Hald, De danske Stednavne paa -um 89.
7   Cf. Agathe Lasch, Mittelniederdeutsche Grammatik § 227.
8   Wolfgang Laur, Die Ortsnamen in Schleswig-Holstein 271.
9   Cf. the map Die Köge Nordfrieslands, in Nordfriesland, Heimatbuch für die Kreise Husum und Südtondern, ed. L.C. Peters, 1929.
10 DgP I 1314 f., J. Kousgård Sørensen, Danske bebyggelsesnavne på -sted 118.

Über die phonematische Wertung von Mundartaufzeichnungen*

Es soll hier versucht werden, einen Beitrag zur Diskussion darüber zu liefern, welche Überlegungen und welche Mittel anzuwenden sind, wenn man sich auf Grund aufgezeichneter Sprachproben von dem Lautsystem einer Mundart Kenntnis verschaffen will. Es handelt sich also nicht um eine Diskussion der sprachwissenschaftlichen *Methode* im engeren Sinne, sondern um eine Diskussion des Verfahrens, das die Beschaffung eines Materials ermöglicht, auf welches die Methode der Sprachwissenschaft anwendbar ist.

Den Ausgangspunkt meiner Überlegungen bildet meine Beschäftigung mit mundartlichem Material, insbesondere mit den Aufzeichnungen aus dem schleswigschen Kirchspiel *Fjolde* (deutsch *Viöl*) bei Husum.

1. Die lautliche Unterscheidungsfähigkeit der Aufzeichner.
In den Aufzeichnungen, die der Begründer der dänischen Mundart-

forschung, K.J. Lyngby, in den Jahren 1858 und 1859 in Fjolde vornahm, ist auslautendes -p von auslautendem -b unterschieden; Lyngby schreibt *tap* "Zapfen" aber ȼab "Schrank"; diese Unterscheidung ist konsequent durchgeführt, auch wenn dasselbe Wort zu verschiedenen Zeiten mehrmals aufgezeichnet ist; sprachgeschichtlich verteilen sich die Zeichen so, dass -p immer altdänischem *pp* entspricht, -b dagegen altdänischem *p* oder *bb*. In den Aufzeichnungen des Herrn Mag. Poul Andersen aus den Jahren 1928 und 1929 und in meinen Aufzeichnungen von 1931 ist diese Unterscheidung dagegen nicht durchgeführt; wir haben beide in der Regel das Zeichen -b verwendet, sowohl in *tab* als in ȼab, und das Zeichen -p, das selten vorkommt, war in unserer Lautschriftpraxis nur ein Zeichen für eine phonetische Variante des auslautenden labialen Verschlußlauts.

Welches ist nun das richtige? Gibt es in der Mundart von Fjolde eine oder zwei auslautende labiale Verschlußlaute?

Man könnte vielleicht diese Frage zugunsten der neueren Aufzeichnungen entscheiden unter Hinweis darauf, daß Poul Andersen und ich eine bessere phonetische Schuling genossen hätten als Lyngby. Man könnte vielleicht auch die phonetische Ehre Lyngbys retten dur ɔ die Annahme, daß die Mundart hinsichtlich der auslautenden Verschlußlaute sich im Laufe der dazwischenliegenden 70 Jahre geändert hätte. Und sollte jemand einwenden, daß die Mundart von Fjolde allen Aufzeichnern, auch Poul Andersen und mir ein völlig *fremder* Sprachgebrauch sei, und daß dieser Umstand unsere phonetische Unterscheidungsfähigkeit beeinträchtigt haben könne, so könnte man auf die große Abhandlung Bernhard Schädels über dieses Thema hinweisen: Über Schwankungen und Fehlergrenzen beim phonetischen Notieren, Bulletin de Dialectologie Romane *II* 1910.

Der Ausgangspunkt Schädels ist eben unser Problem: "Es ist keine Seltenheit", sagt er, "daß zwei Forscher, die unabhängig von einander das gleiche Dialektgebiet bereisten, über den Lautstand eines Ortes oder die Ausbreitung lautlicher Erscheinungen stark divergierende Berichte liefern, oder dass insbesondere der Einheimische und der Ausländer in ihren Mitteilungen sich sehr widersprechen"; und er stellt die Frage, "in welchem Maasse und in welche⸗ Einzelheiten die Schwankungen in der Lautauffassung da⸗   hervorgerufen werden, dass der Beobachtende einer näher- oʋ ʃernerstehenden Sprachgemeinschaft oder der des Sprechenden selbst angehört." Um diese Frage zu beantworten stellte er das folgende Experiment an, wo eɩ selbst und drei Spanier aus Barcelona als Versuchspersonen mitwirkten: Die drei Spanier sprachen nacheinander mehrere Male einen barcelonischen Sprachlaut aus, und alle Versuchspersonen, sowohl der Sprechende als die Hörenden, beschrieben dann gleichzeitig und unabhängig von einander diesen Sprachlaut vermittelst des Jespersenschen antalphabetischen Systems. Nachdem dieser Sprachlaut nach der Aussprache aller drei Spanier so beschrieben worden war, wurde der nächste Sprachlaut in gleicher Weise beschrieben, und so fort, bis alle barcelonischen Sprachlaute beschrieben waren. Ein Vergleich dieser Beschreibungen ergibt eine erstaunliche Übereinstimmung. Die wenigen Unterschiede stellen sich in der Regel als Unterschiede zwischen den Beschreibungen des Sprechenden und denen der Hörenden heraus; und die Unterschiede zwischen den Beschreibungen des hörenden Ausländers und denen der hörenden Spanier sind eben so selten wie die Unterschiede zwischen den Beschreibungen der beiden jeweiligen hörenden Spanier. Hieraus folgert Schädel, daß die erwähnte Divergenz zwischen den Beschreibungen derselben Mundart durch verschiedene Aufzeichner *nicht* dem Umstand zuzuschreiben sei, daß die Muttersprachen der Aufzeichner verschieden sind, sondern ausschließlich dem Umstand, daß ihre phonetische Schulung und Übung verschieden ist.

Dieses Ergebnis wäre vielleicht geeignet, das Vertrauen auf Poul Andersens und meine Aufzeichnungen zu stärken: wenn keiner von uns ein auslautendes -*p* von einem auslautenden -*b* unterscheiden konnte, dann wird es wohl erlaubt sein anzunehmen, entweder daß die Mundart sich geändert hat seit der Zeit der von Lyngby vorgenommenen Aufzeichnungen, oder daß sich Lyngby in seiner Notation von seinen sprachegeschichtlichen Kenntnissen hat irreführen lassen.

Aber dem Experiment Schädels kann aus verschiedenen Gründen kein Wert bei der Beurteilung aufgezeichneten Materials beigelegt werden. Erstens war es bei dem Experiment nicht die Aufgabe der Versuchspersonen festzustellen, welches Phonem ausgesprochen wurde, denn das wußten sie schon im voraus; es handelte sich nur darum, die Aussprache eines gegebenen Phonems zu beschreiben. Zweitens ist das antalphabetische System Jespersens nicht so fein, wie man beim ersten Blick glauben könnte: innerhalb derselben Bezeichnungsweise gibt er einen Spielraum für ziemlich große Variationen. Und drittens ließ man den Sprechenden die Laute sehr oft wiederholen; es war erlaubt, seine Sprechorgane unter allen Gesichtswinkeln zu beobachten, und ihm "eine Stricknadel aus Bein" in den Mund zu stecken um die Zungenstellung zu ermitteln; solche Hilfsmittel kann man sich aber leider nur in bescheidenem Maße bei Mundartaufzeichnungen zu Nutzen kommen lassen.

Das Experiment Schädels hat also nicht unser praktisches Problem, das ja lediglich auf die Unterscheidungsfähigkeit des Aufzeichners in bezug auf die Sprachlaute einer fremden Mundart abzielt, gelöst (das Wort Sprachlaut wird hier vorläufig ohne genauere Definition in der Bedeutung *Lautklasse* benutzt).

Um einer Lösung näher zu kommen, ziehe ich zunächst einige Erfahrungen herbei, die ich selbst bei mundartlichen Aufzeichnungen gemacht zu haben glaube.

Bei Aufzeichnungen, die gleichzeitig von mehreren Aufzeichnern nach demselben Gewährsmann gemacht wurden, habe ich öfters beobachtet, daß gut geschulte und geübte Ohrphonetiker von demselben Einzellaut verschiedene Beschreibungen gegeben haben. Ebenfalls habe ich bemerkt, das ihre Fähigkeit, die Nuancen in der Aussprache desselben Wortes, gesprochen von verschiedenen Repräsentanten derselben Mundart, wahrzunehmen, sehr verschieden ist; besonders fiel mir dieser Unterschied auf, wenn wir Probeaufzeichnungen machten nach Personen, die meine eigene Mundart sprechen; es zeigte sich nämlich oft, daß die fremden Beobachter innerhalb der Aussprache desselben Sprachlauts Nuancen sicher aufzufassen vermochten, die ich nicht hören konnte; wenn es sich aber um Mundarten handelte, die mir fremd waren, hat mir umgekehrt meine eigene Fähigkeit, feine lautliche Nuancen mit Sicherheit aufzufassen, mitunder leise imponiert.

Wie ist es nun um diese feine Unterscheidungsfähigkeit in bezug auf fremde Sprachlaute bestellt? Ich werde ein Beispiel aus meiner eigenen Praxis vorlegen.

Es gibt in der Mundart von Fjolde einen Zischlaut, der mir völlig fremd war. Während meiner letzten Aufzeichnungen in Fjolde, als ich fast 2 Monate lang versucht hatte, mich an die fremden Sprachlaute zu gewöhnen, hörte und bezeichnete ich drei verschiedene Varianten dieses Sprachlauts: am häufigsten habe ich ʂx- geschrieben, sehr oft ʂc-, und seltener sg-. Es handelt sich um ein und dasselbe Phonem — in Fällen wo ein Wort mehrere Male aufgezeichnet wurde, ist die Bezeichnung fast immer inkonsequent; so habe ich z.B. *sgaƚ, ʂxaƚ* und *ʂcaƚ* "(ich) soll" —; meine feine Bezeichnungsweise entbehrt also jeglichen linguistischen Interesses, kann aber illustrieren, auf welche Art und Weise eine solche phonetische "Genauigkeit" erreicht wird: *sg-* ist meine Bezeichnung der Lautverbindung *s* + *k* meines eigenen Sprachgebrauchs, und *șc-* meine Bezeichnung der Lautverbindung *s* + *j* meines eigenen Sprachgebrauchs. Die Anwendung dieser beiden Bezeichnungen besagt also in den einzelnen Fällen · bloß, daß der gehörte Laut mir nicht als ein von meinem eigenen sk- oder sj- verschiedener Laut vorkam. Dagegen bezeichnet *șx- nicht* eine Lautverbindung, die mir bekannt war; diese Bezeichnung habe ich augenscheinlich benutzt, wenn der Laut mir sowohl von meinem s + k als von meinen s + j abzuweichen schien (bezeichnenderweise habe ich auch in diesem Falle den fremden Sprachlaut als eine Lautverbindung und nicht als einen einzelnen Laut aufgefaßt; ich werde weiter unten auf diesen Sachverhalt zurückkommen).

Es hat sich also gezeigt, daß meine Fähigkeit, lautliche Nuancen zu unterscheiden, in diesem Falle ausschließlich davon abhängig war, daß ich die gehörten Laute als identisch mit Lautverbindungen meiner eigenen Muttersprache auffassen konnte. Und ferner hat es sich gezeigt, daß ich nicht imstande war, mich im Laufe zweier Monate an einen fremden Sprachlaut derartig zu gewöhnen, daß ich mich von solchen Identifikationen freimachen konnte.

Gilt Entsprechendes nun auch von anderen Aufzeichnern?

Lyngby hat in Sønderjysk Sproglære für diesen Sprachlaut ebenfalls drei verschiedene Bezeichnungen: *sk-*, *sx-* und *sj-*. In den Aufzeichnungen steht außerdem noch ꝫ-; dieses ꝫ- bezeichnet nach Lyngby denselben Laut wie deutsch *sch-*, ich zweifle aber daran, daß das deutsche sch in Lyngbys Aussprache von der dänischen Lautverbindung s + j wesentlich verschieden gewesen ist. Jedenfalls finden wir bei Lyngby fast dieselbe Einteilung der Nuancen dieses Sprachlauts wie bei mir; auch Lyngby war geneigt, die gehörten Laute mit Lautverbindungen seiner eigenen Muttersprache zu identifizieren; es kommt noch bei ihm die Identifikation mit seiner eigenen Aussprache eines deutschen Sprachlauts hinzu.

Diese Abhängigkeit der Aufzeichner von ihren eigenen Muttersprachen ist mehrmals von erfahrenen Aufzeichnern hervorgehoben worden. Zuerst wohl von den beiden Klassikern Lyngby und Winteler[1], und später von anderen. Die klarsten Worte hierüber findet man wohl bei dem klugen norwegischen Mundartforscher Amund B. Larsen; dieser sagt u.a.[2]: "Die Muttersprache, oder ausnahmsweise die zweite Muttersprache, hat bei jedem Einzelnen ein *akustisches Vorurteil* hervorgerufen, so daß man die fremden Sprachlaute, die man hört, in Beziehung bringt zu den am nächsten stehenden des eigenen

Lautsystems". Und dann folgt ein wirklich gutes Beispiel: "Als ich als junger Student zum ersten Male eine Vorlesung auf Deutsch hörte, war ich in dieser Sprache nicht so weit phonetisch unterrichtet, daß ich darauf vorbereitet war, den Vokal in deutsch *Sohn* anders als in norwegisch *sol* zu hören; ich faßte ihn deshalb sozusagen wechselweise als *o* und als *å* auf — machte mir aber daraus freilich zuletzt die Theorie, daß er eigentlich zwischen den beiden steht." Dies entspricht ja recht genau der Tatsache, daß Lyngby und ich den erwähnten Zischlaut bald als s + j auffaßten, bald als s + k, und bald als einen dritten Laut, an den wir uns ohne allzu großen Erfolg zu gewöhnen bestrebten.

Auf den soeben besprochenen Sachverhalt war Lyngby nicht aufmerksam; er glaubte, wenn er einen Unterschied hören konnte, dann seien auch zwei Sprachlaute vorhanden; dagegen hat er oft hervorgehoben, daß es ihm mitunter schwer falle, Unterscheidungen durchzuführen, die seiner eigenen Muttersprache fremd sind. "Ein Mann in Ladelund", schreibt er z.B.[3], "versicherte mir, den Unterschied zwischen *hus* als Einzahl und als Mehrzahl deutlich hören zu können (ich schreibe *hus, hu̇s,* muß aber in diesem Falle zum Teil nach Analogie verfahren, da die Sache meinem Ohr zu schwierig ist)." Bei Amund B. Larsen findet man mehrere Äußerungen entsprechender Art, z.B. diese[4]: "Im Bewußtsein der Sprechenden ist eine bestimmte Grenze vorhanden zwischen urspr. *i* z.B. in *bidnè* < biðni n. "Faß", und *budnè* < beðnir "gebeten" pt. ptc. plur. (nämlich pl. von beðinn), trotzdem der Unterschied für Ostländer fast unhörbar sein kann".

Es scheint also eine recht gewöhnliche Erscheinung zu sein, daß die Aufzeichner geneigt sind, nicht nur ihre eigene "Sprechweise", wie Winteler sagt, sondern auch ihr eigenes Lautsystem in eine fremde Mundart hineinzuhören. Wie können wir uns aber dann auf Grund eines von fremden Beobachtern aufgezeichneten Materials ein objektives Bild von einer Mundart machen?

Das Hauptmaterial aus Fjolde, dem südlichsten schleswigschen Kirchspiel, dessen dänische Mundart uns bekannt ist, ist von vier fremden Aufzeichnern gesammelt worden, die alle verhältnismäßig kurze Zeit an Ort und Stelle verbracht haben: Lyngby insgesamt etwa 1 1/2 Monate in den Jahren 1858-59, ich 2-3 Monate 1931-32, Dr. Marius Kristensen ungefähr 14 Tage 1913 und 1928-31, und Mag. Poul Andersen 10-12 Tage 1928-29. Sämtliche Aufzeichnungen tragen deutlich das Gepräge davon, daß die Mundart von Fjolde von Sprachgebräuchen, die den Aufzeichnern vertraut waren, be-

trächtlich abweicht; sie enthalten zahlreiche Berichtigungen, Frage-
zeichen und Inkonsequenzen, und sie weichen auch an einzelnen
Punkten so stark von einander ab, daß ich, wenn ich jede Aufzeichnung für sich als Grundlage einer Mundartbeschreibung benutzen
würde, drei oder vier, bei weitgehender Ähnlichkeit immerhin *verschiedene* Mundarten herausbekommen würde. Und da uns vorläufig
jede Berechtigung fehlt, der einen Aufzeichnung vor den übrigen den
Vorzug zu geben, bin ich darauf hingewiesen, alle Aufzeichnungen
heranzuziehen, um das x zu finden, das sich in den Aufzeichnungen
in so verschiedener Art und Weise abspiegelt.

2. Das statistische Verfahren Trubetzkoys.

Den anregendsten Versuch, den ich kenne, eine ähnliche – obwʳ ̇il
schwierigere – Aufgabe zu lösen, bilden die Polabischen Studi̇en von
Trubetzkoy[5].

Die polabischen Sprachreste sind ja von Laien aufgezeichnet, die
– mit einer einzelnen Ausnahme – nicht selbst Polabisch verstanden
und sämtlich sehr verwirrende, auch inkonsequente Bezeichnungsweisen verwendeten. Aug. Schleicher hat ja als erster in diesem
Wirrwarr Ordnung gebracht, und seine Ergebnisse bilden die Dis-
kussionsbasis auch für Trubetzkoy. Obwohl Trubetzkoy Phonologe
ist und auch die Methodik verfeinert hat, ist das Verfahren der beiden Forscher im Prinzip dasselbe. Beide wählen als Ausgangspunkt
die altslavische oder eine andere rekonstruierte vorpolabische Sprache
und untersuchen dann die Entsprechungen der vorpolabischen Phoneme in den polabischen Sprachresten; zeigt es sich nun, daß zwei
vorpolabische Phoneme in den polabischen Quellen in gleicher Weise
vertreten sind, dann stellen sie den Zusammenfall der beiden Phoneme fest, wird aber irgend ein Unterschied der Bezeichnungen gefunden, dann ziehen sie daraus den Schluß, daß die beiden Phoneme
noch im Polabischen unterschieden werden. Das folgende Beispiel
wird einen Eindruck des Scharfsinns geben, der die Ausführungen
Trubetzkoys kennzeichnet.

Vorpolabisches *i* und *ü, e* und *ö* werden in den Wortsammlungen
aus *Lüchow* schön unterschieden. In Hennig von Jessens großer Wort-
sammlung aus *Wüstrow* aber steht fast immer *i* und *e* für sowohl altes
ü, ö als für altes *i, e;* in verhaltnismäßig wenig Fällen begegnen die
Zeichen *ü* und *ö,* ebenfalls sowohl altem *ü, ö* als altem *i, e* entsprechend.
Aus diesem Sachverhalt hat man gefolgert, daß vorpolabisches *ü* mit
i und *ö* mit *e* durch Entrundung zusammengefallen seien in der

Wüstrower, aber nicht in der Lüchower Mundart. Trubetzkoy aber opponiert gegen diese Annahme von folgender Erwägung aus: Die *ü*- und *ö*- Schreibungen sind bei Hennig von Jessen zwar selten, sie verteilen sich aber nicht, wie man es erwarten sollte, gleichmäßig auf altes *i, e* und altes *ü, ö*, sondern sie verteilen sich so:

4% der vorpolab. *i*, aber
22% „   „   *ü* werden durch *ü*- Schreibung, und
1% „   „   *e*, aber
13% „   „   *ö* werden durch *ö*-Schreibung vertreten.

Die Zahlen sind groß genug; bei oberflächlichem Durchlesen zählte ich ungefähr 100 *ü* in der ersten Hälfte des Hennigschen Materials[6]. Die Schwäche des Räsonnements liegt an einem andern Punkte; es setzt nämlich die Behauptung voraus, daß es nur zwei geschichtliche Möglichkeiten gibt: entweder seien sämtliche vorpolabische *ü* und *ö* als *ü* und *ö* erhalten, oder sie seien alle mit *i* und *e* zusammengefallen; es besteht aber eine dritte Möglichkeit: durch kombinatorisch bestimmte Lautänderungen kann ein Teil der alten *ü* und *ö* mit *i* und *e* zusammengefallen sein, während ein anderer Teil erhalten blieb; und da diese Fehlerquelle in ihren Wirkungen unberechenbar ist, ist die theoretische Grundlage der Trubetzkoyschen Anwendung von Wahrscheinlichkeitsberechnungen hinfällig. Trubetzkoy ist selbst auf die Möglichkeit von kombinatorisch bestimmten Lautübergängen aufmerksam gewesen, und führt deshalb zwei Fälle an, wo Hennig in demselben Worte das eine Mal *i*, das andere Mal *ü*, bzw. *e, ö* geschrieben hat. Dadurch wird aber eigentlich nur die Annahme widerlegt, daß kombinatorische Lautänderungen zu einem solchen Zustand geführt hätten, daß die Notation Hennigs in *allen* Fällen richtig wäre.

Es ist sehr wohl möglich, daß das Ergebnis Trubetzkoys richtig ist; die Art seiner Beweisführung, die sprachgeschichtliche Statistik, ist aber nicht zwingend. Nur wenn alles übrige Beweismaterial versagt, kann und soll die Sprachgeschichte in die Diskussion mit einbezogen werden. Denn auch aus einem zweiten Grunde ist es ein mißliches Verfahren, bei der Rekonstruktion der polabischen Sprache von Überlegungen auszugehen, deren Grundlage eine durch Sprachvergleichungen konstruierte vorpolabische Sprache bildet; wenn man nämlich später dieses rekonstruierte Polabisch als Gegenstand der Sprachvergleichungen anwendet — und wozu sollte man es sonst gebrauchen —, läuft man schließlich leicht die Gefahr Zirkelschlüsse zu machen.

3. Gesetzmäßigkeit der lautlichen Unterscheidungsfähigkeit.

Die Ausführungen Trubetzkoys über das polabische *i, ü* und *e, ö* laufen in die folgende Konklusion aus[7] : "Es besteht somit nur eine mögliche Erklärung der Hennigschen Schreibweise: wir müssen annehmen, daß die polabischen etymologischen *ü, ö* auch im Wüstrower Dialekt in allen Stellungen von den etymologischen *i, e* verschieden waren, daß dieser Unterschied jedoch für *Hennigs Gehör nicht immer wahrnehmbar war.* Ob diese Nichtwahrnehmung des genannten Unterschiedes auf rein subjektiven Ursachen beruhte (d.h. darauf, daß Henn., wie viele Deutsche, gegen den akustischen Unterschied zwischen gerundeten und nichtgerundeten Vokalen vorderer Reihe wenig empfindlich war), oder auch objektive Ursachen dabei eine Rolle spielten (indem etwa die Rundung der genannten Vokale im Polabischen überhaupt oder speziell im Wüstrower Dialekt oder schließlich speziell bei Henn.s Gewährsmann verhältnismäßig schwach war) — das läßt sich natürlich nicht mit Sicherheit bestimmen."

Dieser letzte Satz ist nicht so unwiderlegbar, wie er beim ersten Blick scheint. Denn man darf, was auch Trubetzkoy hervorhebt, ohne triftigen Grund keine mundartlichen Abweichungen zwischen den beiden Nachbardörfern Lüchow und Wüstrow annehmen; deshalb müssen die "subjektiven Ursachen" vor den "objektiven" den Vorzug haben, d.h. es muß versucht werden, die Aufzeichnungen aus Wüstrow mit denen aus Lüchow in Übereinstimmung zu bringen unter Rücksichtnahme auf die Verschiedenheit der Aufzeichner.

Über die Aufzeichner der polabischen Sprache ist uns recht wenig bekannt, aber etwas wissen wir. Die Dissertation Selmers[8] gibt Aufschlüsse über die niederdeutsche Sprache der betreffenden Gegend, nicht nur wie sie heute ist, sondern auch wie sie um 1700 war, als die polabischen Aufzeichnungen gemacht wurden; und dieses Niederdeutsch war die Muttersprache der meisten Aufzeichner. Trubetzkoy kennt dieses Buch nicht. Es hätte ihm wahrscheinlich viel Verdruß bereitet, enthält aber Material, das ihm nützlich gewesen wäre. Namentlich wird dieses Material, wie ich glaube, eine Reduktion des von Trubetzkoy aufgestellten imponierenden Phonembestandes veranlassen. Z.B. wird das Phonem *f*, dem Trubetzkoy sogar "ein jedenfalls in unseren Quellen nicht vorkommendes Gegenstück *f̑*" zur Seite zu stellen geneigt ist, wahrscheinlich ausfallen müssen; Schleicher nahm an[9] , daß dem Polabischen ebenso wie dem Polnischen das *f-* fehlte, und daß das *f-* deutscher Lehnwörter durch *v-* substituiert wurde, und er behält augenscheinlich Recht; die Orthographie der

Aufzeichner — sie schreiben in der Regel *w*-, selten *f*-, mitunter im selben Worte sowohl *f*- als *w*- — stimmt mit der Tatsache überein, daß das Wendländer Niederdeutsch um 1700 keinen Unterschied zwischen *w*- und *f*- kannte; daher haben die Aufzeichner wahrscheinlich das *f* als einen in seiner Bedeutung dem *w* gleichen Buchstaben betrachtet (wie in der modernen deutschen Orthographie v mit f gleichwertig ist), und wenn sie z.B. *farbia* mit *f*- schreiben, dann ist das dadurch zu erklären, daß ihnen die Buchstabierung des entsprechenden deutschen Wortes *Farbe* bekannt war.

Was nun *ü* und *ö* betrifft, wird das Ergebnis Trubetzkoys bestätigt, wenn man die Argumentation auf den Muttersprachen der Aufzeichner aufbaut. Parum Schulze — der Krüger aus Lüchow, der die gerundeten vorderen Vokale *nicht* mit den ungerundeten verwechselt — ist bei Lüchow geboren, und aus Selmers Buche geht hervor, daß *i* und *ü, e* und *ö* im dortigen Niederdeutsch unterschieden wurden nicht nur im Jahre 1916, als Selmer die Mundart untersuchte, sondern auch um 1700, als die polabischen Aufzeichnungen gemacht wurden. Dagegen ist Hennig von Jessen — der Pfarrer aus Wüstrow, der die Rundung so selten bezeichnet — nach der Allgem. deutschen Biographie in Jessen bei Oschatz im Königreich Sachsen geboren, und im Königreich Sachsen gibt es keine Unterscheidung zwischen gerundeten und ungerundeten vorderen Vokalen, und gab es auch damals nicht.

Es besteht somit kein Grund, den erwähnten Unterschied zwischen den Lüchower und Wüstrower Aufzeichnungen auf einen Unterschied zwischen den beiden benachbarten Mundarten zurückzuführen.

Es fragt sich nun, ob es überhaupt möglich ist, ausschließlich auf Grund der Aufzeichnungen Mundartfremder den Phonembestand einer Mundart zu finden und die Phoneme der einzelnen Wörter zu bestimmen, ganz ohne Miteinbeziehung sprachgeschichtlicher und sprachgeographischer Betrachtungen.

Das ist m. E. möglich, wenn die Aufzeichnungen drei Bedingungen erfüllen: eine konsequente und gewissenhafte Notation der Aufzeichner, ein umfassendes Material und eingehende Kenntnisse von den Muttersprachen der Aufzeichner; diese Bedingungen werden nach meinem Ermessen von den Aufzeichnungen aus Fjolde erfüllt. Aber die logische Voraussetzung eines solchen Unternehmens bildet das kühne Postulat, daß es einen gesetzmäßigen Zusammenhang gibt zwischen der Muttersprache des Aufzeichners und seiner phonetischen Unterscheidungsfähigkeit.

Ich werde zunächst an Hand eines den soeben erwähnten Aufzeichnungen aus Fjolde entnommenen Beispiels zeigen, daß sich
durch die Annahme einer solchen Gesetzmäßigkeit Ordnung und Klar-
heit in ein scheinbares Chaos bringen läßt.

Es handelt sich um Lyngbys und meine Bezeichnungen des in-
und auslautenden velaren Spiranten. Lyngby hatte schon damals die
Feststellung gemacht, daß dem altdän. *k* in Wörtern wie sak "Sache",
sakær "Sachen" in den nordjütischen Mundarten ein stimmhafter
Spirant *q*, in den nördlichsten südjütischen Mundarten dagegen im
Auslaut ein stimmloses *x* und im Inlaut ein stimmhaftes *q*, und in
den südlichen südjütischen Mundarten endlich sowohl im In- als im
Auslaut ein stimmloses *x* entspricht[10]. Um die genaue geographische
Grenze zwischen dem stimmlosen und dem stimmhaften Spiranten
zu finden, hatte er während seiner Aufzeichnungsreisen immer seine
Aufmerksamkeit auf dieses Problem gerichtet. Aus den Aufzeichnungen aus Fjolde geht aber hervor, daß es ihm hier nicht gelang,
darüber ins klare zu kommen, ob der Spirant stimmlos oder stimmhaft ist. Auch ich suchte vergebens über diese Frage, der ich damals
eine größere Bedeutung beizumessen geneigt war als heute, Klar-
heit zu gewinnen.

Das Material verteilt sich folgendermaßen:

Lyngby
1. Inlaut.
   a) betonte Silbe: Vok. + Spir. + schw. ə   42 *q* (82%)   9 *x* (18%)
   b) unbetonte Silbe: ə + Spirant + ə   1 *q* (90%)   0 *x*
2. Auslaut.
   a) betonte Silbe: Vok. + auslautender Spir. 56 *q* (68%)   26 *x* (32%)
   b) unbetonte Silbe: ə + auslautender Spirant 9 *q* (90%)   1 *x* (10%)

Bjerrum
1. Inlaut.
   a) betonte Silbe: Vok. + Spir. + schw. ə   176 *q* (46%) 205 *x* (54%)
   b) unbetonte Silbe: ə + Spirant + ə   8 *q* (80%)   2 *x* (20%)
2. Auslaut.
   a) betonte Silbe: Vok. + auslautender Spir 91 *q* (18%) 427 *x* (82%)
   b) unbetonte Silbe: ə + auslautender Spirant 3 *q* (4%) 64 *x* (96%)

Das Material enthält eine sehr große Anzahl von Fällen, wo dasselbe Wort mit verschiedener Bezeichnung des Spiranten aufgezeichnet
ist; es handelt sich demnach nicht um zwei Sprachlaute, sondern um

einen; die wechselnden Bezeichnungen besagen also nur, daß die Aufzeichner diesen Sprachlaut bald als stimmhaft, bald als stimmlos aufgefaßt haben.

Wenn wir nun die Bezeichnungen Lyngbys zugrunde legen, müssen wir annehmen, daß die Stimmhaftigkeit deutlicher ist in unbetonter als in betonter Silbe (wobei jedoch die Qualität des inlautenden Spiranten in unbetonter Silbe unaufgeklärt bleibt, da die Zahlen zu klein sind); nach *meinen* Aufzeichnungen ist ein solcher Unterschied wohl im Inlaut vorhanden, im Auslaut aber verhalten sich die Bezeichnungen umgekehrt; nach *meinen* Aufzeichnungen scheint die Stimmhaftigkeit im Inlaut viel deutlicher gewesen zu sein als im Auslaut, bei Lyngby verteilen sich die Bezeichnungen ziemlich gleichmäßig auf In- und Auslaut.

Es gibt zwei Möglichkeiten, diesen Widerspruch zu erklären: entweder haben die Aufzeichner ganz verschiedene Sprachgebräuche aufgezeichnet, oder ihre Wahrnehmungsfähigkeit ist verschiedenartig gewesen. Die erste Möglichkeit ist unkontrollierbar; sie kann also keineswegs abgelehnt werden. Wenn man aber die Muttersprachen und sonstige Sprachbeherrschungen der Aufzeichner untersucht, erweist sich die zweite Erklärungsmöglichkeit als ausreichend.

Was den *Inlaut* betrifft, haben sowohl Lyngby als ich aus unseren eigenen Sprachgebräuchen nur stimmhaftes -q- gekannt; wir haben beide durch unsere Kenntnis der deutschen Hochsprache und — insbesondere — der mittel- und ostschleswigschen Mundarten ein inlautendes -x- kennengelernt; dieses -x- klingt nach meinem Gehör immer noch wie ein stimmloses und besonders stark aspiriertes -q-, d.h. wie mein eigenes -q- + ein Merkmal, und es ist anzunehmen, das ein Gleiches bei Lyngby der Fall gewesen ist. Das mittel- und ostschleswigsche -x- habe ich viel öfter gehört als Lyngby; der Unterschied zwischen den Ziffern des Inlauts kann daher durch die Annahme zwanglos erklärt werden, daß die Fähigkeit, das Merkmal der Stimmlosigkeit (mit verstärkter Aspiration) zu unterscheiden, bei mir wegen der größeren Übung größer gewesen ist als bei Lyngby.

Was den Auslaut betrifft, verhalten sich aber dei beiden Muttersprachen verschieden. Lyngby kannte aus seinem reichssprachlichen Usus nur stimmhaftes -q im Auslaut (er sagte *saq* "Sache", *taq* "Dach" u. dgl.), und von der nordjütischen Mundart, die er als Kind gekannt und zum Teil auch beherrscht hat, gilt das Gleiche. In *meiner* nordwestschleswigschen Mundart dagegen kommt nur stimmloses -x im Auslaut vor, und in meinem reichssprachlichen Usus kommt Vokal + auslautendes -*q* fast nie vor (in Wörtern wie *sa?q* "Sache", *ta?q* "Dach" habe ich Vokal + Stoßton + *q*). Lyngby har durch An-lernen der deutschen Hochsprache und besonders durch Aufzeich-nungen in Südjütland das auslautende stimmlose -*x* kennengelernt, das nach seinem Gehör wie ein -*q* plus ein Merkmal geklungen haben wird. Ich habe durch nordjütische Aufzeichnungen und auch durch die Reichssprache ein auslautendes stimmhaftes -*q* kennengelernt, das nach meinem Gehör wie mein -*x* plus das Merkmal Stimmhaftig-keit (mit abgeschwächter Aspiration) klingt. Einen indirekten Be-weis dafür, daß ich das auslautende -*x* als den normalen Laut, das -*q* dagegen als eine merkmalhaltige Variante höre, erblicke ich in einer Aufzeichnung wie *vå·x* "Wiege" mit langem Vokal + -*x* neben mehrmaligen *voq, vox* mit kurzem Vokal + -*q* und -*x;* die erstange-führte Schreibung ist wahrscheinlich so zu erklären, daß ich das Merkmal Stimmhaftigkeit wahrgenommen aber falsch gedeutet habe, und zwar als Teil des Vokals.

Betrachten wir nun die angeführten Zahlen unter dem Gesichts-punkt: die Fähigkeit der Aufzeichner, eine von ihren angewohnten Sprachgebräuchen abweichende Eigentümlichkeit an dem velaren Spiranten wahrzunehmen, dann verschwindet der Widerspruch, den sie vorher zu enthalten schienen. Da es sich nämlich bei den Bezeich-nungen des auslautenden Spiranten bei mir um ein anderes Merkmal handelt als bei den Bezeichnungen des inlautenden Spiranten bei mir und den Bezeichnungen überhaupt bei Lyngby, ist sowohl der unmittelbaren Vergleichung der Ziffern des Inlauts mit denen des Auslauts wie auch der unmittelbaren Vergleichung der Ziffern bei mir mit denen bei Lyngby der Boden entzogen. Dagegen ist es be-rechtigt, die Ziffern der betonten Silben mit denen der unbetonten Silben zu vergleichen; und in diesen Ziffern tut sich jetzt eine ein-fache und klare Regelmäßigkeit kund: Im Auslaut sind in meinen Aufzeichnungen die Bezeichnungen der Stimmhaftigkeit häufiger in betonter als in unbetonter Silbe; sonst sind überall die Bezeichnungen der Stimmlosigkeit häufiger in betonter als in unbetonter Silbe[11]; mit anderen Worten: beiden Aufzeichnern ist die Wahrnehmung des abweichenden Merkmals in betonter Silbe leichter gefallen als in unbetonter Silbe.

Wenn wir nun den soeben dargestellten Sachverhalt als eine iso-lierte Erscheinung betrachten, können wir die theoretische Möglich-keit nicht ablehnen, daß die angeführten Zahlen durch die Annahme eines — freilich sehr komplizierten — Unterschieds zwischen den Gewährsleuten der beiden Aufzeichner in bezug auf die Verteilung der Stimmhaftigkeit des velaren Spiranten zu erklären wären. Bedenken wir aber, daß entsprechende Gegensätze zwischen den Aufzeichnungen in vielen ähnlichen Fällen vorhanden sind, und daß uns die konsequente Zurückführung dieser Gegensätze auf Unterschiede zwischen den Gewährsleuten zur Annahme einer immer komplizierteren und ganz unerklärbaren, sowohl phonetischen als auch phonematischen, Verschiedenartigkeit innerhalb desselben Kirchspiels zwingen würde, dann müssen wir die obenangeführten Zahlen als einen triftigen Grund hinnehmen, die zweite Erklärungsmöglichkeit als Arbeitshypothese zu wählen; es ist also anzunehmen, daß es eine gesetzmäßige Abhängigkeit besteht zwischen der Muttersprache und der Wahrnehmungsfähigkeit des Aufzeichners, selbst in einem Falle wie dem besprochenen, wo beiden Aufzeichnern reichliche Gelegenheit gegeben war, sich auf die Wahrnehmung der erwähnten Abweichungen von den angewohnten Sprachlauten zu üben.

4. Variation der sprachlichen Merkmale.
Worauf beruht es aber, daß ein solche Abweichung vom Angewohnten durch einen Aufzeicher bald bezeichnet wird und bald unbezeichnet bleibt? Beruht das ausschließlich darauf, daß er in den einzelnen Fällen nicht mit gleicher Intensität gelauscht hat, oder kann es auch auf den gehörten Lauten beruhen? Das erstere würde der Fall sein, wenn die gehörten Vertreter eines Sprachlauts alle akustisch genau gleich wären. Wir wissen aber, daß sie nicht gleich sind.

Der Gedanke, daß die Aussprache eines Sprachlauts innerhalb einer gewissen Variationsbreite (oder ''uttalslatitud'') variiert, ist ja sehr früh bei nordischen Mundartforschern entstanden. Den klarsten Ausdruck hat dieser Gedanke bei Noreen gefunden[12]: ''Unter einem gewissen, qualitativ bestimmten Laute im Gegensatz zu einem anderen verstehen wir gewöhnlich — und im Folgenden — nicht einen unter allen Umständen identisch gleichen Laut. Es ist nämlich ein reiner Zufall, wenn es sogar demselben Individuum gelingt, einen einmal produzierten Laut in vollkommen gleicher Weise zu reproducieren, und selten oder nie dürfte dieser Fall tatsächlich eintreten. Sondern wir verstehen z.B. unter dem neuschwedischen *i*-Laute eine Menge von Lautvarietäten, die sich — akustisch und gewöhnlich auch genetisch — soweit ähnlich sind, daß sie von den Sprechenden und Hörenden entweder gar nicht oder wenigstens mit großer Schwierigkeit als verschieden wahrgenommen werden, und deren Qualitätsdifferenz, wenn sie auch dem Gehör wahrnehmbar sein sollte, jedenfalls nicht für sprachliche Zwecke, d.h. als Träger einer Bedeutungsdifferenz, verwendet wird."

Noreen hat hier zwei Begriffe zusammengeworfen, nämlich den Begriff des Ausdruckselements und den des Sprachlauts. Das Ausdruckselement ist dadurch bestimmt, daß eine Vertauschung des einen Elements durch ein anderes bewirken kann, daß die Ausdruckseinheit eine andere Bedeutung annimmt. Der Sprachlaut dagegen ist eine wahrnehmungspsychologische Einheit, welche, wie Noreen sagt, durch eine Menge von "Lautvarietäten", die von den Sprechenden und Hörenden entweder gar nicht oder wenigstens mit großer Schwierigkeit als verschieden wahrgenommen werden, vertreten wird.

Der Begriff der Variationsbreite spielte für Trubetzkoy keine Rolle, und augenscheinlich auch nicht für Bernh. Schädel, der ja seine Versuchspersonen denselben Sprachlaut mehrere Male wiederholen ließ. Dagegen hat er für die nordische Mundartforschung, z.B. für Wigforss und Lindroth, für Amund B. Larsen, für Marius Kristensen und Brøndum-Nielsen, eine große Rolle gespielt.

Seine klare theoretische Gestaltung hat dieser Gedanke aber erst — und unabhängig von den Nordisten — bei *Zwirner* gefunden[13].

Zwirner hat ja die Dauer der Vokale einer Schallplatte gemessen und dabei gefunden, daß die Langvokale und die Kurzvokale jeder Gruppe für sich durch Laute sehr verschiedener Dauer vertreten sind, daß sich aber die dabei gefundenen Zahlen um zwei Mittelwerte in Übereinstimmung mit der Gaußschen Fehlerkurve streuen. Die Aussprache der Langvokale variiert um einen Mittelwert von 12 bis 13 Hundertstel Sekunden, die Aussprache der Kurzvokale um einen etwa halb so großen Mittelwert, ungefähr 7 Hundertstel Sekunden. Die Variationsbreite reicht bei den Kurzvokalen von etwa 2 bis etwa 12 Hundertstel Sekunden, bei den Langvokalen von etwa 2-3 bis etwa 22-23 Hundertstel Sekunden, und ist bei den Langvokalen also ungefähr doppel so groß wie bei den Kurzvokalen. Die beiden Variationsfelder greifen also in auffallendem Grade ineinander über; die Größe der Variationsbreiten muß aber im Zusammenhang mit der Tatsache gesehen werden, daß Zwirner den Umstand, daß die offenen Vokale nach den Messungen Ernst A. Meyers[14] länger sind als die geschlossenen, unberücksichtigt ließ. Hätte Zwirner sich damit begnügt, die Vertreter von z.B. langem *i* und kurzem *i* zu messen, wären seine Variationsbreiten also nicht so groß gewesen, und die beiden Kurven würden sich nicht in so hohem Graden überschneiden.

5. Die Wahrnehmung der variierenden Laute.
Danach hat aber Zwirner ein wahrnehmungspsychologisches Experiment angestellt, das für unsere Probleme von noch größere Wichtigkeit ist[15]. Er wählte unter den Vokalen der Schallplatte einen Vokal aus, dessen Dauer ziemlich genau dem gefundenen Mittelwert entsprach, und ließ dann einige Versuchspersonen die übrigen Vokale derselben Quantitätsgruppe mit dem Mittelvokal durch Abhören vergleichen; die Versuchspersonen sollten dann in jedem einzelnen Falle beurteilen, ob der gehörte Vokal länger oder kürzer als der Mittelvokal oder von der gleichen Dauer sei. Das Experiment ergab eine bestimmte Schwelle, die überschritten werden mußte, damit die Versuchspersonen die Abweichung mit voller Sicherheit festzustellen imstande waren. Diese wahrnehmungspsychologische Schwelle war bei den Kurzvokalen 3-4 Hundertstel Sekunden vom Mittelvokal entfernt; bei den Langvokalen war sie 6-8 Hundertstel Sekunden, d.h. um das Doppelte, vom Mittelwert entfernt. Da die Variationsbreite bei den Langvokalen doppel so groß war wie bei den Kurzvokalen, wurde also eine Korrespondenz zwischen dem Abstand der Schwelle vom Mittelwert auf der einen und der Variationsbreite auf den anderen Seite festgestellt.

Es soll nun nicht geleugnet werden, daß dies Experiment sich an ein paar Punkten kritisieren läßt. Erstens bleibt die Frage unbeantwortet, ob die Versuchspersonen dasselbe schlesische Hochdeutsch sprechen wie das Hochdeutsch der Schallplatte. Zweitens wäre es auch hier wünschenswert gewesen, das Experiment auf Vokale derselben Qualität zu beschränken; es kann nämlich nicht im voraus als gesichert gelten, daß die Versuchspersonen bei diesen Quantitätsvergleichungen imstande sind, von der Qualität der Vokale zu abstrahieren; nach Ernst A. Meyer müssen wir ja annehmen, daß ein normales *a* länger ist als ein normales *i*; es ist durchaus denkbar, daß eine Versuchsperson mit Sicherheit unterscheiden kann, daß ein *a* einer bestimmten Dauer kürzer ist als das Normal-*a* aber *nicht* hören kann, daß ein *i* derselben Dauer auch kürzer ist als das Normal-*a*. Drittens wäre es für unsere Zwecke besser gewesen, wenn man die beschwerlichen Vergleichungen mit dem Mittelvokal weggelassen und die Versuchspersonen einfach gefragt hätte, ob der jeweilige Vokal verhältnismäßig lang, verhältnismäßig kurz oder normal sei. Es soll hier auf eine Tatsache hingewiesen werden, die es vielleicht wahrscheinlich machen könnte, daß diese Vergleichungen ohne Be-

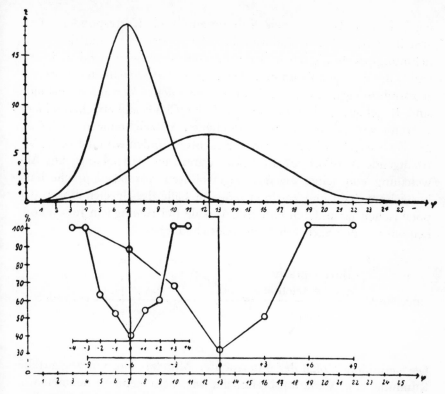

Graphische Darstellung der Streuung der gemessenen Vokale (oben) und der
Verteilung der von den Versuchspersonen gegebenen richtigen Antworten auf
die ihnen vorgelegten Fragen bezuglich der Länge der gemessenen Vokale (unten). Nach E. Zwirner: L'opposition phonologique et la variation des phonèmes
(Archiv für vergl. Phonetik II 143).

lang sind: bei den Langvokalen hat man aus irgendeinem Grunde einen Testvokal gewählt, dessen Dauer dem Mittelwert nicht genau
gleich, sondern 1/2-1 Hundertstel Sekunde länger ist; die beiden
Schwellen liegen aber in verschiedener Entfernung von diesem Testvokal, dagegen aber in *gleicher* Entfernung vom Mittelwert; es ist jedoch kaum anzunehmen, daß die Genauigkeit der Messungen und die
Anzahl der gemessenen Vokale groß genug ist, um Schlüsse auf Grund
so kleiner Abweichungen zu gestatten.

Hoffentlich werden wir in Zukunft weitere wahrnehmungspsychologische Ergebnisse aus der Werkstatt Zwirners erwarten dürfen; auch
zu unserer praktischen Frage nach der lautlichen Unterscheidungsfähigkeit sprachfremder Beobachter wird uns ein weiteres Vordringen
auf dem Wege, den Zwirner uns gebahnt hat, wahrscheinlich weit-
reichende Aufschlüsse geben können. – Vorläufig aber ist als Haupt-

ergebnis des Zwirnerschen Experiments eine Korrespondenz festgestellt zwischen der Variationsbreite und dem Abstand der wahrnehmungspsychologischen Schwelle vom Mittelwert. Und es ist erlaubt, dieses Ergebnis unserer Wertung des aufgezeichneten Materials
zugrundezulegen, solange wir durch ein solches Verfahren imstande
sind, Regelmäßigkeit zu finden, wo früher Chaos zu herrschen schien.

Wenn wir nun die oben besprochenen Aufzeichnungen im Lichte
des Zwirnerschen Experiments betrachten, finden wir eine völlig be-
friedigende Antwort auf die Frage, warum ein Aufzeichner eine Abweichung von seiner eigenen angewohnten Normalaussprache bald
bezeichnet, bald unbezeichnet läßt. Im Falle der Bezeichnungen der
polabischen gerundeten vorderen Vokale bei Hennig von Jessen können wir uns den Sachverhalt so veranschaulichen:

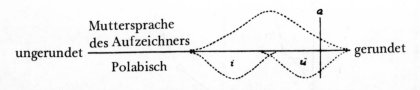

Der gerundete Vokal der untersuchten Mundart hat in bezug auf die
Rundung eine Variationsbreite, die wir nicht kennen; nehmen wir
aber an, daß auch das Merkmal der Rundung nach der Gaußschen
Fehlerkurve variiert, dann steht diese Kurve in einem bestimmten
Verhältnis zu der wahrnehmungspsychologischen Schwelle des Auf-
zeichners für die sichere Unterscheidung der Rundung (a), und diese
Schwelle korrespondiert mit der Variationsbreite seines eigenen
Sprachgebrauchs. Nach dieser Betrachtungsweise ist es verständlich,
warum die Vertreter des polabischen *ü* von Hennig verschieden aufgefaßt werden *mußten*.

Durch ein entsprechendes, nur ein wenig kompliziertes Bild können wir uns den Fall der Bezeichnung des velaren Spiranten durch
Lyngby und mich veranschaulichen:

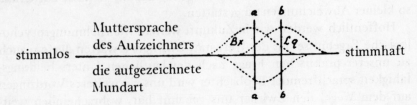

Der auslautende velare Spirant der untersuchten Mundart hat in bezug auf die Stimmbeteiligung eine Variationsbreite, die wir nicht kennen, die aber in einem bestimmten Verhältnis steht zu den psychologischen Schwellen bei Lyngby und mir für bzw. Stimmlosigkeit (a) und Stimmhaftigkeit (b), und diese Schwellen korrespondieren mit den Variationsbreiten unserer eigenen Sprachgebräuche. Es ist verständlich, daß wir die meisten Vertreter des fremden Sprachlauts verschieden auffassen mußten.

In allen drei Fällen hat der Beobachter eine falsche Einteilung der gehörten Einzellaute vorgenommen, weil er sie bald als Vertreter der Sprachlaute seiner eigenen Muttersprache, bald als etwas abweichende Laute hören konnte und mußte.

6. Die Anwendung der wahrnehmungspsychologischen Gesetzmäßigkeit auf die Aufzeichnungen.
Es ist mithin der Mühe wert zu untersuchen, ob ein Vergleich zwischen mehreren *verschiedenartigen* Einteilungen uns ermöglicht, die richtige Einteilung zu finden, ohne Einbeziehung sprachgeschichtlicher Argumente. Die erste Schwierigkeit eines solchen Unternehmens, die Unterscheidung zwischen falschen und richtigen Einteilungen, läßt sich in den meisten Fällen ziemlich leicht überwinden; eine falsche Einteilung gibt sich nämlich bei mehrmaliger Aufzeichnung desselben Wortes in der Regel durch die Nichtübereinstimmung der Bezeichnungsweisen kund.

Das Verfahren bei einer solchen Untersuchung läßt sich am leichtesten an einem Beispiel erhellen, und zwar nehme ich meine Einleitungsfrage wieder auf: Gibt es in der Mundart von Fjolde einen oder zwei auslautende labiale Verschlußlaute? Ich habe bereits erwähnt, daß Lyngby ein auslautendes -p von einem auslautenden -b unterscheidet; auch bei mehrmaliger Aufzeichnung desselben Wortes ist er so gut wie immer konsequent, ich habe nur einen Fall der Inkonsequenz gefunden. Lyngby kannte aus seiner eigenen Muttersprache nur *einen* auslautenden labialen Verschlußlaut; in einigen nordjütischen Mundarten, z.B. der Mundart von Vendsyssel, hatte er aber die Gelegenheit gehabt, ein "weiches" *b*, wie er sagt, zu beobachten. Er wußte genau, daß das "weiche" *b* altdänischem *p* und *bb*, das "harte" dagegen altdänischem *pp* entspricht, und er hat in seinen Schriften und in Briefen mehrmals gesagt, daß er in seiner Notation mitunter "nach Analogie" verfuhr, d.h. sich von seinen sprachgeschichtlichen Kenntnissen leiten ließ. Zur Kontrolle dieser Fehlerquelle fehlt uns vorläufig jedes Material; es ist aber denkbar, daß uns die übrigen Aufzeichnungen ein solches Kontrollmaterial bieten. Die Aufzeichnungen Marius Kristensens verhalten sich in diesem Punkte genau wie die Lyngbys und geben uns also keine weiteren Aufschlüsse. Poul Andersens Aufzeichnungen und meine ersten Aufzeichnungen sind in dieser Hinsicht einander ähnlich und weichen von den beiden anderen beträchtlich ab. Wir kannten damals beide aus unseren eigenen Sprachgebräuchen und aus den Mundarten, die wir damals kannten, nur *einen* auslautenden labialen Verschlußlaut; wir hatten uns beide daran gewöhnt, diesen Verschlußlaut in der Regel durch -*b*, im Falle der deutlich wahrnehmbaren Behauchung aber durch -*p* zu bezeichnen, glaubten aber beide, daß es sich nur um Varianten desselben Sprachlauts handelte; keiner von uns hat sich also in diesem Falle von der "Analogie" leiten lassen. Eine nähere Prüfung des Materials ergibt nun, daß wir fast nie -*p* geschrieben haben in Wörtern, die in den übrigen Aufzeichnungen mit -*b* geschrieben sind, daß wir dagegen sowohl -*p* und -*b* haben, wo Lyngby und Mar. Kristensen -*p* schreiben. Schon diese Verteilung deutet darauf hin, daß Lyngby und Mar. Kristensen die gehörten labialen Verschlußlaute richtig eingeteilt haben, während unsere Einteilung falsch ist. Hinzu kommt aber noch, daß wir beide ein anderes Merkmal (Abweichung vom Normalen) als die Behauchung wahrgenommen haben: Poul Andersen hat einmal das Subst. *Skab* "Schrank" mit -*b* niedergeschrieben und dann durch ein in Klammern hinzugefügtes *ƀ* angegeben, daß ihm die Aussprache dieses -*b* einem bilabialen Spiranten ähnlich schien; und ich habe einmal das Subst. *Gab* mit -*v* geschrieben; in diesem Falle habe ich augenscheinlich eine Abweichung vom meinem -*b* wahrgenommen, aber falsch gedeutet. Da Lyngby und Mar. Kristensen in den beiden genannten Wörtern immer -*b* haben, wird also die Zweiteilung dieser beiden Aufzeichner durch unsere falsche Dreiteilung durchaus bestätigt. Eine weitere Bestätigung ergibt sich aus meinen bisher nicht erwähnten Aufzeichnungen aus dem folgenden Jahre. Ich hatte mir damals durch nordfriesische Aufzeichnungen eine gewisse Übung erworben, den auslautenden stimmhaften Verschlußlaut vom stimmlosen zu unterscheiden. Und auch in Fjolde kam es mir jetzt mitunter vor, als ob eine leise Stimmhaftigkeit des auslautenden Verschlußlauts in einem Worte wie *ʂxab* "Schrank" wahrnehmbar wäre. Ich stellte dann ein Verzeichnis einiger Testwörter auf und bat meine Gewährsleute, die ja der dänischen Orthographie unkundig sind, diese Wörter zu buchstabieren. Es stellte sich dabei heraus, erstens daß sie nur in ein paar Fällen über die Antwort auf die Frage *p* oder *b* in Zweifel gerieten, zweitens, daß sie mit Ausnahme eines vereinzelten Falles in bezug auf die Buchstabierung einig waren, und drittens, — was mich damals besonders freute — daß zwischen ihrer Buchstabierung und der Orthographie altdänischer Texte die schönste Übereinstimmung herrschte. Es gelang mir nie, das Merkmal der Stimmhaftigkeit auch nur einigermaßen sicher zu unterscheiden; bei den folgenden Aufzeichnungen mußte ich sehr häufig zum Verfahren des Buchstabierens greifen, und in vielen Fällen mußte ich eine Bezeichnung verwenden, die besagte, daß ich nicht zu entscheiden vermochte, ob der eine oder der andere Verschlußlaut gemeint sei. Trotzdem hat ein Vergleich zwischen diesen Aufzeichnungen aus 1932 und den übrigen Aufzeichnungen den endgültigen Beweis dafür erbracht, daß zwei Sprachlaute vorhanden sind, d. h. daß die Sprecher und Hörer zwischen zwei Klassen von auslautenden labialen Verschlußlauten zu unterscheiden vermochten. Diesen beiden Sprachlauten sind auch zwei Ausdruckselemente zuzuordnen, obwohl es meines Wissens nur ein Wortpaar gibt, auf welche die Vertauschungsprobe (Kommutationsprobe) anwendbar ist, nämlich *lɔb* "der Lauf": *lɔp* "der Floh".

7. *Zwei weitere Faktoren: Übung und Erwartung.*
In diesem Falle bewährte sich also die Regel von der Abhängigkeit zwischen der Muttersprache und der lautlichen Unterscheidungsfähigkeit der Aufzeichner. Zugleich sind aber zwei weitere Faktoren in die Erscheinung getreten. Erstens hat es sich herausgestellt, daß ich durch Übung imstande war, die Schwelle dem Mittelwert ein klein wenig näher zu rücken. Daraus folgt, daß wir unser Augenmerk auf die im Laufe einer Aufzeichnung vollzogenen Änderungen der Notation richten müssen. Zweitens stellt sich — zu unserer Überraschung vielleicht — bei den Aufzeichnern eine Neigung heraus, sich beim Notieren von ihren sprachgeschichtlichen oder sonstigen sprachlichen Kenntnissen beraten zu lassen, so daß sie bei einem gegebenen Worte im voraus eine bestimmte Lautung *erwarten*. Wenn eine solche Erwartung vorhanden ist, dann muß eine Abweichung vom normalen Laute vermutlich größer sein, um wahrgenommen zu werden, als wenn eine solche Erwartung nicht vorhanden ist.

Daraus ergibt sich die Notwendigkeit, Material zu finden, das uns darüber Aufschlüsse geben kann, welche Rolle dieser Faktor spielt. Und hierbei genügt es nicht, sich ein Urteil über die einzelnen Aufzeichner im allgemeinen zu bilden, sondern ihre Einstellung zu jedem einzelnen sprachlichen Unterschied muß gesondert untersucht werden.

Lyngby schreibt im Frühling 1857 — also bevor er nach Fjolde kommt — in einem Briefe an den Mundartforscher Eiler Hagerup über die palatalisierten *n*- und *l*-Laute folgendes[16] : "Für einen, der nicht selbst die Sprache sprechen kann, ist es sehr schwierig, diese Laute von reinem *n* und *l* zu unterscheiden; ich kann wohl im allgemeinen hören, daß *n̦* und *l̦* vorhanden sind, kann es aber nicht in den einzelnen Wörtern hören." Nach dem Gehör Lyngbys waren also die palatalisierten Laute merkmalhaltig, und es fiel ihm schwer, das Merkmal zu unterscheiden. Lyngby hat ja als erster die Entdeckung gemacht, daß diese Laute altnordischem *nn*, *nd* und *tn* und altnordischem *ll* und *ld* entsprechen. In welchem Grade haben nun die sprachgeschichtlichen "Analogien" seine Fähigkeit, die Palatalität wahrzunehmen, in den einzelnen Fällen beeinflußt?

Es gibt in den Aufzeichnungen aus Fjolde einen einzigen Fall, wo Lyngby eine mit Unrecht erwartete Palatalität bezeichnet hat; es handelt sich um das Wort *jæmən̦* "Heimat", wo das *n* in unbetonter Silbe steht; dieses Wort hat in anderen jütischen Mundarten, auch in meiner nordschleswigschen Mundart, palatalisiertes *n̦*, ich habe aber in Fjolde mehrere Male *n* in diesem Worte gehört. — Dagegen hat Lyngby in mehreren Fällen, wo er *n̦* und *l̦* erwarten mußte, *n* und *l* aufgezeichnet; er schreibt *iəl̦* "Feuer", aber gleich danach *iələn̦* "Feuerung"; er schreibt sowohl *vin̦ən̦* als *vinən̦* "Fenster", und es gibt einige Fälle mehr. In Wörtern, wo er nicht wissen konnte, welcher Laut zu erwarten sei, schreibt er meist *n* und *l*, auch in Fällen, wo ich *n̦* und *l̦* habe (aus den Ausführungen weiter unten wird hervorgehen, warum wir meinen Bezeichnungen in *dieser* Beziehung einen besonderen Wert beimessen müssen): er schreibt z. B. dreimal *bal* "bald" (in meinen Aufzeichnungen kommt das Wort sehr oft vor, immer in der Schreibung *bal̦*), und einmal *bil* "Bild" (ich habe mehrere Male *bil̦* geschrieben). — Auf dieser Grundlage können wir uns über die Aufzeichnungen Lyngbys in bezug auf die *n*- und *l*-Laute mit großer Sicherheit folgendes Urteil bilden: Lyngby hat das Merkmal der Palatalität nur dann bezeichnen wollen, wenn er es tatsächlich hörte; die Wahrnehmung dieses Merkmals ist ihm aber etwas leichter gewesen im Falle der Erwartung als im Falle der Nicht-Erwartung.

Poul Andersen kannte aus seiner eigenen Muttersprache wie Lyngby nur einen *n*- und einen *l*-Laut, und wie Lyngby hat er die Palatalität nicht immer wahrgenommen; in der Regel aber hat er sie gehört, aber in höchst verschiedener Weise bezeichnet, am häufigsten durch einen *i*-Vokal + das Zeichen des palatalisierten *n* oder *l;* nach dem

Gehör Poul Andersens waren aber nicht nur n_j und l_j merkmalhaltig, sondern auch das velarisierte t, und auch dieses Merkmal wird fast immer wahrgenommen, aber sehr verschieden bezeichnet, in der Regel durch Vokal + l oder t; z.B. hat er das Adj. *gul* "gelb" zu verschiedenen Zeiten folgendermaßen geschrieben: *gu·ət, gu·t, gu·Ol*. Bei der Wahrnehmung dieser Merkmale hat aber die Erwartung bei ihm keine Rolle gespielt: die Fälle, wo er nicht wissen konnte, was sprachgeschichtlich zu erwarten sei, verhalten sich genau so wie die Fälle, wo er es wußte. Deshalb muß man bei der Beurteilung des Phonembestandes der einzelnen Wörter in diesem Punkte auf die Bezeichnung Poul Andersens großes Gewicht legen.

Ich selber war anders eingestellt als die übrigen Aufzeichner, weil ich aus meiner eigenen Mundart den sprachlich relevanten Unterschied zwischen den beiden n-Lauten und den beiden l-Lauten kenne. Deshalb sind die palatalisierten Laute nach meinem Gehör nicht merkmalhaltig in dem hier gebrauchten Sinne dieses Wortes. Dieser Umstand hat sich mitunter sehr deutlich kundgegeben, wenn ich mit Kollegen, die aus ihren eigenen Sprachgebräuchen nur ein n und ein l kennen, zusammen aufgezeichnet habe. Während einer solchen Aufzeichnung machten wir in einem mittelschleswigschen Kirchspiel die Entdeckung, daß der Gegensatz zwischen den beiden n- und den beiden l-Lauten in gewissen Stellungen nach geschlossenen Vokalen aufgehoben ist; diese Entdeckung wurde aber nicht von mir gemacht, sondern von meiner mundartfremden Mitarbeiterin, Mag. Ella Jensen, die in einem Worte wie *mil* "milde" keine Palatalität des l unterscheiden konnte; mir dagegen fiel es schwer, den Unterschied zwischen diesem l und meinem eigenen palatalisierten l_j desselben Wortes zu hören. Nach meinem Gehör war also in diesem Falle die Nicht-Palatalität das vom Normalen (und Erwarteten) abweichende Merkmal.

Auch in Fjolde habe ich die Laute als Vertreter meiner eigenen vier Sprachlaute aufgefaßt; und in meinen Aufzeichnungen herrscht durchgehends die schönste Konsequenz. Die Frage ist nun, wieviel diese Konsequenz wert ist; denn in den allermeisten Fällen konnte ich es ja nicht vermeiden, einen bestimmten Sprachlaut zu erwarten, und diese Erwartung kann meine Fähigkeit, das abweichende Merkmal wahrzunehmen, herabgesetzt haben. Glücklicherweise habe ich ein paar Fehler gemacht, die uns einer Beantwortung dieser Frage auf die Spur setzt. In meiner Mundart hat das Partizip des Präsens palatalisiertes n_j, auch in der Verwendung als nomen actionis. In

Fjolde erwartete ich in solchen Formen natürlich auch palatalisiertes *n̦*, und schrieb dementsprechend auch *n̦* in den allerersten Aufzeichnungen: zuerst *ba·qən̦* "das Backen"; hier steht aber in Klammern hinzugefügt: "mit sehr schwach palatalisiertem *n̦*; dann *vn* bʀæ̨ŋən̦ jɛʀeg "eine brennende Hitze" (wo das letzte *n* in der schwierigst möglichen Position steht: in unbetonter Silbe nach *n̦* und vor *j*) und *sma.xən̦* "schmackhaft"; dann aber, ein wenig später, *vn sdɛgən jɛʀeg* "eine stechende Hitze" und *sedən* "sitzend"; und in den folgende Aufzeichnungen habe ich nur in ein paar vereinzelten Fällen *n̦*, sonst immer *n* geschrieben. Es hat sich also in diesem Falle gezeigt, daß ich mit ziemlich großer Sicherheit auf eine Abweichung vom Erwarteten reagierte.

Es gibt aber ein paar andere Fälle, wo solche Reaktionen bei mir ganz oder teilweise ausblieben. Als letztes Beispiel werde ich den einen Fall kurz besprechen, der besonders interessant ist, weil er eine recht unerwartete Erscheinung illustriert: Wir haben gesehen, daß ein ungewohnter lautlicher Unterschied einem Aufzeichner Schwierigkeiten bereiten kann:

Muttersprache
des Aufzeichners

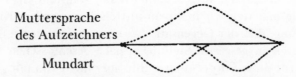

Mundart

Die Erkenntnis des umgekehrten Sachverhalts, daß nämlich die untersuchte Mundart einen lautlichen Unterschied, der in der Muttersprache des Aufzeichners vorhanden ist, nicht kennt, kann aber noch schwieriger sein:

Muttersprache
des Aufzeichners

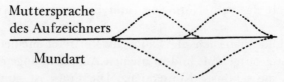

Mundart

Eine Zweiteilung eines einzelnen Sprachlauts durch den Aufzeichner *sollte* sich ja eigentlich bei mehrmaliger Aufzeichnung desselben Wortes durch eine große Anzahl von Inkonsequenzen bekunden, und tut es in der Regel auch. Wenn aber solche Inkonsequenzen in einigen Fällen weniger zahlreich sind als erwartet, muß das erstens der Schwierigkeit, eine Abweichung vom Erwarteten wahrzunehmen, zugeschrieben werden; zweitens aber spielt dabei der Umstand auch eine Rolle, daß ein Aufzeichner, wenn er etwas Unerwartetes gehört zu haben glaubt, in der Regel den Gewährsmann das Wort wiederholen läßt; und wenn man die Variation der sprachlichen Merkmale in Betracht zieht, ist es eigentlich nicht verwunderlich, daß solche · Wiederholungen sehr häufig zuletzt zur vollen Zufriedenheit des Aufzeichners ausfallen.

Die meisten dänischen Sprachgebräuche besitzen ja ein langes e· und ein langes $æ$·; in der Mundart von Fjolde entsprechen zwar die Diphthonge iˀ und eꞯ dem altdänischen $\bar{e}$ und $\bar{æ}$; es gibt aber eine Anzahl von Wörtern, die im Altdänischen kurzes i und kurzes $æ$ haben, wo alle Aufzeichner ein e· und ein $æ$· erwarteten. Einige inkonsequente Schreibungen sind vorhanden (Lyngby hat z.B. $e·n$ꞯ und $æ·n$ꞯ ''Ende'', $be·st$ und $bæ·st$ ''Biester''), aber sie sind nicht sehr zahlreich. Außer e· und $æ$· haben Poul Andersen und ich auch das Zeichen $ɛ$· verwendet; dieses Zeichen wird wenigstens in meinen Aufzeichnungen als Ausdruck dafür verwendet, daß ich in dem betreffenden Falle nicht zu entscheiden vermochte, ob das Wort e· oder $æ$· hatte. Meine Anwendung dieses Zeichens wurde nach und nach immer häufiger, und als mir dies zuletzt zu sehr auffiel, fragte ich meine Gewährsleute nach ihrer Meinung und gelangte zuletzt zu der Überzeugung, daß die Mundart nur *einen* ungerundeten offenen Vorderzungenvokal besitzt. Zwei Gewährsleute — die jüngsten und schlechtesten — sprachen freilich in einigen niederdeutschen Lehnwörtern ein niederdeutsch klingendes e^i; es zeigte sich aber, daß diese beiden als die einzigen meiner dänischen Gewährsleute in ihrem Niederdeutsch den gewöhnlichen niederdeutschen Unterschied zwischen $\bar{e}$ und $\bar{ę}$, $\bar{o}$ und $\bar{ǫ}$ anerkannten; sie sagten also $nę̄^gn$ $xę̄lə$ $sd\bar{e}n$ ''neun gelbe Steine'' und $sǭbm$ $xr\bar{o}nə$ $b\bar{o}mə$ ''sieben grüne Bäume'' mit verschiedenen e- und $ö$-Lauten, während die ältesten Gewährsleute in diesen Wörtern denselben e-Laut und $ö$-Laut sprachen. Diese Erhebungen konnten nur meine Ansicht bestätigen, daß auch die dänische Mundart in Fjolde den Unterschied zwischen e· und $æ$· nicht kennt. Nun gibt es aber eine Quelle, die ich im Vorhergehenden nicht erwähnt habe, weil sie zur Lösung der behandelten Probleme keine wesentlichen Beiträge liefert. Das sind die Briefe Lorenz Petersens an den Mundartforscher P.K. Thorsen aus dem Jahre 1901[17]. Lorenz Petersen war Volksschullehrer auf Bornholm, aber gebürtig aus dem Kirchspiel Fjolde. Die Briefe enthalten nur ein dürftiges Material; da Lorenz Petersen aber der einzige Eingeborene ist, der Wörter dieser Mundart niedergeschrieben hat, verdienen seine

Aufzeichnungen natürlich große Aufmerksamkeit. Es zeigte sich nun, daß Lorenz Petersen zwischen langem *æ·* und langem *e·* unterscheidet: 13 Wortformen sind mit langem *æ·*, 15 mit langem *e·* geschrieben; z.B. schreibt er *brænt* "gebrannt", aber *kent* "gekannt" und *rent* "gerannt". 1935 stellte ich zur Kontrolle meiner Ergebnisse ein Verzeichnis von ein paar hundert Testwörtern auf; hier schloß ich nun einige Wortpaare mit ein, wo der Unterschied zwischen einem *e·* und einem *æ·* eventuell sprachlich gültig sein *könnte*. Mag. Ole Widding und ich fragten zwei Gewährsleute, ob *sælge* "verkaufen" von *Sele* "Pferdegeschirr", *stjæle* "stehlen" von *skille* "scheiden" und *Vejr* "Wetter" von *vide* "wissen" lautlich verschieden seien; die Gewährsleute erklärten, die Wörter seien paarweise gleichlautend, und das war auch nach unserem Gehör der Fall: *stjæle* und *skille* wurden als *ʂxe·t*, *sælge* und *Sele* als *se·t* und *Vejr* und *vide* als *ve·ı* aufgezeichnet. Eine erneute Untersuchung von Lorenz Petersens Material ergab nun, daß *æ* nur in solchen Wörtern steht, die in der damaligen dänischen Orthographie mit *æ*, – *e* dagegen nur in Wörtern, die mit *e* geschrieben wurden; Lorenz Petersen hat also augenscheinlich diese beiden Buchstaben als Zeichen desselben Sprachlauts verwendet, in gleicher Weise wie Parum Schulze aus Lüchow 200 Jahre früher *w·* und *f·* als gleichbedeutende Zeichen benutzte.

8. Die syntagmatische Gliederung der wahrgenommenen Lautmassen.
Das oben Dargestellte betrifft nur die *paradigmatische* Einteilung der Sprachlaute; dagegen ist noch nichts gesagt über die Frage nach der *syntagmatischen*[18] Gliederung des Redestroms.

Trubetzkoy ist dieser Frage mit seinen Regeln über die monophonematische und polyphonematische Wertung von Lauten und Lautverbindungen[19] nicht auf den Grund gegangen. Denn die Laute, die bei Trubetzkoy monophonematisch bzw. polyphonematisch gewertet werden, sind schon durch schriftliche Zeichen gegliedert. Aber einem schriftlichen Zeichen ist ein Sprachlaut nicht ohne weiteres zuzuordnen, auch nicht wenn es sich um ein sogenanntes Lautzeichen handelt. Und erst recht nicht, wenn das Lautzeichen von einem fremden Beobachter niedergeschrieben ist; denn eine von einem fremden Beobachter niedergeschriebene Reihe von Lautzeichen besagt nur, daß die und die Person auf eine bestimmte Lautmasse so und so reagiert und die Lautmasse so und so gegliedert hat.

Diese Gliederung einer gehörten Lautmasse durch einen fremden Aufzeichner erfolgt in der gleichen Weise wie die Wahrnehmung fremder Laute überhaupt: in Übereinstimmung mit irgend einer Gliederung bekannter Sprachen, insbesondere derjenigen seiner Muttersprache. Die Gliederung einer Lautmasse der Muttersprache geschieht wohl in der Regel in Übereinstimmung mit dem orthographischen System der Schriftsprache und braucht nicht die best mögliche zu sein, d.h. sie braucht nicht die in der betreffenden Sprache bestehenden sprachlich relevanten Unterschiede zwischen Lautmassen auf die möglichst einfache Formel zu bringen — das ist Aufgabe des Sprachforschers —; aber sie muß diese Unterschiede auf irgend eine Formel bringen, die genügt, um sie als Unterschiede zwischen Sprachlauten und nicht als Unterschiede zwischen ungegliederten Lautmassen aufzufassen.

Der Aufzeichner hört also eine fremde Lautmasse, als ob sie Vertreterin einer Reihe ihm bekannter Sprachlaute wäre. Ein fremder Sprachlaut wird deshalb, wenn es geht, in zwei Stücke zerschlagen, d.h. als Vertreter zweier aufeinanderfolgender bekannter Sprachlaute aufgefaßt, oder jedenfalls als Vertreter eines Sprachlauts plus ein "Gleitlaut". Dabei spielt aber die Variation eine besonders große Rolle: Eine geringe Änderung kann bewirken, daß ein gehörter Laut nicht mehr als Vertreter zweier Sprachlaute, sondern als Vertreter eines einzelnen Sprachlauts aufgefaßt wird. Deshalb enthalten die Aufzeichnungen gerade in Hinblick auf die syntagmatische Gliederung besonders zahlreiche Inkonsequenzen. Beispiele sind oben S. 90 f. und S.108 angeführt, z.B. aus den Aufzeichnungen Poul Andersens die Schreibungen des Wortes *gul* "gelb": *gu·Ol* (wo das velarisierte *t* als Vokal + "normales" *l* aufgefaßt ist), *gu·t* (als velarisiertes *t*), *gu·ət* (als Gleitlaut + velarisiertes *t*). Solche Schwankungen in bezug auf die von den Aufzeichnern vorgenommenen Gliederungen der wahrgenommenen Lautmassen sind auf dieselbe Weise wie die übrigen Schwankungen zu überprüfen und unter Anwendung entsprechender Überlegung mit einander in Übereinstimmung zu bringen.

9. Schluß.
Die oben angeführten Beispiele sind natürlich deswegen ausgewählt worden, weil die Aufzeichnungen in diesen Fällen besonders weit auseinandergehen und deshalb in diesem Zusammenhang besonders aufschlußreich sind; in den meisten Fällen stimmen sie vollkommen überein; aber auch mit dieser Einschränkung dürfte aus den Beispielen hervorgehen, daß die Aufzeichnungen in Fjolde für sämtliche Auf-

zeichner eine besonders schwierige Aufgabe gewesen sind: Keinem von uns ist es durch unmittelbare Beobachtung gelungen, das Lautsystem der Mundart zu erfassen. Sie beweisen aber auch, daß der Wert einer Aufzeichnung nicht davon abzuhängen braucht, ob die Bezeichnungsweisen widerspruchslos sind oder nicht; Konsequenz der Bezeichnungen *kann* nämlich dadurch erzielt worden sein, daß es dem Aufzeichner schwergefallen ist, Abweichungen vom Erwarteten wahrzunehmen. Unbedingt notwendig ist nur eine gewissenhaft durchgeführte Notation, die nur das bezeichnet, was tatsächlich wahrgenommen wird; an Hand solcher Aufzeichnungen wird es uns gerade durch die Erkenntnis, daß die Wahrnehmungsfähigkeit der Aufzeichner beschränkt ist, und durch die Behauptung, daß sie in gesetzmäßiger Weise beschränkt sei, ermöglicht, die scheinbaren Widersprüche aufzuheben und ohne Zuhilfenahme der Sprachgeschichte das x zu finden, das sich in den Aufzeichnungen in so verschiedener Art und Weise widerspiegelt.

Das x, das wir durch die oben vorgeschlagenen wahrnehmungspsychologischen Erwägungen finden können, ist freilich noch nicht das System des sprachlichen Ausdrucks einer gegebenen Mundart, sondern nur die "Sprachlaute"; diese bilden aber das unentbehrliche Rohmaterial, aus welchem wir durch Anwendung der eigentlichen sprachwissenschaftlichen Methode dieses System erarbeiten können.

ANMERKUNGEN.

*Vorgelegt in der gemeinschaftlichen Sitzung der Gesellschaft für nordische Philologie und des Kopenhagener Linguistenkreises vom 14. November 1939.

1   S. z.B. K.J. Lyngby: Bidrag til en sønderjysk Sproglære (1858) s. 38; J. Winteler: Die Kerenzer Mundart des Kantons Glarus (1876) s. 35ff.

2   Sognemaalene (1922) s. 40.

3   Sønderjysk Sproglære S. 38 f.

4   Sognemaalene S. 54 f.

5   N. Trubetzkoy: Polabische Studien (Sitzungsberichte der Akademie der Wissenschaften in Wien, phil.-hist. Klasse B. 211, 1929).

6   Nach P. Rost: Die Sprachreste der Draväno-Polaben (1907) S. 87 ff.

7   Polabische Studien S. 53.

8   E. Selmer: Sprachstudien im Luneburger Wendland. 1918.

9   Laut- und Formenlehre der polabischen Sprache S. 152.

10   K.J. Lyngby: Bidrag til en sønderjysk Sproglære S. 5, 37.

11   Zur *Grösse der Ziffern* ist folgendes zu bemerken: Die Zahlen bei Lyngby 1b sind naturlich zu klein; alle ubrigen Zahlen sind (nach Berechnungen, denen ich Herrn Dr. Groth-Petersen, Kopenhagen, verdanke) gross genug, um die genannten Vergleichungen durchzuführen; im ungünstigsten Falle (bei den Zahlen des Auslauts bei Lyngby) ergab die Wahrscheinlichkeitsberechnung eine Sicherheit von 95%.

12   Adolf Noreen: Vårt Språk I p. 407.

13 S. namentlich: E. Zwirner und K. Zwirner: Aufgabe und Methoden der Sprachvergleichung durch Mass und Zahl (Zeitschr. f. Mundartforschung XII 65 ff.), E. Zwirner und K. Zwirner: Grundfragen der Phonometrie (1936), und K. Zwirner: L'opposition phonologique et la variation des phonèmes (Archiv fur vergl. Phonetik II 135 ff.); vgl. auch L. Hjelmslev: Neue Wege der Experimentalphonetik (Nordisk Tidsskrift for Tale og Stemme II 153 ff.).

14 E. A. Meyer: Englische Lautdauer (Skrifter utg. af K. Vetenskaps-Samfundet i Uppsala VIII 3) S. 39 f.; Zur Vokaldauer im Deutschen (Nordiska Studier tillägnade Adolf Noreen, 1904) S. 354 f.

15 E. Zwirner im Archiv fur vergl. Phonetik II 142 f.; G. Linke: Problemgeschichtlicher Uberblick uber Quantitäts- und Lautdauermessungen (Archiv fur vergl. Phonetik III) S. 115 f.

16 Blandinger udg. af Universitets-Jubilæets danske Samfund I S. 56.

17 Im Archiv des Udvalg for Folkemaal, Kopenhagen.

18 Die beiden Wörter paradigmatisch und syntagmatisch werden hier in der Hjelmslevschen Bedeutung benutzt; s. z.B. L. Hjelmslev im Archiv fur vergl. Phonetik II S. 131 f.

19 N. Trubetzkoy: Anleitung zu phonologischen Beschreibungen S. 10 ff, Grundzüge der Phonologie S. 50 ff.

The unstressed vowels
in Danish runic inscriptions
from the period c. 1000 - c. 1250

Introduction.

There is an unfortunate lacuna in our knowledge of the history of the Danish language, namely the period between c. 1000 or c. 1050, the time when the runic period proper was coming to an end, and c. 1250 or 1300, the time when the so-called MS period was beginning. Only a few meagre linguistic records survive from these two or three hundred years, i.e. some medieval runic inscriptions, mostly on tombstones and similar articles, and the Danish personal and place-names which are found in Latin charters, necrologies etc.

This lacuna is all the more unfortunate because in the course of the period in question a number of linguistic developments took place which resulted in the splitting up of the earlier unified Danish language area into at least three different dialect areas. One of the ways in which this division is revealed is in the development of the vowels of unstressed syllables. It is these vowels which are the subject of this article.

In viking age runic inscriptions the usage with respect to these vowels was identical over the whole of the Danish area. There were three different vowels, namely | i, ɲ y and ┼a. It is, of course, impossible for us to know with certainty how these vowels were *pronounced* but we do know that they were different from each other and that they were different in the sense that the substitution of one for another would give a different meaning: faþir nom.: faþur obl. case; kuna nom.: kunu obl. case; tufi nom.: tufa obl. case.

In the present article Hjelmslev's term *commutation* will be used to indicate this kind of distinction and vowels that differ in this way will be called commutables. A difference which is not a commutation will be called a *variation,* and vowels which differ from each other without being commutables will be called *variants.*

The Danish law texts from the period around 1300 reveal that there were already three distinct dialect areas, Scania, Zealand and Jutland.

In texts from Scania there are *three* commutables in unstressed syllables and each of these commutables can be written in two different ways, that is to say has two variants: i/e, u/o, a/æ. There is, then, variation and not commutation between i and e, between u and o, between a and æ. The variants fall into two series: i u a and e o æ. These two series alternate with each other in accordance with a well-known principle called Scanic vowel harmony. This has been described in detail by Brøndum-Nielsen in articles in APhS 2. Scanic also has another kind of unstressed syllable, in which only one vowel appears. This sound can be represented in several ways, either by æ or by the vowel of the preceding stressed syllable: bøndær / bøndør, skiutær/skiutur, acær/acar (verb and subst.) etc. These syllables are, then, those containing a so-called svarabhakti vowel.

The state of the language in Zealand is represented by the oldest MS of Erik's Zealand Law, AM 455 12°. This has *three* commutables: a/æ, u/æ, i/æ. Whereas it is normally æ that appears, with the result that the three commutables coincide, there are a few instances of a, u(o), i: alla, haua; tiughu 'hayfork' (obl. case), thumul fingær, houoth; hini (masc. pl. nom.), suni (dat.). In addition i often appears in the neighbourhood of certain consonants, notably k and g. Apart from this the principle behind the variation would seem to be a special Zealand vowel harmony which differs from the Scanic one (cf. Brøndum-Nielsen's GG I 391 ff.).

Finally, in Jutlandic only one vowel is found in the syllables in question. This is normally represented by æ but, when not followed by a consonant, it can be omitted altogether. In Jutlandic, then, there is alternation between æ and zero.

In this brief survey of the language in the three dialect areas no account has been taken of complications which arise in certain specific situations, e.g. the unstressed diphthongs ia and iu present particular problems. Since these are not relevant to the present survey, however, it seemed reasonable to leave them out of consideration.

The question now is: what changes had taken place in the language during the period between about 1000, when the runic inscriptions show that the linguistic situation was uniform throughout the country, and about 1300, when the MSS of the laws reveal the different situations in the three dialect areas?

The development of the unstressed vowel in the period in question is normally referred to by the term *vowel weakening*. The form þene instead of the expected þeni on the Hanning stone from Jutland, which is from c. 1100, has thus been taken to be an exceptionally early instance of Jutlandic vowel weakening. The term vowel weakening, however, is unfortunate for two reasons. Firstly because it is a *phonetic* term; whether or not it is an apposite phonetic term will not be discussed here, it is at any rate a phonetic term and hence presents the problem in an inconvenient way. Inconvenient, because the problem is, in principle, insoluble. As has been mentioned above, it is impossible for us to know *anything definite* about the phonetic pronunciation of the vowels in the medieval period. And we ought, of course, here as elsewhere, to restrict ourselves to problems which, in theory at least, can be solved. This means first and foremost questions to do with the structure of the language, in particular the number of commutables and the rules for their manifestation. Secondly because the term vowel weakening combines two phenomena which ought to be kept separate, namely a reduction of the number of commutables and a change in their *manifestation*. The first phenomenon occurs in the Jutlandic Law, the second in AM 455 12°, where there is a partial but not complete merging of the three commutables: a/æ; i/æ; u/æ.

I intend, then, to attempt to answer two questions with the aid of the material available: How many commutables are found in unstressed syllables in a certain linguistic situation? And by what laws is their manifestation determined?

In theory it should be possible to answer these questions. In practice, however, it is not always possible to do so because the material available is so meagre and uncertain that we are unable to determine with certainty what linguistic structure underlies any given text. The fragments of text surviving only allow us to determine which solutions are feasible and which are not. From among the feasible solutions it should then be possible to select the one that fits most conveniently into a linguistic-historic system. Our prime task, however, and the most important one must be to discover the structural possibilities which are offered by the texts. It is in this sense and in this sense only that diachrony presupposes synchrony, that the history of the language presupposes the description of the language.

In the following an attempt will be made to answer the two questions for each of the three periods: 1000-1050, 1050-1150, 1150--1250. As far as the second question is concerned, special attention will be paid to the possibility of *vowel harmony* (i.e. the law according to which the variation of the unstressed vowel is determined by the vowel of the preceding stressed syllable) and of *vowel balance* (i.e. the law according to which the variation is determined by the length of the stressed syllable, where the distinction is between a *short* syllable, containing a short vowel followed by a single consonant, and a *long* syllable, containing either a short vowel followed by a consonant group or double consonant or a long vowel with or without a following consonant or consonants). In both cases the determination can be *exclusive,* i.e. under the one condition the one vowel *always* appears and under the other condition *always* the other vowel, or *inclusive* or *participative,* i.e. under the one condition the one vowel *always* appears, while under the other condition *now* the one vowel appears and *now* the other. Because of the meagreness of the material available, no account is taken of the unstressed diphtongs ia and iu.

It will be necessary to begin by giving a short description of the texts that survive.

From medieval Denmark in the period c. 1000 - c. 1250 we have altogether close on 250 runic inscriptions but a great number of these are either indecipherable or uninterpretable. Chronologically they are distributed as follows[1] : Period 1. c. 1000 - c. 1050 with over 100 inscriptions: period 2. c. 1050 - c. 1150 with about 50 inscriptions of which 37 are from Bornholm; period 3. c. 1150 - c. 1250 with over 100 inscriptions. As far as their orthography is concerned, the following comments on the vowels in unstressed syllables must be made[2] : A special e-rune, different from the i-rune († : |) comes into use c. 1000; in stressed syllables the i-rune can be used instead of the e-rune but the reverse process does not occur; the use of the e-rune, however, becomes more common with the passage of time. A special o-rune, different from the u-rune (ᚴ : ᚿ) comes into use c. 1100; in stressed syllables the two runes are normally kept apart. A special æ-rune, different from the a rune (ᛏ : ᚼ) comes into use c. 1150; in stressed syllables these two runes are also normally kept apart from each other.

The inscriptions from Scania and Bornholm.
In the earliest period we have three commutables in unstressed syllables. Two of these always appear as a and o respectively, since there was as yet no possibility of distinguishing between a and æ and between o and u. The third commutable appears sometimes as e and sometimes as i, for the e-rune had already come into use. The special e-rune still only makes rare appearances, however, even in stressed syllables; a typical example is the Holmby stone, DR no. 328: suin risþi stina þesi ef(t)iʀ þurgiʀ faþur sin. In unstressed syllables e only appears in a single inscription, namely DR no. 329 Gårdstånga 1 : þulf ʀ uk ulf ʀ risþu stina þise ufter asmut liba felaga sin.

From among the many possible explanations for the appearance of e in þise and ufter there are three which are worthy of mention here. Firstly, this use of e agrees with the normal Scanian laws for vowel harmony. The i in þise probably indicates the vowel æ, and the u in ufter the vowel ø. Secondly, the use of e (þæss- being a long syllable) agrees with a law about vowel balance which says that a short syllable must be followed by i, a long syllable by e. There is, however, no means of checking this, since from the period in question not a single word survives with a stressed short syllable followed by the vowel i/e. This is because in Old Danish there are many more stressed long syllables than stressed short syllables. Thirdly, there could have been free interchange of i and e.

In the second period, 1050-1150, the majority of the inscriptions are from Bornholm. There are still three commutables. The one is always written a, the second sometimes i and sometimes e, the third sometimes u and sometimes o. The special e-rune is still rare. In unstressed syllables it is only found in two inscriptions, namely in DR no. 383 Vester-Marie 1:. . . bruþ(i)ʀ . . . raist[u] kumbl þitsi . . . afteʀ as . . . bruþuʀ sin, and in DR no. 400 Klemensker 2: brune auk þeiʀ bruþr let . . . eftiʀ þurlak foþur sin auk eskiʀ bruþur sin. The third vowel is almost always represented by u; o appears only once, in DR no. 392, Øster-Marie 3: (b)ar(n)i auk tofi ok askutr letu resa sten eftiʀ siba (b)roþor sin.

In this period it is hardly possible to ascribe the alternation to the workings of vowel harmony, since the personal name brune is probably derived from the ODan adj. brūn "brown" and e ought not to be found after u. On the other hand, there may be vowel balance, since e and o in afteʀ, brune and broþor occur after long syllables.

From the period 1150-1250 we have comparatively few runic inscriptions from East Denmark. There are still three commutables, all represented in DR supplement no. 5, bone fragment from Lund 4: bondi ris ti mal runu. arar ara æru fiaþrar[3]. The first is always written as a, the second as both i and e, the third as both u and o. The e-rune appears in five identical inscriptions on fonts from Scania from the end of the twelfth century (DR nos. 320, 322, 326, 327, 332): marten mik giarþe and marten mik giarþi; and possibly also in DR no. 336, which is only known from Skonvig's drawing: hær ligr hilþulf suin sun uoþær. In DR the last word of this inscription is assumed to be an error for unþær "under" (Skonvig may have read ᚴ as ᚴ); since it is impossible to distinguish Skonvig's representations of the runes ᚬ æ and ᛐe from each other, however, (see DR atlas no. 781), the word ought perhaps to be read as unþer. The o-rune only occurs in DR no. 347 Nörra Åsum: krist mario sun hiapi þem ær kirku þe . . . [g]erþi[4] absalon ærki biskup ok æsbiornmuli.

This use of e and o does not correspond to the laws for vowel harmony. It is true that marten and giarþe can be made to agree with the laws for vowel harmony evidenced in the last part of MS B 74 of the Scanic Law[5] but this does not apply to mario (and unþer). On the other hand, there could be vowel balance, for e and o always occur after a long syllable; in this case the rule must be that a long syllable can be followed by i, u and e, o, but a short syllable only by i, u. The material is so meagre, however, that other possibilities must also be taken into account, e.g. free interchange or a combination of vowel harmony and vowel balance[6].

This result is in full agreement with the one reached by Brøndum-Nielsen on the basis of his examination of the oldest sections of Libri Datici Lundenses, which contain name forms such as Sibbe, Sune, Unnæ[7]. It is possible, but not certain, that there was vowel balance in the Scanian dialect in the twelfth and thirteenth centuries.

The inscriptions from the Danish islands.
From the period between 1000 and 1050 there are only two inscriptions, DR no. 229 Sandby 3 and no. 238 Fjenneslev. Both of these have three commutables, represented by a, i and u.

From the period between 1050 and 1150 there are three inscriptions, DR no. 200 Ørsted, no. 201 Allerup and no. 212 Tillitse. They have three commutables (cf. the concluding portion of the long Tillitse inscription: toki risti runaʀ ef (tiʀ) [þ](o)ru stiubmoþur sina kunu koþa); the two first of these always appear as a and i, while the third is found as both u and o. The o-rune is only found in the last part of the Allerup inscription, which is only known from Skonvig's drawing (DR atlas no. 476): sati aft faþur [o](k) moþor (the following (t)on(o) is uncertain).

In this period we may have vowel harmony or vowel balance or a combination of the two, besides other possibilities.

In the following period, 1150-1250, there is a difference between the inscriptions from Zealand and those from Funen. From Zealand there are the following inscriptions: DR nr. 222-23 Allerslev, 235 Tårnborg, 240-41 Asminderup, 257 Søborg, There are three commutables, although there is only one certain instance of a: st(ina) in no. 235; u always appears as u (misu, mæsu, runu, ræhnldu) and i normally as i (risti, raþi, toki, lani, garþi) but probably once as æ, namely on the brick from Søborg, which has been dated to the close of the 12th century: þæn fyrstæ. If we accept DR's interpretation of these words as "the first (brick)" (i.e. the first brick to be burnt), then the adj. must be in the masc. sg. and presumably in the nom. case. There is no reason why the originally acc. form þæn should not be found for the nom. as early as this, for in the contemporary inscription from Allerslev, DR no. 222, þæn appears as the nom. of the demonstrative pronoun: raþi þæn ær kan. It is thus possible, and indeed probable, that æ here is a manifestation of i. On the other hand, it ought not to be impossible for þæn fyrstæ to be in the acc. and in that case æ would be a manifestation of a.

In either case we may have vowel harmony or vowel balance, besides other possibilities.

This result can be compared with the material provided by the oldest MSS from Zealand. There are three main sources: 1. the oldest documents in the Esrum Cartulary, 2. the cadastre of King Valdemar, and 3. two charters from c. 1200 in the register of donations to Næstved (printed in SRD IV 403 f. with numerous errors that have been corrected in the following).

In the oldest documents in the Esrum Cartulary[8] it is doubtful whether two or three commutables are found. One is represented by a and e (æ occurs extremely rarely); a occurs particularly after a and ā, e.g. in the place-names Tanga (1151, 1162, 1178, 1211), Hafraholm (1184, 1193, 1211); cf. also Hafreholm 1189, 1211, and the form Hauerholm 1178, 1228, which is probably to be ascribed to the scribe), and Cracadal[9] (1189, 1193, 1211; also Crakedal 1211); on etymological grounds a would have been expected in, e.g. Hiarnethorp (1189, 1193); a is also found, however, although less frequently, after u, o, ō, ø, ø̄, æ, ē, e.g. in Tumathorp (1189, also Tomethorp 1178 and 1211, Tumethorp c. 1170, 1184, and Tummethorp 1211), Notaboda (1228 beside Nøthebothe 1246), Eplaholt (1211-14), Herleua (1228, but e.g. Frithisleue 1162-66). Where i would be expected on etymological grounds, e almost always appears; i is only found before s and ng and in masc. names of the weak declension, e.g. Birgisholm (1178), Byrgisholm (1184), but Karlestorp (1178), Sune Ebbi filius (1162-66). Where u would be expected on etymological grounds, e always appears after both short and long syllables, e.g. in Mulnethorp (1178), Mulneholt (1178, 1211), Lathebo (1228) and probably also in Worethorp (c. 1170).

We find exactly the same state of affairs in the cadastre of Valdemar (which survives in a transcript, most of which was written by the same scribe as AM 455 12°)[10] : Here, however, it is more certain that there are three rather than two commutables. a interchanges with æ and e; a is found particularly after a, e.g. in Hamarsheret (and Hamersheret), Faxaheret (and Faxæheret), Slangathorp (and Slangæthorp, Slangethorp), Saxakopingh, Nacascogh; rarely after ū, ō, ø̄: Tvnaheret (and Tunæheret), Sothathorp, Sotathorp, Logaheret (and Løghæheret[11]); when i and u would be expected on etymological grounds, æ, e normally appear indiscriminately; i is only found after k, g and before s, ng, and in a few weakly declined masc. names such as Frændi, Vbbi; and u is only found in the endings -um and -ung(i), the latter form alternating with -ing(i), -yng(i) in one and the same name (thus differing from the ending -ing(i), which is never written -ung(i)).

The situation in these two sources recalls most of all the typically Zealand vowel harmony which has been shown by Brøndum-Nielsen to be found in AM 455 12° (GG I 391 ff.).

A different impression is given by the third source, the two letters from the register of donations to Næstved. They only survive in an abstract from 1528 but it is clear that the scribe has retained the orthography of his originals; e.g. the use of ch in the two place-names Tochatorp and fulchulsø (the first l must be due to anticipation) to represent k and g respectively corresponds exactly with the orthography of other sources from c. 1200, e.g. in personal and place--names in Saxo, in Libri Datici Lundenses and in the Esrum Cartulary, where k is represented by k, c, ch, and g by (h), g and ch[12]. In these letters the three unstressed vowels almost always appear as a, i and u, e.g. in the place-names Jarandaleph, Siælstoffta, Hildistada, Withahagi, Rinchsabøli, Holstada, Tochatorp, Euiuby, Strychunes. There are only three exceptions, namely two instances of e for i and one of æ for a: Engeboli (the first el. is the collective ængi n. which occurs in other place-names), Merethueth (the second el. is the subst. thwēt f. and the first el. the comparative mēri, which ends in -i in the fem. sg. in all cases) and Østofftæ (the second el. is a fem. a-stem derivative of the subst. toft, cf. Siælstoffta above). Since the material is so limited, however, this distribution of æ and e may merely be accidental, as is the case with the use of æ and e in the Esrum Cartulary and the cadastre of King Valdemar. Even so, the divergence from the Esrum Cartulary and the cadastre is so great and the resemblence to the oldest MSS of the Scanic Law so striking that it is tempting to assume that the charters were written by a monk from Scania. Such an assumption would however, conflict with the above-mentioned form fulchulsø, the first el. of which is the gen. of the masc. name Fughl. Fulchuls has full vowel harmony in the svarabhakti vowel in agreement with forms such as DR no. 14 Bjolderup c. 1200 ligir pres. sg. "lies"[13], Valdemar's cadastre Sthorsakar (error for Thorsakar, Jutland), Swansakar (Langeland) and probably also Alaslef (Zealand; presumably an error for Alafs-, gen. of masc. name Alf), and finally the Næstved calendar c. 1200 Asal, masc. name Asl[14]. Vowel harmony in the svarabhakti vowel can thus be detected in sources from Jutland and the Danish islands as early as c. 1200. In the sources from Scania, however, it does not appear until c. 1300 (cf. GG I 407 f.). It is never found in the oldest sections of Libri Datici Lundenses and Necrologium Lundense, which only have name forms such as Asl (twice), Asel (several times) and Gisl (once). The two charters from the Næstved register of donations ought, therefore, to be treated as Zealand sources on an equal footing with the runic inscriptions, the charters from the Esrum Cartulary and the cadastre of Valdemar.

As far as the vowels in unstressed syllables are concerned, the material discussed here can be described as follows: There are three commutables, the first represented by a, æ, e, the second by i, æ, e, and the third by u, æ, e. As regards their representation, there is the difference between the runic inscriptions on the one hand and the cadastre of Valdemar and the Esrum cartulary on the other, that the former prefer a, i, u, the latter æ, e. To judge from the geographical distribution of the runic inscriptions, this difference is rather to be explained as a difference between archaic and modern usage than as a difference between dialects. The variation of the vowels in the runic inscriptions may have been determined by either vowel balance or vowel harmony, in the MS sources only by vowel harmony.

The runic inscriptions from Funen from this period all derive from between 1200 and 1250; they are DR no. 184 Bregninge, 186 the Svendborg knife, and the censers from the south of Funen, nos. 175, 179, 183. They normally have æ, rarely e, in unstressed syllables; there is only one instance of etymologically expected a: the second æ in læmæþe, and also only one of expected u: sazær, gen. of the masc. name Satsur; for expected i we have e and æ: unde (prep. "under"), aræ, helge, toke (the three last being the nom. case of masc. names), læmæþe, ristæ, gyorþæ, kørþæ, gørþæ, gøræ, køptæ (alle 3rd pers. sg.), mærge, hæftæ (both neut. i-stems). This material resembles that found in the Esrum Cartulary but is not incompatible with the contemporary material from Jutland.

The inscriptions from Jutland.
To the first period, 1000-1050, probably belong DR no. 46 Oddum, 62 Sjelle, 66 Århus 4, 68 Århus 6, 83 Sønder-Vinge 2, 97 Ålum 4[15]. They have three commutables, which are always written a, i, u.

From the following period, 1050-1150, there is only one inscription, namely the much-debated DR no. 48 Hanning: ua. . tofa su(n) rsþi sten þene eftir gyþu moþ[u]r sina.

There are three commutables, of which the two are represented by a and u and the third by both i and e (that -e in þene represents i and not a is deduced from the fact that þani, þæni is the normal younger Jutlandic form of the masc. sg. acc. of sāsi, as distinct from East Danish þana, þena (cf. DR col. 708). The principle behind the variation is quite uncertain. There is a possibility of either vowel balance (since þænn- is a long syllable) or vowel harmony.

In the following period there seems to be a difference between the inscriptions from northern Jutland and those from the rest of the peninsula.

As North Jutlandic inscriptions are reckoned DR nos. 147 Gudum (Himmerland, just south of Limfjord), 148 Søndbjerg, 156 Thisted, 157 Hillerslev (the last three from Thy), 163 Ø.-Brønderslev, 165 Børglum (these 2 from Vendsyssel). In these inscriptions there are 3 commutables. The first is always written, a, e.g. resa, kirkia, germuntar, misguntar. The second is written as i, e, æ (i in uþuakins, tufi, e in kristne (dat.), huiler, and æ in uulæ "caused", gurþæ "made", hæræ ? "here"), and the third as u, o (u in faþur, o in manom, mario (gen.)). Here there cannot be vowel harmony but only vowel balance.

Unfortunately it is not possible to compare these inscriptions with MSS from the same or the suceeding period since the abbey and cathedral archives from North Jutland only survive in very young and corrupt registers.

The inscriptions from the rest of Jutland present a completely different picture from those from North Jutland. The inscriptions concerned are the following: DR nos. 14 Bjolderup, 16 Hoptrup, 24 Holsted, 28 Vamdrup, 33 Ål, 51 Handbjerg, 59 Øm, 73 Kragelund, 74 Vejerslev, 92 V.-Velling, 111 Gesing 1, 142 Vitskøl[16]. From this evidence it would seem that there were only two commutables, the first corresponding to older a, the second to i and u. The first commutable is written a and æ: iuar, runa, þesa (no. 74); urnæ (no. 14), lakhæ (no. 111), this last is probably the acc. of the by-name Lāghi "the low". The second commutable is written i and æ; 1. for etymologically expected i: ketil (masc. name, nos. 14, 59), gæþi ("made", no. 111), þæni (no. 111), gæti (pres. subj. 3rd sg., no. 111)[17]; yvær (no. 74), yfæ ("over", no. 111), loþæns (gen. of the masc. name Lothin, no. 92); 2. for expected u: asir (interpretation open to doubt; DR proposes the nom. of the masc. name Atsur, no. 142); broþær (acc., no. 74). The runic material is, of course, much too slight to exclude the possibility that there may have been a third commutable, among other reasons because the above-mentioned form asir is uncertain and because there is a lack of examples of etymological u after a short root syllable and after root syllables containing e.g. u, i, y. We do, in fact, have an instance of surviving u in a charter from 1203 (only preserved in a 15th-century transcript in the Århus book, SRD VI 404): Saxwæl Ruthu, Saksild Rude, the acc. of the subst. ODan *rutha, OSwed ruþa f. "clearing". Here u is found in what must be the position most favourable for survival, namely after u in a short root syllable (cf. the fact that the youngest instance of surviving Primitive Scandinavian -u is sunu acc. sg. on the Helnæs stone). As late as about 1300 we have a single instance of -u in this position, namely the form referred to by Brøndum-Nielsen in GG I 395 flughu, pl. "flies" in the Stockholm MS of Harpestræng (Marius Kristensen's ed. 9[3]).

It is not possible to establish a law for the variation of the vowels. The last-named example is consistent with both vowel balance and vowel harmony but the previous ones are hardly consistent with either.

The MS material from Jutland is inferior to that from the islands and Scania. The best register is probably Ribe Oldemor but this has very little material from before 1250. It will only allow us to state that æ is written for etymologically expected a in e.g. lundæwra (1214), harthæsyslæ, almundsyslæ, warwithsyslæ (all 1234), and u for expected u in almund- (1234).

Conclusion.
A survey of all the relevant material with the answers to the questions formulated on p. 118 can be presented as follows:

	South Jutland	The islands	North Jutland	Scania-Bornholm
1000- -1050	3 commutables vowel bal. poss.[18] vowel harm.poss.	3 commutables vowel bal. poss. vowel harm.poss.	÷	3 commutables vowel bal. poss. vowel harm.poss.
1050- -1150	3 commutables vowel bal. poss. vowel harm.poss.	3 commutables vowel bal. poss. vowel harm.poss.	÷	3 commutables vowel bal. poss. vowel harm.im- poss.
1150- -1250	3 commutables vowel bal. imposs. vowel harm imposs.	3 commutables vowel bal. imposs. vowel harm.poss.	3 commutables vowel bal. poss. vowel harm. imposs.	3 commutables vowel bal. poss. vowel harm. imposs.

The results of the survey can be summarised as follows: The complete merging of the three vowels in unstressed syllables must be dated to the period around 1300. It occurs earliest in southern Jutland (it is only possible for us to talk about the sources which are known; we can know nothing about the spoken language). A little later, at the beginning of the fourteenth century, we find merging of the vowels in the sources from Zealand.

Apart from this the most marked difference between sources from southern Jutland and those from Zealand is that vowel harmony cannot be demonstrated in the Jutlandic sources, whereas Zealand sources from c. 1150 show clear signs of it.

The sources from northern Jutland differ from those from southern Jutland and resemble the ones from Scania-Bornholm. Like these, they have strong indications of vowel balance in the period 1150-1250. It seems likely that this represents the survival of an old feature of the Danish language and that in earlier periods there had also been vowel balance in Jutland and the islands. Such an assumption does not, as we have seen, conflict with the evidence offered by the texts but it has not been possible to prove that it is correct.

There are two differences between the sources from Zealand and those from Scania-Bornholm. Firstly, the rules for vowel harmony in Zealand are different from those in Scania, and secondly, full vowel harmony in the svarabhakti vowel appears earlier in Zealand than in Scania.

NOTES:

1 According to DR.
2 Cf. DR cols. 935 ff.
3 The dating of the inscription, however, is uncertain.
4 DR reads [g]erþo but an examination of the papier-maché impression taken by Wimmer, which is in the Royal Library, Copenhagen, by Erik Moltke and the present author revealed that the only possible reading is [g]erþi; cf. below p. 150 n. 35.
5 Cf. Brøndum-Nielsen in APhS 2. 177.
6 The medieval but not more precisely datable inscription from Listerby (DR no. 362, atlas no. 843), which is only known from Skonvig's drawing, reads: touæ (masc. name, twice), giorþæ and gorþæ "made"; here the appearance of æ (or e?) can be explained as either vowel harmony or vowel balance.
7 In APhS 2. 183 f.; GG I 387.
8 Account has been taken here of charters from c. 1150 to c. 1230. As far as the representation of the unstressed vowels is concerned, it has not been possible to demonstrate any difference between the older and the younger charters within this period, nor between papal bulls and native documents.
9 The first el. is the gen. sg. of the ON subst. kraki m. "pole" or the younger gen. pl. of krāka f. "crow".
10. Attention is only paid to names from Zealand, Lolland and Falster.
11 Forms with -a seem to retain more traces of the original orthography than do forms with -æ; cf. Loga- with Løghæ- with o = ø and g = gh, and Sotha- with th = t.

12 Marius Kristensen in DSt (1929) 66 ff.; Brøndum-Nielsen in GG II 104 f.; Poul Diderichsen in APhS 12. 131 f.

13 It might be possible to explain sinnæbuuhr on DR no. 175 Hesselager censer as an error in carving (or copying) for suinburuh.

14 In DgP I 70 this name has been confused with the related name Asli; these two names are kept apart in the sources except that Libri Datici Lundenses Sueno f: Asal must be an error for Asla, since the bearer of the name is identical with Suenonis f: Asla in Necrologium Lundense.

15 Account is only taken of inscriptions containing the special e-rune.

16 No account is taken of DR nos. 38, 39, 47, 103, because these inscriptions cannot be dated on archaeological grounds and they are probably younger than c. 1250. DR no. 146 Ferslev (North Himmerland) ought, perhaps, to be included among the inscriptions from North Jutland: . . . sti runar . . .

17 Masc. names in -i have changed their declension. They almost always end in i, not only in the nom.: imi (no. 16), tuki (no. 24), isli (no. 51), æsi (no. 73) − blomæ (no. 33) is the only exception − but also in the acc.: skalmi (no. 74); in the gen. they end in -i or -is: æbissun (no. 28), æbi sun (no. 111), cf. the North Jutlandic amdis son (no. 156) and the Zealandic Sune Ebbi filius (Esrum cartulary 1162-66); the latter probably represents a Danish Ebbi sun or Ebbis sun.

18 By this is meant that it is possible to explain all the unstressed vowels in the text by vowel balance alone.

Verbal number in the Jutlandic Law

I. Introduction.

1. 1. Among students of Scandinavian philology it is, presumably, the general opinion that the spoken dialects of Jutland abandoned numerical inflection of verbs already in the Middle Ages. This opinion is founded upon the fact that we find finite verbs in the singular instead of the plural in cases when the latter is to be expected (but practically never in the plural when the singular is to be expected) in the Jutlandic Law — the oldest mss of which date from about 1300 — and in other texts from Jutland more frequently than in the other Old Danish texts.

The origin and growth of this view will become apparent through an examination of the following treatments of the subject: K.J. Lyngby, *Udsagnsordenes böjning i jyske lov og i den jyske sprogart* (1863) p. 38 seq. (the instances of the singular instead of expected plural forms found in the Jutlandic Law are explained away); Edvin Jessen in *Tidskrift for Philologi og Pædagogik V* (1865) pp. 200-205 (the singular form of the verbs gradually ousted the plural form, and in the spoken language of Jutland and the Danish islands the numerical inflection disappeared altogether before 1600, but later than 1500, whereas the written language retained it till the modern period); Oluf Nielsen, *Gamle jydske Tingsvidner* (1882), intr. p. XXIII ("the verbs have lost all plural inflection" in the Jutlandic dialects of the 15th century); Hjalmar Falk and Alf Torp, *Dansk-Norskens Syntax* (1900) p. 13 (several dialects, particularly those of Jutland, abandoned the plural forms of the verbs in the 14th century); Verner Dahlerup, *Forelæsninger over første bog af jyske lov* (1920) p. 54 (the plural of the verbs may have been "a dying form" in the spoken language of Jutland about 1300); Peter Skautrup, *Dansk Sproghistorie I* (1944) p. 273 (the singular form had undoubtedly become the only one used in the spoken language of Jutland already about 1300).

The answers offered by these writers to this question depend upon their attitude to the general problem of the relation between the language of the Old Danish mss and the spoken language of the same period. Lyngby was of opinion that the difference between them must have been negligible at the time of the oldest mss of the Law (*Udsagnsordenes böjning* p. 3). By way of protest against this assumption, Jessen pointed out the quite considerable difference between the language of the oldest mss of the Jutlandic Law and the language of the contemporary ms of the Flensborg By-Laws. The latter difference can only be explained on the assumption that already by ab. 1300 a difference existed between the spoken Jutlandic dialects and a traditionally evolved written standard which the individual scribes tried to observe with varying success. Jessen's opinion prevailed. It was supported, among others, by V. Såby (*Årbøger for nordisk Oldkyndighed* 1872) and especially by Oluf Nielsen in his important edition of Jutlandic assize-records from the 15th and 16th centuries, a collection of texts the language of which can only be explained as a fusion of the dialects spoken by the scribes with a written standard. During the subsequent period investigators of the language of the Danish medieval mss have shown a singularly strong tendency to explain peculiarities in the text by means of hypotheses concerning the contemporary spoken language.

1.2. Thus the question we are dealing with, − viz. whether the Jutlandic dialects abandoned the numerical inflection of verbs about 1300 − gives rise to two other questions, one of a special nature, the other of a general nature: 1°. Does the description of the numerical inflection of verbs in the Jutlandic Law necessitate the establishment of two sets of rules, one applicable to a standard of written language, the other to the Jutlandic dialect spoken by the scribes, or is it possible to describe the text by means of a single set of rules? 2°. Under what circumstances is it possible to substantiate the thesis that the description of a text requires more than one set of rules, that is, under what circumstances is it possible to maintain that there is more than one linguistic structure behind a given text?

1.3. We shall try to answer the former of these questions first. For our textual material we choose the ms NkS 295 8°, which has been printed as the main text (A^1) in *Danmarks gamle Landskabslove*, vol. II. In addition, attention is given to the mss A^2, A^{13}, B^1, D^1, E, and G, i.e. all old mss up to ab. 1350 except those mss that belong — entirely or in part — to the I-group, the language of which is influenced by Scanic (cf. key to abbreviations in *Danmarks gamle Landskabslove*, vol. II p. CXXV seq.). Besides, a Latin translation made from a ms of the A-group (ab. 1300) and printed in *Danmarks gamle Landskabslove* vol. IV is taken into consideration. The main ms lacks the preface and the concluding (and younger) chapters on witchcraft, and these two parts, as well as the textually dubious headings, are therefore left out of consideration.

Whenever a quotation is cited it is accompanied by the corresponding passage of the Latin text mentioned above whenever the latter seems to be called for; when the Latin translation is too free it is replaced by a literal English translation.

1.4. There is no difference between the singular and the plural of verbs in the Jutlandic Law under the following conditions:

1°. When the verb is in the subjunctive (*han, the gialdæ* 'he, they pay'); 2°. When the verb is in the passive voice (*han, the finnæs* 'he is found, they are found'); 3°. When a verb of the weak conjugation is in the preterite tense (*han, the gørthæ* 'he, they did'). Consequently, the investigation may be confined to those sentences in which the verb is in the indicative mood, the active voice, and the present tense, and to such sentences as contain a strongly conjugated verb in the preterite indicative active. In these cases the plural ends in *-æ* or zero (the latter only in the present tense of verbs the roots of which end in double vowels, e.g. *mæn boo* 'men dwell'), and the singular form ends in either *-ær* or zero (the latter only in the preterite of strong verbs, in the present tense of preterite-present verbs, and in the present tense of certain verbs the roots of which end in *l, n, r,* or *s,* e.g. *dyl han* 'if he denies').

2. Sentences without Subjects.

2.1. In the first place we shall try to answer the question whether the endings mentioned above are to be regarded as expressions of the numerical content found in the subject (i.e. whether the numerical content of the subject is simply expressed twice, both in the formant of the subject and in that of the verb). If this question is answered in the affirmative, the task in hand will be an examination of the relation between an expression and its content. If the answer is in the negative, the numbers of the verbs must be conceived of as elements of content, and then we are confronted with the much more difficult task of defining the relations between these elements of content and other elements of content.

The question, however, can only be answered in the affirmative on condition that all sentences of the text in question have a subject. Accordingly, at the outset we shall have to find out whether it is possible to interpolate by catalysis a subject in all those sentences in which an explicit subject is missing[1].

2.2. With regard to the occurrence of sentences with a subject and of sentences without one in the Jutlandic Law the following three rules may be established:

1°. When *terminus a quo* for the action of the finite verb is indefinite there is no subject, e.g. *of thæm skil vm. . .* 'si discordant . . .', literally: 'if (it) separates them about. . .'; *hwænnær swo timær at . . .* 'if so happens that. . .'; *skiftæ mællæ aruing* 'then you must distribute (it) among the heirs'.

2°. When it is clearly indicated by the context what is the agent of the action implied by the verb, the subject may be lacking. Thus e.g. in a great many subjunctive sentences preceded by conditional sentences, cf. *hauær bondæ hafth kirkins iorth fivghærtivghæ wintær i hæfth, w æ r æ logh løøs for kirki. æn hauær kirkin hafth bondæns iorth thretvghwintær i hæfth vkærth, w æ r æ logh løøs for bondæn* (102³) 'si aliquis habuerat terram xl annis in possessione, *debet* eam absque omni lege tamquam iusto titulo possidere. Set si ecclesia triginta annis fuerat in possessione absque querela, *optinebit* terram absque omni lege'; all the old mss lack subjects in the two subjunctive sentences, *finnæ thæ at hun ær mæth barn. s i t æ fram i æghæn til barn wrthær fød* (24²) 'et si cognouerint eam inpregnatam, *resideat* sicut prius in bonis usque ad partum'; G has *tha sitæ hun*².

3°. When terminus a quo is not indefinite, and when it is not indicated unambiguously by the context what is the agent of the action implied by the verb, the sentence always has a subject in cases where it is necessary for the proper understanding of the statutory provision in question to know what the agent is; cf. *æn sæl bondæ siin kunæ iorth. oc køpær annæn iorth. takæ h u n af køpæ iorth fulling e mæthæn til ær* (86[6]) 'item si maritus uendiderit terram uxoris et emerit aliam, *ipsa* recipiet plenum restaurum de terra empticia, quam diu terra illa suffecerit'. G has *tha takæ hun.* But the subject may be lacking in this type of sentence, too, when the proper understanding of the text does not necessitate knowledge of the identity of the agent. The following example is illuminating: *hwa sum hauær slækæfrith i garth mæth sik. oc g a n g æ r opænbarlich mæth at souæ, oc h a u æ r laas oc lykki, oc s ø k æ r atæ oc dryk mæth opænbarlich i thre wintær. hvn skal wære athælkunæ oc ræt hwsfrø*[3] (68[6]) 'whoever has a concubine in the house with him, and goes openly to sleep with, and has lock and key, and seeks openly food and drink with for three years, she shall be wedded wife and lawful mistress of the house'[3]. It is seen that there are no subjects for the three verbs *gangær, hauær,* and *søkær* ('goes', 'has', and 'seeks'). Only as regards the second verb is it possible to infer the identity of the agent, seeing that the supervision of lock and key belonged to the women by rights. But it is quite uncertain who is the agent in the two other sentences. Some of the mss, and the Latin translation as well, have tried to find out, but they have arrived at different results (which constitutes a proof that the original ms had the same construction, without subjects, as A[1]). The Latin translation has: 'quicumque habuerit secum concubinam in curia et uadit *cum* ea manifeste dormitum, et *ipsa* habet seras et claues, et commedit *cum ea* et bibit manifeste in tribus annis, hiis elapsis ipsa debet esse legittima'. Corresponding to the 'cum ea' of the first sentence some (younger) mss have *mæth hænnæ* ('with her'), others have *mæth hanum* ('with him'); corresponding to the 'ipsa' of the second sentence E and some younger mss have *hvn* ('she'); in contradistinction to the 'cum ea' of the last sentence, E and a good many younger mss have *mæth hanum.*

A similar uncertainty is in evidence with regard to *hauæ hemæ giald* (89[2]). Here some younger mss have *(tha) hauæ hun,* but the Latin translation has 'ambo dampnum sustineant'. Neither in this nor in the preceeding quotation does the understanding of the provision necessitate exact knowledge of the identity of the agent in the sentences in question.

Accordingly, the last sentences cited must be considered ambiguous as regards the identity of the agent. In the first quotation the phrase *oc hauœr laas oc lykki.* . is neutral in relation to the identity of the agent[4], whereas *oc hvn hauœr las oc lykki* (the phrase used in E) decides in favour of one possibility. Presumably, the other sentences without subjects ought to be subjected to a similar interpretation: in a state of isolation they remain neutral in relation to several possibilities; it is only by their being placed in a context that they choose one of them.

Consequently, it is permissible to state for certain that sentences without a subject change their meanings when a personal pronoun is added as a subject. But this implies that it is impossible to interpolate a personal pronoun as a subject in this kind of sentence.

2.3. It might be objected, however, that it is not a personal pronoun pure and simple that ought to be interpolated, but one – or a number – of the constituent parts of the content of a personal pronoun. The content of *hun*, 'she', might be divided up into the following constituent parts: "nominative" (as distinct from all other cases) + "the third person" (as distinct from the first person and the second person) + "the singular" (as distinct from the plural) + "definiteness" (as distinct from "indefiniteness" in a pronoun like e.g. *œnnœn*, 'some one') + "the feminine gender" (as distinct from the masculine gender and the neuter). Thus the three first of the constituent parts mentioned (i.e. "nominative" + "third person" + "singular") might be interpolated in the sentence *oc hauœr*, and yet it would remain different from *oc hun hauœr*, which contains the additional constituent parts of "definiteness" + "feminine gender"[5].

If, however, we consider sentences of the type *of thœm skil vm. . .,* and if we assume that the interpolation of a pronominal subject (in this instance *thœt* 'it', 'that'[6]) would bring about a change in the content of this type of sentence, we find that here it would be precarious to catalyse by means of a subject consisting of "nominative case" + "the third person" + "the singular" + "indefiniteness" (i.e. a subject different from *thœt*, which contains "definiteness" instead of "indefiniteness"). For in contradistinction to the type of sentence discussed in the preceding paragraphs, the latter type of sentence does not involve any clear notion whatever of an agent, whether in the singular or in the plural. If we are to interpolate a subject in this type of sentence we have to infer its number from the formant of the verb, and in all these cases the formant is a singular-formant. So, the relevant question will be whether the existence of a singular-formant in the verb warrants the conclusion that the subject is in the singular. The following examination of the relation between the number of the verb and the number of the subject will show that such a conclusion is not permissible: the singular of the verb may be combined with both the plural and the singular of the subject.

Hence it may be stated that it is impossible to interpolate a subject with a numerical content expressed by the number-formant of the verb in all sentences without a subject. Consequently, the numbers of the verb must be dealt with as elements of content.

It will thus be our task to define the correlation between these elements of content, and on the other hand their relations to other elements of content, in order to be able to determine their proper place in the system of language.

3. Verbal Number in Sentences with Subjects in the Jutlandic Law[7].
3.1. Generally, there is concord between the number of the subject and the number of the verb in such sentences[8]. When the cases mentioned in 3.3 below are left out of consideration, there are the following modifications of this main rule:

When a subject in the singular is placed *before* the verb the latter is invariably in the singular[9], but when a subject in the plural is placed before the verb the latter is in the singular in the following four cases: *hoor børn t a k æ r æftær fathær ækki. . . vtæn han saldæ t h æ m nokæt i hændær førræ æn han døthæ* (65[6]) 'filii adulterini nichil post patrem recipiunt. . . nisi ante mortem suam assignauerit eis aliquid'; this is the reading of 2 old mss, 3 others have *hoor børn takæ* (i.e. plur. + plur.), and two have *hoor barn takær* (i.e. sing. + sing.); only one of the latter mss has *thæt* 'it' instead of *thæm* 'them' in the next sentence. *alt thæt the æ r laghlik til kraft* (148[4]) 'ad que fuerint laghlik til krafth'; 3 old mss have the plural form *æræ. ængi andræ raan m a wæræ minnæ æn half marks costæ* (218[5]) 'pro minori non potest adiurari raan quam pro re ualente dimidiam marcham denariorum', literally: 'no other robberies may be less than. . .'; 5 mss have the plural form *mughæ. thær han wæntær at hans costæ æ r til kummæn* (309[8]) 'ad quam credit res suas uenisse'; 2 old mss have *æræ*. To this may be added an example found in two other old mss: *svm limæ lvtæ oc røtær r i n n æ r* 'quantum frondes et radices extenduntur'; most of the mss have *root rænnær* 'radix extenditur'.

3.2. When a subject in the singular is placed *after* the verb the latter is never in the plural[10]. On the other hand the verb is in the singular when placed before a subject in the plural in 7 cases (out of ab. 200), e.g. *til hwar by a mæth rættæ fivghær wæghæ at gangæ* (130[4]) 'to every village has by rights four roads to go'; a few younger mss have the plural *aghæ. for thy at thæræ s c a l thry thing til* (146[5]) 'quia ad hoc debent esse tria placita'. *tha s c a l skyrthæs mæn* (379[3]) 'tunc debent styræsmen'; only A[1] and A[2] have the singular *scal*[11].

3.3. In the Jutlandic Law one noun has the plural form, but acts as a word in the singular, viz. *logh* 'law, legal case'. After some prepositions it appears in the dative plural, *loghum*, e.g. *mæth loghum* (72[2], 212[1], 342[6], 370[2], 410[2]); *at loghum* (172[3], 243[2], 319[2], 425[4]), but otherwise the word is in the singular: *thæn samæ logh ær vm fiskæ garth* (136[3]) 'eadem lex est de sepibus, qui dicuntur fiskægarthæ'. *for thy at meræ logh takær e thæn minnæ burt* (171[2]) 'quia maior iusticia semper preiudicabit minori'.

A special case is the noun *man* 'man', which displays an exceptional freedom with regard to concord. Thus *man* (sing.) + a verb in the plural occurs three times[12], and *mæn* (plur.) + a verb in the singular occurs three times[13]. It is a moot point whether *man, mæn* is used as an indefinite pronoun of the same denotation as the Modern Danish *man* 'one' in the main text of the Jutlandic Law; one tolerably certain example of this use of the word is found in the preface: *tha thyrftæ men ekki logh with* 'then one did not need any law'; other old mss have *man*[14]. In any case it may be justifiable to attribute a content including both an element of the plural and one of the singular to *man* and to *mæn* as well.

Similarly, the noun *folk* 'people' has a verb in the singular in some mss, in others a verb in the plural in the sentence *oc æ r æ folk a* (489[2]) 'and if there are people on (the ship)'[15].

3.4. Finally, mention has to be made of the cases in which the subject consists of two or more nouns connected by means of *oc* 'and' or *æth* 'or'. In these cases there are two possibilities: the number of the verb may either be in concord with the number of the word closest to it, or the verb may be in the plural; the former possibility is most frequently chosen when the verb is placed before the subject, the latter when the verb is placed after the subject. Cf. 1°. *s i t t æ r bondæ oc hwsfrø samæn i fælagh* (31[4]) 'if a farmer and his wife *sits* together in community'; 2 old mss have the plural

138

sitæ. oc æ r stivpmothær oc stivpbørn æftær (34[1]) 'and *is* the step-mother and the stepchildren left'; 2 old mss have the plural *æræ*. *tha ær fathær brothær. æth mothær brothær. brothær børn. æth systær børn. allæ æm næær* (28[3]) 'then is the father's brother or the mother's brother, the brother's children or the sister's children all equally near'. *mæthæn han l i u æ r oc mothær* (47[3]) 'as long as he lives and his mother'. − 2°. *thær theræ fathær oc mothær d ø ø* (48[4]) 'et pater et mater postea moriuntur'; 2 old mss have the sin-gular form *døør. klostær man. oc flætførth man. oc thræl. m u g h æ æi wæri wæræ* (66[4]) 'item seruus naturaliter et flætføring et clau-stralis non possunt esse tutores'; one old ms has the singular *ma*. *æn bondæ sun æth dottær i fællagh mæth theræ fathær m u g h æ ækki af hændæ* (446[1]) 'quod nec filius bondonis nec filia existentes in communitate cum patre eorum nichil possunt alienare'[16].

3.5. An examination of the sentences with subjects thus yields the following results: 1°. When the subject is in the singular the verb may be either in the singular or in the plural, the latter however only when the subject is a collective *(man, folk)* and when the subject consists of two or more nouns connected by means of *oc* or *æth*. Perhaps it is justifiable to say that in these two cases the subject contains both an element of "plurality" and one of "unity"; if that is the case a subject in the singular can only be combined with a verb in the plural provided that it contains an element of "plurality". 2°. When the subject is in the plural the verb may be either in the plural or in the singular, the latter not only when the subject is a collective *(mæn)* or consists of two or more nouns connected by means of *oc* or *æth*, but also in cases where it is impossible to maintain that the subject contains an element of "unity". Conse-quently, the relation between the number of the verb and the con-tent of the subject with regard to "plurality" and "unity" may be shown in the following diagram (provided that the interpretation of the collective and complex subjects suggested above proves valid).

When the subject contains:

	the number of the verb may be	
	plur.	sing.
"plurality" only	+	+
both "plurality" and "unity"	+	+
"unity" only		+

From this it is seen that the presence of an element of "plurality" in the subject does not imply the presence of the plural in the verb, and that the presence of "unity" in the subject does not imply the presence of the singular in the verb (under certain circumstances "unity" may be combined with the plural in the verb). Furthermore, the presence of the singular in the verb does not imply the presence of "unity" in the subject; but the presence of the plural in the verb does imply the presence of "plurality" in the subject.

This last relation of dependence ("selection", in Hjelmslev's terminology[17]) is sufficient demonstration that there is no confusion between the singular and the plural of verbs in the text under discussion. Indeed, the correlation between the singular and the plural of verbs is not that of mutual exclusion, but that of participation[18] so that, everywhere, the singular can act as a substitute for the plural, but not vice versa.

4. Verbal Number in Sentences without Subjects in the Jutlandic Law.

4.1. In "impersonal constructions" into which it is impossible to interpolate any subject (cf. p. 135 above) the verb is invariably in the singular, e.g. *skil børn with mothær* (51⁵) 'si mater et pueri discordant', literally: 'if (it) separates the children from the mother'. *æn worthær oc swo at. .* (247²) 'if so happens that. .'. *for draap of dræpæt waar. for saar of særth war* (402¹) 'for homicide if killed was, for wound if wounded was'. *swo sum foor wrthær mælt* (395⁵) 'as is agreed previously'.

4.2. In a few cases, a subject whose content is of an indefinite nature similar to that of *man, mæn* (p. 137 above) may be interpolated in the sentence, that is, a subject containing both "unity" and "plurality". In these cases the verb may be both in the singular and in the plural: *af the a grøthæ thær taknæ æræ. oc æi af the thær liggæ a iorthæn æth sa s c a l* (386³) 'from the crops which have been taken, and not from those that lie on the ground or sow shall (sing.)', כ : 'and which you must sow, which are to be sown'; 3 old mss have the plural *sculæ. til scapæth clæthæ oc gørth andboth oc til wapnæ. . . sculæ win til hauæ* (308⁴) 'for (the purchase of) cut cloth and manufactured tool and weapon. . must (plur.) have a witness' כ : 'you have to have a witness'; 2 old mss have *sculæ* without a subject, 5 old mss *sculæ mæn* 'must men'.

4.3. Finally, there are a great number of cases in which the agent has been mentioned previously. If there is more than one agent the verb is in the plural, no matter whether the agents in question are in the plural or in the singular in the preceding sentences[19] : *sittær bondæ oc hwsfrø samæn i fælagh oc k ø p æ iorth oc h a u æ [æi] børn samæn* (31[4]) 'if a farmer and his wife sits[20] together in community and buy (plur.) land and have (plur.) no children together'. *brytær man skiip oc æræ folk a. oc k u m m æ liuænd til landz* (489[2]) 'if a man is shipwrecked and people are on board, and come (plur.) alive to shore'; 3 old mss have *ær folk* 'people is' (cf. p. 138), but these mss also use the verb *kummæ* in the plural in the next sentence, which is in agreement with the fact that subsequently the shipwrecked persons are referred to by means of a pronoun in the plural. In one case the agent is a collective ('money'); although it has been referred to previously by means of a noun in the plural, the verb is in the plural only in some of the mss; in others it is in the singular: *sæl man sinæ iorth for rethæ pænning og w r t h æ æi lauth i iorth* (93[5]) 'if a man sells his land for cash money (*rethæ pænning* is the plural form) and *are* not laid in land'; 2 old mss have the plural *wrthæ*, one ms has *worth the* ('they are'), 4 old mss have the singular *warthær*.

By far the greater number of cases coming under this heading are constituted by relative clauses without relative pronouns[21]. Generally speaking, the verb is in the singular when the word to which the clause refers is in the singular, and in the plural when the word in question is in the plural. There are, however, cases without concord.

In three cases the verb is in the plural, although the clause refers to a noun in the singular. In two of these cases the plural form may be explained by reference to the influence of a numeral in the next sentence: *æn æræ æi tolf mæn i by: tha sculæ mæn takæ af thæn by thær thæm æ r æ næst e til tolf æræ* (122[3]) 'et si in uilla non sunt xij, recipiantur tot de uilla proxima, donec xij fiant', literally: 'from the village which are nearest to them'. Only A[1] has the plural *æræ*, the other mss have the singular *ær*. Undoubtedly the plural form is a scribal mistake caused by the fact that the scribe has been thinking of the men who were to be appointed. *win ær thæt witnæ thær with w a r æ at thæt køp køftæs. thæt ær æi minnæ æn twa mæn* (308[5]) 'amicus est testimonium alicuius fidedigni, qui *affuit* et *uidit* quando illud emebatur, et ad hoc sufficiunt duo boni homines'. Most mss — and among them 4 of the old mss dealt with in the investigation — have the singular *war*, but 3 old mss have the plural *waræ*, which may be explained by the fact that in this case the collective *witnæ* refers to two men, as appears from the subsequent sentence. The plural form is also explicable in the third case: *thæt ær thre·mæn af hwar fiarthing thær i thæt hæræth æ r æ* (492⁴) 'that is, three men of every fiarthing (which) *are* in that hundred'; the A-B--group and the ms G (including 4 old mss) have the plural *æræ*, the other mss have the singular *ær*. In the A-B-group (and G) there may be confusion with the phrases *hwar theræ fiarthing* 'each of the fiarthings', and *allæ the fiarthing* 'all the fiarthings' the noun *fiarthing* having no plural ending in the Jutlandic Law.

In about 80 cases the relative clause refers to a noun or a pronoun in the plural. In these cases the verb is generally in the plural. The singular is found in 12 cases. 3 of these cases may be explained away, whereas 9 cases cannot possibly be explained away²² ; cf. *til hwar by a mæth rættæ fivghær wæghæ at gangæ. thær af æræld ær til gangæn* (130⁴) 'to every village has by rights four roads to go, (which) *has* gone there from olden times'; only A¹ and A² have the singular *ær*, the other mss have the plural *hauæ*, 'have'; *ængi man ma swornæ wægh lukkæ æth menæ thær til køping. æth things æth strand æth til scogh æ r lauth* (132⁴) 'nullus potest uias ex antiquo iuratas impedire uel claudere, que *ducunt* ad uillas forenses uel ad placitum uel ad siluas uel ad litus maris'; all the old mss have the singular *ær;* 2 old mss have the singular *sworæn wægh* 'via iurata'. *the samæ thing høring thær thæm t o o k wt* (312⁵) 'the same thing-hearers (who) took (sing.) them out'; of the old mss only A¹ and A² have the singular *took*, the others have the plural *tokæ. tha sculæ the sannænd mæn til. thær thæræ ær i bygd* (450²) 'then those true men must assist who *is* in that district'; 2 old mss have the plural *æræ*² ³. *the costæ thær [i] hws w r t h æ r funnæn* (320⁵) '(pro) rebus furatis, que inuente *fuerint* in domo'; one old ms has the plural *warthæ*, 2 old mss have the passive form *finnæs* (in the passive voice there is no distinction between the singular and the plural, cf. p. 132). *vtæn the thær hanum s æ c t æ r* (354⁴) 'exceptis illis qui eum impetunt'; 3 old mss (A¹, A², G) have the singular *sæctær*, the others have the plural *sæctæ*²⁴. The following example from other mss may be cited: *æn hauær hin two brøthær thær frith løs ær flytth. thær sialf h a u æ gotz* (185³) 'item si ille habuerit duos fratres, qui pace priuatus est, qui per se *habent* bona'; 3 old mss have the singular *hauær*.

4.4. The result of this examination of verbal number in sentences without subjects are in exact agreement with the results achieved by the previous examination of sentences with subjects: 1°. When a sentence without a subject is related to a noun or a pronoun in the singular the verb may be either in the singular or in the plural; yet the plural only occurs when the sentence in question refers to a collective *(folk, witnæ)*, that is, only when it is possible to interpolate a subject which contains both "plurality" and "unity" (according to our assumption on p. 138 above)[25]. 2°. When a sentence without a subject is related to a noun or a pronoun in the plural the verb may be either in the plural or in the singular, the latter not only when the sentence refers to a collective *(costæ, rethæ pænning)*, but also in other cases. 3°. When a sentence without a subject is not related to any noun or pronoun the verb may be either in the singular or the plural if it is possible to interpolate a subject containing both "plurality" and "unity" *(scal, sculæ (mæn))*. But if it is impossible to interpolate any subject in the sentence the verb can only be in the singular *(skil børn)*. This affords corroboration of the thesis of participation arrived at on p. 139: the verb can only be in the plural when a subject containing the element of "plurality" may be interpolated, but the singular may act as a substitute for the plural in any case.

4.5. With these considerations in mind it should be possible to determine the proper place of the category of number within the system of the language[26].

For our starting-point we may take the unit which Hjelmslev has named a "nexia" (i.e. roughly a sentence or a sentence + the clauses belonging to it). We are now in a position to define the category of number as a category of *morphemes.* For a category of morphemes is defined as a category one item of which, at least, is capable of *direction;* direction is a unilateral or bilateral dependency that implies the presence of a "nexia". The very selection we found between the verbal plural and a certain element within the subject is a direction, because it selects a "nexia". Furthermore, morphemes may be divided up into *fundamental morphemes* and *converted morphemes:* a category of morphemes is a fundamental category if at least one of its items may be directed. As the plural of the subject is directed by the plural of a verb, the plural is a fundamental morpheme, and by virtue of this fact the entire category of number is a category of fundamental morphemes[27].

We may now proceed to subdivide the categories of fundamental morphemes according to their mutual dependencies. A category of selecting morphemes is called a *marginal* category, a category of selected morphemes is called a *central* category, a category of selecting *and* selected morphemes is called a *semi-central* category. In exact correspondence with this a division can be made of the minimal elements of expression within the theme of the syllable (i.e. the syllable without its accent); the result of such a division is a distinction between marginal units (consonants), central units (vowels), and semi-central units (semi-vowels): the presence of a consonant implies the presence of a vowel, but not vice versa; a semi-vowel may act as a consonant and as a vowel as well. The division of the fundamental morphemes yields a similar result; thus, in the language which is the subject of the present analysis, case is a category of marginal morphemes, mood and tense are categories of central morphemes (the presence of a case implies the presence of a mood and a tense, but not vice versa); and number is a category of semi-central morphemes, that is to say, it is a category containing both selecting and selected variants, the former forming part of the characteristic of the nouns and pronouns, the latter forming part of the characteristic of the verbs.

4.6. After this we are able to answer the first of the questions put on pp. 131-32: it has proved possible to describe verbal number in the Jutlandic Law by means of a single set of rules. Thus nothing has been found to necessitate an explanation of the text by means of the hypothesis of two systems of language, one including numerical inflection of the verb, the other without numerical inflection, the former being the standard of a written language, the latter the Jutlandic dialect spoken by the scribes. It might be asked whether any features of the rules arrived at might make it logically desirable to assume two linguistic structures behind the text. Presumably, the answer is that such an assumption is desirable if it can be demonstrated that the correlation between the singular and the plural of the verbs ought to be one of exclusion, not one of participation. For if that were the case, the description of the text might be based upon the hypothesis of a written language which upholds the state of exclusion on one hand and a spoken language which lacks distinction of verbal number entirely on the other hand.

The question, then, is whether such an assumption concerning a "normal" correlation between the singular and the plural of verbs can be substantiated. This leads to the second problem outlined on p. 132, viz.: under what circumstances does the description of a text require the setting up of more than one linguistic system?

The general answer to this question is bound to be this: a given text can never contain features which make it *necessary* to explain the text on a basis of more than one linguistic structure unless universal rules can be established as to what a linguistic structure ought to look like. Such universal rules, however, would have to be made out inductively, that is, by means of an examination of all existing linguistic structures. Our knowledge of these structures must needs be fragmentary and accidental and it will therefore never become possible to formulate structural rules which, strictly speaking, may be called universal.

(To be sure, criteria can — and ought to — be set up as to what we want to call language and what we want to call non-language. But that kind of general criteria ought not to be mistaken for universal rules. Within the field of such objects as have been defined as language the general theory of language must make it possible to describe any structure whatever. One of the chief advantages of Hjelmslev's theory of language is the very fact that its creator is consistent in his endeavour to make it so general that it is suitable not only for describing known linguistic structures, but also for dealing with all logical possibilities. Among the possibilities thus taken into consideration is the very possibility — which, by the way, is very often realized — that the items within a category are interrelated participatively, not exclusively).

While it is impossible, as we have seen, to set up really universal rules concerning linguistic structures, it is at any time possible to establish rules concerning such linguistic structures as *have already been analysed*. And from such rules it might be possible to produce evidence which — in a given situation — might make it desirable to explain a given text by two systems of language, each of which contains only such features as are known from elsewhere.

This kind of situation is present whenever a given text complies with the following two conditions: 1°. In some respects the text differs from other texts originating from the same region and the same period. 2°. The text in question can be explained by means of two linguistic structures of which one, at least, is found in other texts from the same region and period.

We therefore have to find out whether there exists an Old Danish written language in which the correlation between the singular and the plural of verbs is one of exclusion, and whether other texts necessitate the hypothesis of the existence of an Old Danish spoken language which lacks verbal number altogether.

In order to elucidate this question we shall proceed to describe briefly the language of other Old Danish texts, foremost among which we take the Scanic Law (together with the Scanic Ecclesiastical Law), a text in which most investigators, so far, have found "concord" between the number of the verbs and the number of the subjects.

5. Verbal Number in the Scanic Law and other Old Danish Texts.

5.1. For our starting-point we take the ms B.69 which has been printed in *Danmarks gamle Landskabslove*, vol. I. I. and I.2. as text II, but at every turn we intend to make comparisons with other mss.

5.2. The Scanic Law differs from the Jutlandic Law in that the difference between the singular and the plural is only abandoned in the subjunctive *(han, the gialdi* 'he, they pay'), whereas the passive voice *(gifs* 'is given' *gifwas* 'are given') and, normally, also the preterite of weak verbs *(han wildi* 'he would', *the wildu* 'they would') retain the difference.

On the whole, this text is on a par with the Jutlandic Law as regards sentences containing grammatical subjects. If a subject is placed *before* the verb there is almost always concord between the number of the subject and the number of the verb. The only exception is found on p. 244[31] : *tolf hors æ r stoth* 'twelve horses is a stud'; most mss have the singular *ær;* A[1] has the plural *gøræ* 'make'[28]. When a subject is placed *after* the verb the plural is never found instead of the expected singular; but the opposite situation is in evidence four times, e.g. *æn um thæt w i l dylia arfwa hans* (869[27]) 'but if that will (sing.) deny his heirs' : 'if his heirs will deny that'[29].

When a subject consisting of more than one noun connected by means of *oc* is placed *after* the verb, the number of the latter is dependent upon the number of the noun closest to it, e.g. *oc sigir hun oc hænna frændær* (203[2]) 'and says she and her kinsmen'[30]. When a verb is placed *after* this type of subject, the Scanic Law may have the singular in the verb (a feature never found in the Jutlandic Law), e.g. *ælli oc siukdom gar them a hændær* (211[17]) 'age and illness attacks them'[31].

With regard to sentences *without* a subject the Scanic Law also displays the same characteristics as the Jutlandic Law. There are no examples of the plural instead of the singular when the latter is to be expected, but there are two[32] certain examples (and one doubtful one) of the singular used instead of the plural[33] : *ware the nest witu ær allum w i l wita til handa* (208[13]) 'be those next to proof who *will* (sing.) prove it at disposal of all' : 'then those are to have a priority of proving their case who want to prove that it belongs to everybody'[34]. *oc hini ær eig w i l d i til cumma oc skifta fa æncti skifti* (218[26]) 'and those (who) would (sing.) not come and partition, shall have no partition'[35].

In conclusion of this examination we may state that verbal number is subject to the same rules in the Scanic Law as in the Jutlandic Law.

5.3. An examination of other Old Danish mss from the 14th century yields the same result. Not a single text from this period could be explained by means of an assumed linguistic structure with an exclusive correlation between the singular and the plural of verbs. Nor does any text make it desirable to suggest the establishment of a linguistic structure without numerical inflection of the verbs. Special attention ought to be given to the fact that two Jutlandic texts from this period, the Leech-Book of Harpestræng, and the Flensborg By-Laws, correspond exactly with the Jutlandic Law in this respect, also from a statistical point of view.

Not till we come to texts from the 15th century do we find a language that differs from the one described above. And here the texts fall into two groups, clearly distinguished from each other. One group is represented by diplomas written in the royal chancellery, the other group is that of assize-records written by Jutlandic county clerks. But as I see it, the difference is not one of structure, but one of usage. In the Jutlandic assize-records we find more examples of verbs in the singular after subjects in the plural than in the Jutlandic Law, but also very frequent examples of verbs in the plural. A verb in the plural is however never found in connexion with a subject in the singular (with the exception of collectives). Consequently, the text cannot be explained on the basis of a language devoid of numerical inflection of verbs. In the royal letters we find a tendency towards a correlation of mutual exclusion between the plural and the singular of verbs. During the subsequent period this tendency, which is presumably caused by influence from Latin, becomes more and more pronounced in written Danish. But in the 15th century we still find a few examples of singular verbs in connexion with subjects in the plural, so that there is still a participative correlation between the singular and the plural. Accordingly, the difference between the two groups is not due to a difference of linguistic structure, but solely to a difference in usage.

5.4. It has thus become apparent that the Old Danish texts certainly do not differ so much from each other that the situation mentioned on p. 145 above can be said to exist. Accordingly, no logical advantage whatever is gained by the assumption that the spoken language of Jutland abandoned the numerical inflection of verbs already in the Middle Ages[36].

Of course, this does not imply evidence of the contrary hypothesis, viz. that the medieval Jutlandic spoken language had a numerical inflection of the verbs. Our knowledge of this spoken language derives only from conclusions from discrepancies between the texts; and, as we have seen, a word of warning against hasty conclusions is called for here. An adequate analysis of the texts may make the supposed discrepancies disappear.

NOTES:

1 On catalysis v. Hjelmslev, *Omkring Sprogteoriens Grundlæggelse* p. 83 seq.
2 Subjunctive sentences headed by *tha* or a similar conjunction almost always have subjects. (Cf. Diderichsen, *Sætningsbygningen i Skaanske Lov* p. 22).
3 The construction *hwa sum. . hvn skal* is not necessarily to be regarded as an anacoluthon. The following constructions are frequent in the Jutlandic Law: *Hwa sum. . .han scal* (e.g. 430⁴), *hwa sum. . . tha scal han* (e.g. 108⁵, 237⁴), *hwa sum. .kummæ han æth hans both* (59⁷), *hwa sum sæl. . . latæ wt wærth in ær saldæ* (95⁴). (Cf. Diderichsen, *Sætningsbygningen i Skaanske Lov* p. 120 with notes).
4 From the point of view of the linguistic structure it is quite accidental that we know from external information that the agent must be a woman.
5 A similar analysis would seem to be applicable to verbs in the imperative, with or without pronouns. As there are no imperative forms at all in the Laws we may cite the Old Norse texts as a case in point. According to M. Nygaard (*Arkiv for Nord. Filologi* X (1894) p. 3) the difference between *bið* and *bið þú* is this: in the latter sentence "the person addressed is emphasized". Probably, a preciser way of putting it is this: *bið* may be addressed both to a definite person and to an indefinite one, whereas *bið þú* can only be addressed to a definite person. This implies that a subject consisting of "nominative case" + "the second person" + "the singular" might be interpolated, whereas *bið þú* contains the additional concept of "definiteness".

148

6   There are no examples of *thæt* being used as a subject in this kind of sentence.

7   Some of the following rules have been outlined quite briefly by Edvin Jessen *(Tidskrift for Philologi og Pædagogik V* p. 201).

8   The number of the verb is never determined by the number of the predicate: *klostær mæn. oc lærthæ mæn. thæt ær præstæ. oc diacon. oc subdiacon* (79[6]) 'monastic men and learned men, that *is* priest and deacon and subdeacon'. — When the subject is an integer higher than 1 the verb is in the plural: *æn swæræ sex ent. oc sæx ant* (123[2]) 'set si sex unum iurauerint. et alii sex aliud'; here, presumably, a subject in the nominative case of the plural ought to be interpolated after the numeral, e.g. *mæn* 'men'.

9   The noun *aghæ* 'fear' is followed by a verb in the singular in some mss, in others by a verb in the plural. It is a masculine *an*-stem, and in the language of the Jutlandic Law its form in the singular is therefore identical with that of the plural. (Cf. Brøndum-Nielsen, *Gammeldansk Grammatik III* 209).

10 In the sentence *oc willæ hans withær saak æi boot takæ* (182[4]) *withær saak* is an apocopal form of *withærsakæ* (thus most of the mss). This form may with equal justification be taken to be either the singular or the plural of a masculine *an*-stem *withærsaki*, v. Brøndum-Nielsen, *Gammeldansk Grammatik III* 209. In G it is taken to be the singular, in the other old mss the plural; thus also the Latin translation: 'et aduersarii sui emendam habere noluerint'.

11 The other 4 cases are: 49[2], 55[1], 117[2], and 246[1]. 209[4] is dubious.

12 120[1], 244[4], 321[2].

13 147[1], 303[1], 485[4].

14 The question has been treated by Wimmer in *Navneordenes Böjning* p. 86 seq., Dahlerup, *op.cit.* p. 43, Diderichsen, *op.cit.* p. 25.

15 Besides, the word *folk* occurs in 490[3] (in the singular) and in 491[1] (the number is dubious). — The noun *fæ*, on the other hand, is always a neuter in the singular.

16 Additional examples are found in 80[1], 316[5], and 440[3].

17 v. *Omkring Sprogteoriens Grundlæggelse* p. 31-37.

18 On exclusion and participation v. Hjelmslev, *La catégorie des cas I* p. 102.

19 If there is only one agent the verb is in the singular; there is only one exception to this rule, viz. *rættæ* (plur.) instead of *rættær* (sing.) in a single ms. As, however, the scribe of this very ms has forgotten the next word it is probable that this form may be dismissed as a scribal mistake.

20 Here the text has the singular in conformity with the rule in 3.4. above.

21 Usually, these clauses are headed by the adverb *thær*, rarely by the conjunction *sum*, and still more rarely there is no introductory word at all *(the eghær a thæn mark boo* (504[5]) 'the owners (who) dwell on that field'). In the old Danish legal texts no relative pronouns, properly so called, are to be found. Cf. Diderichsen, *Sætningsbygningen i Skaanske Lov*, p. 121.

22 The phrase *thær sauth ær* (186[3], 398[3], 399[3]) may be translated: 'of which has been spoken'; yet 344[4] has *thær fyrræ ær r æ sauth* 'that have been mentioned before'. — In the following case the relation between the clause and the noun is ambiguous: *rættæ saar bøtær thær æi ben hoggæt ær oc æi gømæn stungæn* (415[2]) 'pro omni uulnere, quod non est benhogæt nec perforatum'.

23 *ær* and *took* might be interpreted as plural forms, seeing that a few
examples of apocope of final *-æ* in dissyllabic words are to be found in the
Jutlandic Law (cf. *swornæ wægh* instead of *swornæ wæghæ*, above);
that is how they are explained by Lyngby, *op.cit.* p. 38. But as such
monosyllabic forms with apocope of *-æ* are rare, it is hardly probable
that all the cases mentioned above can be explained in this way.

24 Moreover, there are two examples with *gialdær* (219^6 and 220^5).

25 As already stated, *fiarthing* (492^4) may be regarded as the plural form,
and *æræ* (122^3) may be considered a scribal error.

26 The following attempt is based upon Hjelmslev's *Essai d'une théorie des
morphèmes (Actes du IVme Congrès International de Linguistes, Copenhague* 1938, p. 140 seq.) and (especially as regards the latter part) on the
same author's *'Sprogteori. Resumé'* (1943-46, not yet in print). Cf. also
the paper by Diderichsen in *Recherches structurales* (1949) p. 134 seq.

27 In his recent paper *Le verbe et la phrase nominale (Mélanges I. Marouzeau*
p. 263) Hjelmslev maintains that the numbers of the Latin verb are
converted morphemes, i.e. unities forming parts of the verbal themes. This
may be true of Old Danish too. If we keep the number of the noun and
the number of the verb apart (because they constitute not one, but two
paradigms), we may registrate the former as a category of fundamental
morphemes, but not the latter: the singular of the verb can neither be
directing nor directed, and the plural can only be directing, hence none
of them can be directed. According to this view, the number of the nouns
is a category of *marginal* morphemes. (Added in the proofs).

28 In one case (241^1) the verb is in the plural instead of the singular as
expected (*calla* instead of *callar*); as all other good mss, however, have
callar, the form *calla* is most likely to be classed as a scribal error.

29 Some of the mss have the plural, A^1 has the singular. The other cases are
238^{11}, 262^{21} (A^1 has the plural *takæs*, BCD have the singular *taks*), 872^{16}.

30 Other examples are 203^{10}, 206^{22}, 208^6, 210^{16}.

31 The runic inscriptions from Skåne and Bornholm provide several examples
of the plural in sentences of this type: *þulfR uk ulfR risþu stina* 'Tholf and
Ulf raised (plur.) the stones', (v. Jacobsen-Moltke, *Danmarks Runeindskrifter*, nos 271, 321, 329, 337, 339, 343 (Skåne) and nos. 371, 384,
392, 403 (Bornholm). Yet in Bornholm there is one doubtful example of
the singular, viz. no. 387: *trebinu syni auk skogi suek saklausan*, which
ought, perhaps, to be translated 'Træbene-Sønne and Skoge (personal names) deceived (sing.) the guiltless'. A couple of other rather artificial
translations have been suggested, apparently on account of the supposed
difficulty presented by a verb in the singular being placed after a subject
consisting of more than one noun (cf. Moltke in *Danske Studier 1934*, p.
13: "otherwise the runic inscriptions are very meticulous in observing the
numerical inflection of verbs", "as, however, *suek* is in the singular, it can
only have one subject." The latter statement requires some qualification).

32 For statistical reasons it ought to be kept in mind that the Scanic Law
(together with the Scanic Ecclesiastical Law) is only half the length of
the Jutlandic Law: it contains about 35 relative clauses referring to a
noun or a pronoun in the plural, as against about 80 in the Jutlandic Law.

33 The doubtful example is *bøtæ hinum ær sak s ø k æ r* (206^8) 'pay to those
(who) sues'; all the old mss have the singular in the verb; *hinum* might be
the dative singular, but it is made clear by the subsequent sentence that
there is more than one plaintiff.

34   A[1] and several other mss have the plural *wiliæ*, A[2] and D[1] have the singular *wil*.

35   The other mss have the plural. — Presumably, the oldest Scanic example of this construction is found on a runic stone from Norra Åsum (ab. 1200) in the eastern part of Skåne, where the numerical inflection of verbs has been retained till the present day. The inscription ought probably to be read in the following way: *krist mario sun hiapi þem ær kirku þe... [g]erþi absalon ærki biskup ok æsbiornmuli* 'Christ, Mary's son, help those (who) made (sing.) this church, Absalon the archbishop, and Æsbiorn Muli'. Though expressing some doubt as to the correctness of their conjecture Wimmer (*De danske Runemindesmærker* I 2 p. 162) and Jacobsen-Moltke (*Danmarks Runeindskrifter* no. 347) read [g]erþo, probably only because they take it for granted that the verb ought to be in the plural. As far as I can see, only I *i*, not Å *o* can be read on the stone (cf. the photograph in Jacobsen-Moltke, *Atlas*, nr. 800).

36   The participative correlation between the two numbers may give rise to misunderstandings in the usage. An example of this is provided by the sentence cited on p. 141 above: *æn hauær hin two brøthær thær frith løøs ær flytth. thær sialf hauæ gotz*; the second clause is unambiguous: the plural form of the verb makes it clear that the clause must refer to a noun in the plural (i.e. *brøthær*), but many mss have the singular form *hauær* which makes the sentence ambiguous, so that it is only by means of the context and factual knowledge that we can infer that the clause refers to *brøthær*, not to *hin* (outlaws have no property). The first clause is ambiguous: we can only assume that it refers to *hin*, not to *brøthær*, because we know that the paragraph in question deals with the relations between an escaped outlaw and his family. The ambiguity of the clause has caused a misunderstanding in 3 younger mss (from 1450-1500). In these mss *ær* has been corrected into *ære* which makes the clause refer unambiguously to *brøthær*. This and other examples might, perhaps, give rise to the assertion that, in a certain sense, the participative correlation is unpractical, and that it might be expected to survive only for a short period, quickly to be replaced by an exclusive correlation, or perhaps even by a complete abolition of verbal number. Such an assertion would, however, be premature. In answer to my inquiry concerning verbal number in the dialect of Bornholm, Mr. Rohmann, M.A., who spoke this dialect as a child, about 1910, has supplied information showing a striking conformity with the rules applying to the Scanic Law mss of about 1300.

Excerpts from the Grammar
of the language of the Scanic Law[1]

INTRODUCTION.

I. The manuscript.
MS B74 in the Royal Library Stockholm contains the Scanic Law
(ScL) and the Scanic Church Law (ScChL). Johannes Brøndum-Nielsen has demonstrated in ANF 34 that the MS falls into two sections,
the scribe having changed his exemplar at a point near the beginning
of the Scanic Law[2]. The language in the first section differs greatly
from that in the second and this fact suggests that the scribe must
have copied his two exemplars slavishly. In the present grammar
attention is confined to the last part of the MS, firstly because this
is the larger section and secondly because the language in it gives an
impression of greater age than that in the first part.

Only a few short excerpts from the MS are to be found in print[3].
The MS used as the basis for the printed text in Danmarks gamle
Landskabslove (Denmark's old provincial laws) I, which contains the
Scanic Law and the Scanic Church Law, is Codex Runicus. Variants
are quoted from B74 in the same way as from other old MSS, for
B74 was then assumed to derive from c. 1300. After a close palæo-

graphical analysis of the MS, however, Erik Kroman has since proved[4], that it must have been written c. 1250, perhaps even earlier. The handwriting in the MS would seem to be in the process of transition from Carolingian minuscule to Gothic script; a is always written a and never a (with a closed loop at the top as in Gothic bookhand), d still appears as both d and ƌ (the latter symbol is the only one to occur in Gothic book-hand), t is written as ꞇ and not Gothic t, and ę and ǣ are still written with a cedilla. B74 shares all these characteristics with the municipal law of Tønder, which was written down in 1243.

This palæographical dating agrees closely with the dating that is suggested by an analysis of the language.

B74 is the oldest of our law MSS and hence also the oldest work of Danish literature of sufficient length to make a reasonably full description of its language feasible. It is, therefore, a good starting point for a study of Early Middle Danish (EMD).

No description has been made of the language of the MS as a whole but some features of it have been treated, notably by Brøndum-Nielsen in ANF 34, APhS 2, and GG, particularly volume III. In addition, Paul Diderichsen makes occasional references to the MS in his Sætningsbygningen i Skånske Lov (Sentence structure in the Scanic Law) (APhS 15. 1-252) and in Probleme der altdänischen Orthographie (APhS 12. 116-169).

2. Problems of method.

In 1918 Brøndum-Nielsen published the above-mentioned article in ANF 34. In this he presented some of the results which had so far been obtained from an examination of the MSS of the Scanic Law that had been undertaken in connection with the preparation of the great edition of the medieval laws. This article was still being read with enthusiasm ten years later, when I was a student. This was not only because of its many perceptive contributions to textual criticism but also because the trend in it was very much to our taste.

Brøndum-Nielsen's theory ran as follows: *"The language of the laws as it is recorded in the old MSS is to a very high degree a literary language.* It contains a mass of archaic inflexional forms that the scribes were unable to manipulate correctly. This language was probably further removed from the contemporary spoken language than are the language of the bible and of old-fashioned sermons from the

ordinary spoken Danish of today. It was the refined and literary
language of a single class, the language of the "lawmen" ". This
theory was supported by a number of observations which revealed
that under certain circumstances linguistic units could become confused. Thus the neut.sg. of *slic* can be either *slict* or *sligt* (with g
for k before t); both *mæth sæ* and *mæth sic* occur (with acc. instead of dat.); the gen. of *annar man* "another man" can be either
annars mans or *annar mans* (with nom. or acc. of *annar* instead of
gen.); in sentences with a pl. subject the verb is normally in the pl.
but not infrequently in the sg. The interpretation laid on these phenomena, then, is that the one of the two linguistic units (in the
instances above the first-named one) is the correct written form,
while the other (the last-named one) is incorrect if considered as a
written form but correct in the spoken language. By studying the
language of the laws very closely, then, and noting the offences
assumed to have been committed by the scribes against the grammar
of the spoken language, it ought to be possible to gain an impression
of the living spoken language in the Middle Ages.

(For some reason or other we tended to refer to spoken languages
as "living" and written languages as "dead" or at least "creaking".
I cannot claim, however, that these mythological terms had any
clear significance for us.)

Since then the great reorientation in linguistics has caused more
stringent demands to be made of a description of language. This in
turn has drawn our attention to a phenomenon that cannot be
reconciled with the conclusions we drew in the old days about the
spoken language in the Middle Ages. It has been discovered that it
is not unusual for two linguistic units to be related to each other in
such a way that the first can assume the function of the second,
while the second cannot assume the function of the first. This is
what Hjelmslev calls a participative relationship between two members of a paradigm, that, for example, the acc. in a given language can
be used instead of the dat. but not vice versa, that the ind. can be
used for the subj. but not vice versa, that the sg. can be used for the
pl. but not vice versa. It has also been realised that it is not unusual
for two units which are normally kept distinct from each other to
coalesce under certain circumstances; that, for example, the distinction between g and k in a given language is suspended when there is
an immediately preceding t in the same syllable, or that the distinction between nom. and acc. in substantives is suspended when the
subst. is in the pl.

Such phenomena occur not only in the written language but also in the spoken language. In the spoken language, however, they can sometimes be difficult to spot, as can be demonstrated by the following example. When I was engaged in dialect field-work in South Slesvig, it would sometimes happen that one of my informers would say *du kand* or *du skal* instead of *du kat* or *du skat*. Since I knew that the modal verbs have a personal conjugation in the South Slesvig dialect, I usually asked whether it should not be *du kat* or *du skat*, and when the informants had politely admitted this, I would write it down thus. Fortunately, however, I sometimes forgot to ask and thanks to my negligence the material collected cannot be described by means of a rule which runs: When the subject is in the 1. or 3. pers. sg., the verb is in 1./3. pers. sg., and when the subject is in the 2. pers. the verb is in the 2. pers. sg. It is now necessary to formulate a participative rule which runs: When the subject is in the 1. or 3. pers. sg., the verb is in 1./3. pers. sg., and when the subject is in the 2. pers. sg., the verb can be either in the 2. pers. sg. or in the 1./3. pers. sg.

(It is important to realise that it is not an *irregularity* in the language that has been discovered as a result of my negligence. It is *possible* to formulate a correct rule and in respect to such a rule the dialect in question is perfectly regular. It is only in respect to an incorrect rule that the dialect could be called irregular.)

We have thus had to admit that two linguistic units can overlap. If we now, having admitted this, look back at the old argumentation which led us to formulate hypotheses about the differences between the written and the spoken language in the Middle Ages, we find that it was based on a postulate which assumed that the relationship between two members of a paradigm must always be exclusive: In positions where we have a dat. it is not possible in the same language to have an acc., and vice versa; where we have the pl. in the verb, it is not possible to have the sg., and vice versa; and where we have k, it is not possible to have g, and vice versa. Otherwise it would not have been possible for us to assert that *mæth sæ* is a feature of the written language, while *mæth sic* is a feature of the spoken language, that *tolf nøt æra hiorth* represents the written language but *tolf hors ær stod* the spoken language, or that *slict* is written language and *sligt* spoken language, etc. etc.

It would also be possible to describe our old stand-point as follows: We formulated a meta-rule — a rule about rules — which said that of two possible descriptions of a language, the one to be selected, as presumably being the simplest, is the one that always describes the relationship between two members of a paradigm as exclusive rather than the one which sometimes describes the relationship between two members as participative. If we accept this rule about rules, however, we make it impossible to describe a text with the aid of one simple set of rules. Experience has shown that in all the texts that have been studied in detail up to the present time – including the results of dialect field-work – there are cases where we have to choose between registering a participation or formulating two sets of rules, i.e. describing two languages. As far as I can see, it would be inexpedient to renounce a priori the possibility of describing a text with the aid of one single set of rules.

This does not mean, however, that it should not be permissible to describe a text with the aid of two sets of rules. Both methods can be employed, where this is expedient. As far as I can see, however, the latter method can only be expedient when the following condition is fulfilled: Of the two sets of rules, one at least must be sufficient in itself to describe another text from the same area and period. For example, official charters from the beginning of the 15th century have been described with the aid of a single set of rules. Afterwards the same rules are applied to some Jutland court reports from the same period. This procedure reveals certain features to which the rules do not apply. These features are then described with the aid of another set of rules. After this it might be possible to claim that something is known about the spoken language in Jutland in the 15th century.

When we are studying B74, the above-mentioned condition is *not* fulfilled. We do not have one text from the 13th century that can tell us what the Scanian written language was like at the time and another different text that might perhaps give us some information about the spoken language. We have only the one text and we are therefore precluded from knowing anything with certainty about the relationship between the spoken language and the written language in the 13th century.

Does this really matter so much, however? There is after all one thing we *can* do and that is to describe the text we do have.

In the present grammar the text has been treated in principle as an *open text*, i.e. a part of a larger text, the rest of which is unknown.

There are, therefore, occasional conjectures (e.g. pp. 173 and 174) about the language in the unknown parts of the text. (These conjectures are synchronically based. Forms with an asterisk should not be taken to be diachronically based constructions.) In general, however, it has been assumed that the text is representative of the larger text and the description has then been confined to a registration of the forms occurring in the text.

The grammar falls into two main sections, the treatment of expression and the treatment of content. The first section contains two chapters, which deal with the vowel system and the consonant system respectively. The second section contains two longer chapters, which deal with noun declensions and verb conjugations respectively. The treatment of content has thus been arbitrarily restricted to a presentation of the system of morphemes, while no attempt has been made to describe the themes and the derivatives.

The grammar is intended for the use of university students of Danish in the early stages of their course and should serve as an introduction to the study of Middle Danish texts. It is greatly indebted to recent linguistic works — not all of which have been named in the text — notably Hjelmslev's linguistic theory.

The material on which the grammar is based is a transcript made by the author from photographs of B74 in the Royal Library Copenhagen.

The procedure which has been followed during the compilation of the grammar could be referred to as the method of tentative hypotheses: On the basis of a provisional knowledge of the text, a rule is formulated about some detail of, e.g. the verb system. This rule is then confronted with the text (or with a collection of slips containing all the verbal forms in the text) and it will soon be revealed that the rule does not fit the text, i.e. that the author would have to contradict himself if he were both to assert that the rule was true and to respect the data, the forms actually found in the text. Then a new rule will be formulated. This, too, will prove to conflict with the text. The procedure will be repeated again and again until a rule has been found which cannot be disproved with the aid of the forms in the text.

Such a rule must fulfil two conditions with respect to the data of the text before it can take its place in the grammar: 1. It must not conflict with the text (i.e. it must not be falsified); 2. It must be formulated in such a way that it would in principle be possible for

it to conflict with the text (i.e. it must be falsifiable; this last condition implies that the rule must neither be tautological nor ambiguous:
a rule must not be expressed in such vague terms that it would for
that reason alone be impossible for it to conflict with the text).

The rule must also fulfil two exactly comparable conditions in
its relationship to the other rules of the grammar. A very simple
example of the kind of difficulty that can arise in this respect is the
following: In B74 the forms *kuna* and *kunu* are employed indiscriminately. If this problem is treated in the section on the treatment of
expression as a coalescence of the vowels a and u, we come into
conflict with another rule that says that these two vowels are always
kept distinct from each other. If, on the other hand, the problem is
treated in the section on the treatment of content as a case of syncretism between two cases, the rule agrees with the other rules about
the nominal case-system. The grammar must be built up of an incontrovertible hierarchy of rules.

This hierarchy of rules ought also to satisfy two new requirements.
It ought to be exhaustive and it ought to be the simplest one possible.
The first requirement is not satisfied in this grammar because the
most difficult part of the description (the analysis of themes and
derivatives) has been arbitrarily omitted. The author will not venture
to judge with what success the second condition has been fulfilled.

The question might finally be asked whether a rule is correct
when it fulfills the conditions laid down above, whether my description of the language is a true one. The answer depends on the meaning which is attached to the words correct and true. These words
are employed spontaneously by all of us several times a day in a
meaning which can be defined as follows: A sentence is said to be
true, when it is in agreement with reality. Or transferred to a grammar: A rule is correct, when it is in agreement with the language in
question. This definition, however, requires that we either know,
or are in a position to learn, the truth. Or transferred to the grammar,
that we know, or are in a position to learn, the language. We do not
know the language, however. What is immediately available to us is
not a language but a text or rather — as long as we do not have a
description of it — a chaotic collection of letters and meanings.

That is the reason why many scholars take up an attitude to their
material which differs from the naive realistic one that has been
discussed above. They aim merely to construct an incontrovertible
and simple hierarchy of sentences, with the aid of which it is possible

to control the data in question, but they refrain from postulating a reality corresponding to this hierarchy.

A story is told about a French astronomer who discovered that by postulating the existence of a planet with a certain mass, a certain orbit and a certain period of revolution, the orbits of the other planets could be described in a much simpler way than had previously been possible. Many years after he had made this discovery, a couple of younger astronomers observed some small planets in the very position where the postulated planet was supposed to be. This pleased them enormously and they went to the old master to tell him that his hypothesis had been confirmed. The story goes, however, that the master did not find their discovery at all interesting: The observation of small planets was without significance for the confirmation of his theory. His description of the orbits of the planets *was* the simplest yet and for this very reason his postulate had to be correct. The fact that small planets could now be observed through the telescope was quite curious but, all things considered, it was no more than a curiosity.

I must confess that I sympathise with the scholarly attitude which this morose Frenchman maintained with such impressive consistency.

EXPRESSION

I. The Vowel System.

A linguistic *sign* consists of an expression and a content. The linguistic significans can be taken to be built up of a limited number of minimum units, each of which is without a content; and in the same way the linguistic significatum can probably be taken to be built up of a limited number of minimum units, each of which is without an expression.

The minimum units of expression can be didived into two categories, vowels and consonants. When the object of an analysis is a written text, it is most convenient to define the vowel category as consisting of the units of expression which are able on their own to form the expression of a word, together with the units of expression that can enter into the same combinations as these. In B74 *i* and *a* are vowels because each of them on its own forms the expression of a word (namely the expression of the prepositions "in" and "on") and, e.g., *e* is a vowel because it can enter into the same combinations as *i* and *a*, e.g. a combination with a preceding r and a following th (*ritha, ratha, retha*).

Two units of expression within the same category are said to be *commutables* when the substitution of the one for the other can involve a change on the plane of content. For example, *i* and *e* in B74 are commutables because by replacing *i* in *ritha* "ride" by *e* we get a new sign, i.e. a sign with a different content, namely *retha* "comb, disentangle". On the other hand, *i* and *j* are not commutables but freely interchangeable; they are said to be variants of the same commutable.

An analysis of B74 reveals that the vowel category contains altogether 8 commutables, namely:

a, always written *a*.

æ, generally written *æ*, less frequently *ę*.

e, generally written *e*, less frequently *ę*[5].

ø, always written *ø*.

o, always written *o*.

i, generally written *i*, less frequently *j;* i and j are graphic variants in the Latin orthography.

y, almost always written *y*, once in ScChL, however, as *ui: gælquiræ* (originally "tax collecter", the royal official of highest rank in Scania).

u, written *u* and *v*, which are graphic variants of the same letter. *Never w, however;* the preposition "about" appears as *um* and *vm* but never as *wm*.

Generally speaking the eight vowels are kept distinct from each other. In a few cases, however, there is a partial *coalescence* of two vowels. This applies particularly to æ and e: e can namely be used instead of æ, e.g. in *melt* "spoken" (generally *mælt*). On the other hand, æ cannot deputise for e. æ and e cannot, therefore, be said to be variants of one and the same vowel: substitution of æ for e can produce a change in the content, e.g. *sæ* dat. "(to) himself": *se* inf. "to see", the latter word never appears as *sæ*.

Correspondingly, *y* occasionally appears for *i;* we have, for example, *lynda bot* and *ljnda bot* "belt fine" (a particularly severe fine that was exacted from a freed man who had not been admitted into a free family).

This vowel system with 8 vowels is characteristic for EMD in general and not just for this MS. There are, in fact, only two features that are peculiar to B74. Both of these are connected with syncretisms. A *syncretism* occurs when a commutation between two invariants *under certain circumstances* is suspended.

In the majority of Middle Danish MSS there is syncretism of a and o when there is a preceding w: *waghn, woghn* "wagon"; *twa, two* "2". In B74 there is not a single instance of this alternation between a and o; "2" is always *twa* and "wagon" is always *wagn*. This feature is one of the reasons for assuming the MS to be very old.

Equally characteristic for B74 is a syncretism which is very rare in other MSS, namely an alternation between *a, æ* and *i* when the following consonant is g or k followed by i, e.g.

ofna stæfnu dagi, dat.sg. "on the assembly day" (ScL),

at thæm stæfnu dægi, dat.sg. "on that assembly day" (ScL),

at døtha digi, dat. sg. "on the death day" (ScChL),

taki and *tæki*, pres.subj. 3. pers.sg. "let him take".

In other medieval Danish law MSS vowel length is often indicated, either by dittography or by a length-mark above the vowel symbol. From these MSS we conclude that all the 8 ODan vowels with the exception of e could be both long and short, while e could only be long. An isolated study of B74, however, will not lead to an assumption of two vowel quantities (or rather to the registration of a difference between a single vowel and a double vowel). An accent symbol consisting of a slanting stroke above the vowel symbol does occur but it is very rare and only appears above the letters a and e, almost only in the following words: the prepostion *á* "on", the pres.sg. *á* "owns", and the adverb *é* "always".

The following diphthongs occur:

ia, which before single l can alternate with *iæ: sialuær* and (rarely) *siæluær*, masc. nom. sg. "self"; *brofial* and *brofiæl*[6] "plank leading from road to house"; there is a syncretism of a and æ, then, when there is a preceding i and following l.

io, written io and (since y can replace i) yo: *hiona* and *hyona* "staff of servants".

iu, written iu and (since y can replace i) yu: *biuthær* and *byuthær* pres. 3. pers. sg. "commands".

And finally *æy*, always written *æy*, only found in the adverb *æy* "not".

The above-mentioned 8 vowels are only kept distinct from each other in one type of syllable, namely the root syllables, the ones that correspond to stressed syllables in the modern spoken language. There would seem to be two kinds of terminal syllables, i.e. syllables which correspond to unstressed syllables in the modern spoken language.

Firstly, there is a group of terminal syllables which are characterised by the fact that 3 and only 3 vowels occur in them, all of which are syncretisms, namely

a/æ, which is written now a and now æ,

i/e, which is written now i and now e, occasionally, however, æ,

u/o, which is written now u and now o.

The three syncretisms can be manifested, then, sometimes by the letters a i u and sometimes by the letters æ e o. This alternation is in accordance with certain rules which Brøndum-Nielsen has presented in his paper in APhS 2. on vowel harmony and vowel balance in B74. Some of the main rules will be summarised here:

After a root syllable containing i, y or u, i and u appear, e.g.

in subj. forms such as	*wili* "will", *witi* "prove",
	bindi "bind", *nyti* "use",
	fylli "fill", *dyli* "deny",
	biuthi "command", *mugi* "may",
	cummi "come",
in pret. pl. ind. as	*fingu* "got",
in the sg. of ōn-stems as	*mylnu* "mill", *kunu* "woman",
	vku "week".

After root syllables containing e, ø or o, e and o appear,

e.g. in subj. forms such as	*hete* "be called", *wete* "yield",
	bøte "pay a fine", *føre* "lead",
	thole endure".
in the dat. sg. of u-stems as	*coste* "goods",
in the sg. of ōn-stems as	*lego* "rent", *frithløso* "outlawry"
in the dat. sg. of ō-stems as	*iortho* "earth".

After root syllables containing a or æ, appear now e and o, now i and u,

e.g. *bathe* masc. nom. pl. "both", *bæthe* neut. nom. pl. "both",

waro pret. pl. ind. "were",

but *bani* nom. sg. "slayer", *bætri* comparative "better", *allu* neut. dat. sg. "all".

This regular alternation between the variants of the terminal vowels indicates that there was a difference between two kinds of a and two kinds of æ. On the basis of this text alone it is not possible to learn anything about the nature of this difference; a comparison with other MDan texts, however, shows that a and æ followed by e, o correspond to the long a and æ in these texts (or rather double a and double æ), while a and æ followed by i, u correspond to the short (single) a and e in these texts.

By employing this terminology borrowed from other texts, it is now possible to supplement the above-cited main rule by the addition of the following exception:

After a short a or æ preceding r or a consonant combination such as rth, rn, rk, ld, nd, ng, however, e and o generally appear,

e.g. in the subj. forms *vare* "be", *gialde* "pay", *stande* "stand", *gange* "go, walk", *gærthe* fence",

and in the dative *marco* "field",

more rarely i in, e.g. *vari, gangi.*

Whereas the alternating manifestation of the syncretisms i/e and u/o is thus dependent on the quality and quantity of the preceding vowel (such a dependency is known as vowel harmony), the alternating manifestation of the syncretism a/æ is dependent on the quantity of the preceding root syllable (such a dependency is known as vowel balance):

A *short* root syllable is always followed by a,

e.g. in the infinitives *fara* "go", *gifua* "give", *bæra* "bear"; but a *long* root syllable can be followed by either a or æ (rarely the latter),

e.g. in pres. ind. 3. pers. pl. *brista* and *bristæ* "break", masc. nom./acc. sg. *annar* and *annær* "another";

immediately following i, however æ can also be found after a short root syllable,

e.g. in the infinitives *swæria, sværia, sværiæ* "swear", *bithia, bithiæ* "ask for".

Secondly, there would seem to be a kind of terminal syllable in which the vowel differences do not seem to have any linguistic significance. These "syllables" all end in -r and the "vowel" is manifested by several different letters according to the following rules of vowel harmony:

The normal manifestation is *either* æ (or e) *or* the same vowel symbol as the one which is the manifestation of the vowel in the preceding root syllable.

Thus, e.g.,*akær* and *akar* subst. "field", *sialuær, sialuer* and *sialuar* masc. nom. sg. "self";

soter and *sotor* pret. part. masc. nom. sg. "sought";

biuthær and *biuthur* pres.sg. "commands",

gifuær and *gifuir* pres.sg. "gives", *withær* and *vithir* prep. "at, by".

After a root syllable with æ, ø or y, a can also appear.

Thus, e.g., *brændær* and *brændar* pres.sg. "burns", *ræter* and *rættar* adj. masc. nom. sg. "right"; *bøtær, bøter* and *bøtar* nom./acc. pl. "fines"; *brytær* and *brytar* pres.sg. "breaks".

This unit, which philologists have called a svarabhakti (or supporting) vowel, should perhaps be considered as an example of what Hjelmslev has called a *connective*[7], i.e. as a unit that does not represent a vowel but is merely an indication of the presence of a certain type of consonant combination.

CONTENT

It may perhaps prove possible some time in the future to describe the linguistic content, in the same way as the linguistic expression, as being built up of a limited number of minimum units. As yet, however, it has not been possible to carry out an analysis of content corresponding to the analysis of the expression. Only one section of the content has been subjected to as penetrating an analysis as that which has been accorded to the expression, namely the section which has been called *the characteristics.* These can be given a preliminary and vague definition as those units of content whose expressions are inflexional endings such as *-rnes* in Mod.Dan *endelsernes* "of the endings" or *-s* in Mod.English *runs.* These characteristics have been analysed into minimum units, none of which corresponds to an expression, i.e. units such as "genitive", "plural", "definiteness", "present", "singular", "3. person", "active" and "indicative". Such minimum units of characteristics are called *morphemes.* The analysis of the remaining units of content, *the themes,* remains largely a task for scholars of the future.

It has long been realised that morphemes such as sg., pl., subj., ind., etc. enter into certain unilateral or bilateral dependencies that presuppose the existence of a sentence, either interdependency of two examples of the same morpheme (as when sg. linked to a nominative presupposes the presence of sg. in the verb), or dependency between a completely different unit and a morpheme (as when a certain conjunction presupposes the presence of a certain mood in the verb); in the first case we talk of concord, in the second case of rection. Hjelmslev has proposed that the morpheme should be defined by means of these sentence-establishing dependencies. Number, case, gender, tense, mood and person would then be certain instances of morphemes in B74, while definiteness, comparison and voice may perhaps not be morpheme categories.

Definiteness and voice will be included in the present discussion but comparison will be omitted, partly because the available evidence about it is exceptionally slight.

The morpheme categories can be divided into three kinds: nominal morpheme categories, verbal morpheme categories and morpheme categories that can be both nominal and verbal. In our text the category of number belongs to this type. It has proved most practical however, to deal with number in nouns together with the nominal morphemes and number in verbs together with the verbal morphemes. The discussion of content can thus be divided into two sections, declension and conjugation.

A few preliminary remarks will be made at this point about the methods employed in examining the relationship between the members of a content category.

In his Navneordenes Bøjning (The declension of nouns) p. 16, Ludvig Wimmer gives the following paradigm:

    sg. nom. þiufær, þiuf
    acc. þiuf
    dat. þiufi
    gen. þiufs

This reveals that Wimmer considered that the ending zero in þiuf could indicate both the nom.sg. and the acc.sg. It is clear that the reason for his doing this is the fact that the form þiuf in Codex Runicus of ScL is employed not only in syntactic positions where an OIcel text would also have a form with zero ending, e.g. in the sentence þa ma man hængia þiuf "then the man may hang the thief", but also in positions where an OIcel text would have a form in -r, þiófr, e.g. in the sentence æn þo ær han ok þiuf "but nevertheless he is also a thief" (in such instances Codex Runicus most frequently employs a form in -ær, e.g. in the sentence at hin ær þiufær hans "that the latter is his thief").

In a synchronic description it seems to me to be most correct to postulate the simplest possible correspondence between ending and characteristic, i.e. between significans and significatum. That is why I assert that we have the unit of content nominative when, and only when, the ending is -(æ)r, and that we have accusative when, and only when, the ending is zero. Sentences of the type æn þo ær han ok þiuf must in accordance with this theory be explained as being due to the fact that the unit of content accusative can deputise for the unit of content nominative (but not vice versa). I would then, give the following paradigm:

    sg. nom. thiufær
    acc. thiuf
    dat. thiufui, thiufi
    gen. thiufs

(The problem is in one respect analogous to the problem with the orthographical form *melt* "spoken" above p. 159, except that in that case it was a matter of the relationship between manifestans and manifestatum and not of that between significans and significatum. The relationship between the vowels æ and e and the letters æ, ꜫ, e, ę could be presented in the following way:

æ, generally written æ, less frequently ꜫ or e
e, generally written e, less frequently ę,

The two vowels would then have a common manifestans, namely the letter e. In this case I chose to postulate the simplest possible correspondence between manifestans and manifestatum and therefore asserted that we have the vowel æ when, and only when, the text has the letter æ or ꜫ, and the vowel e when, and only when, the text has the letter e or ę; the relationship between the two vowels had then to be described by saying that the one vowel (e) can deputise for the other vowel (æ), but not vice versa).

CONJUGATION

This includes the following 5 morpheme categories: Tense, Number, Person, Mood and Voice.

1. The tense category has 2 members, *Present* and *Preterite*.

There is commutation between the 2 tenses in all conjugations, as will appear from the principal parts given below. These include not only the pres.act. ind. 3. pers.sg. and pret.act.ind.3.pers.sg. but also such parts as inf.act., past.part. etc.[8].

The weak verbs.
can be divided into 4 classes on the basis of the formants.
These correspond to the Primitive Germanic ōn-, i̯an-, ian- and ēn-verbs.

166

I (ōn-verbs).	inf.act.	pres.act.ind. 3.pers.sg.	pret.act.ind. 3.pers.sg.	past.part.
	calla	callar (and kallar)	callathe costathe	
	orka	orcar		m.nom.sg. scapather
	tapar		(pass. tapathæs)	n.nom./acc.sg. tapat

The pres.ind.3.pers.sg. always ends in a/æ + r.

II (įan-verbs).	inf.act.	pres.act.ind. 3.pers.sg.	pret.act.ind. 3.pers.sg.	past.part.
	kræfuia	kræfuær		m.nom.sg. crafthær
	sælia	sæl	salde	m.nom.sg. saldær
	synia		syndi (pass. sundis)	n.nom.sg.[9] sundt
		bær		m.nom.sg. barthær
	gøra	gør	giorthe	n.nom.sg. giort
	sætia,	sætær,		m.nom.sg. sattær,
	sæthia	sætar		sattar

When their root ends in l, n, r or s, strong verbs and įan-verbs have no ending in the pres.act.ind.3.pers.sg. Otherwise they have a svarabhakti vowel + r. In the inf. and pres. įan-verbs have an i-mutated vowel; in the pret. and past.part. they all (with the exception of synia) have a non-i-mutated vowel.

III (ian-verbs).	inf.act.	pres.act.ind. 3.pers.sg.	pret.act.ind. 3.pers.sg.	past.part.
	mæla	mæler		n.nom.sg. mælt
	bøta	bøter, bøtær		n.nom.sg. bøt
	weta	veter, weter, wetær	wete, wette, vette	

liusa		liusdi	f.nom.sg. liusd
søkia	søker, søkir		m.nom.sg. sotor, soter,
stæfna	stæfnir	(næfndi)	m.nom.sg. stæfndær
fæsta	fæstir	fæsti	n.nom.sg. fæst
	hitir, hittir	hitti	

The ending in the pres.act.ind.3.pers.sg. is generally i/e + r. In some verbs, however, the ending of the ian-verbs, svarabhakti vowel + r, is also found, e.g. in bøtær, wetær, løsør (beside bøter, weter, løser). The ending is never lost after l, n, r, s (mæler, kærer, løser, løsør). With the exception of søkia all the ian-verbs have the same vowel in all their principal parts, almost always showing i-mutation.

IV (ēn-verbs) inf.act.	pres.act.ind. 3.pers.sg.	pret.act.ind. 3.pers.sg.	past.part.
hafua	hafuir	hafthi	
sigia	sigir		n.nom.sg. sagat

The ending in the pres.act.ind.3.pers.sg. is i/e + r (in sigir it can be either i/e or a svarabhakti vowel, since the svarabhakti vowel can be represented by the same letter as the preceding vowel; in hafuir, however, it can only be i/e).

Together with the ēn-verbs can be considered:
lægia, læggia, lægger, læggær, lægthi, lagthi, n.nom.sg. lagat.

The strong verbs
can be divided into a large number of classes on the basis of the root vowels of the principal parts. Examples of the most important classes are given below. The most commonly employed philological terms for these classes have been added in brackets for the convenience of the reader.

inf.act.	pres.act.ind. 3.pers.sg.	pret.act.ind. 3.pers.sg.	pret.act.ind. 3.pers.pl.	past.part

(Class 1)
bitha "wait"

rithær
bitær

168

(Class 2)

biutha	biuthær,	bøth	subj.3.pl.	f.acc.pl.
	biuthur		buthi	buthna
	brytær,	brøt		m.nom.sg.
	brytar			brutin

(Class 3)

binda	bindær			f.acc.sg.
				bundna
	brændær,	bran	subj.3.pl.	
	brændar[10]		brynni	
	bristær,			
	bristir			
gialda	gialdær	galt	subj.3.pl.	
			guldi	
vartha	varthær,			n.acc.sg.
	warthær,			vrthit
	warthar			

(Class 4)

bæra	bær	bar	baro	m.nom.sg.
				boren
stiala	stial	stal		m.nom.sg.
				stolen
cumma	cumbær	cum		

(Class 5)

dræpa	dræpær,	drap	subj.3.sg.	m.nom.sg.
	dræper		drape[11]	dræpin
gifua	gifuær,	gaf		m.nom.sg.
	gifuir			giuin, gifuin
vara,	ær	var	varo, varu	n.nom.sg.
wara				varit
waræ				

(Class 6)

taka	takar	tok		m.nom.sg.
				takin
fara	far	for	subj.3.sg.	
			fore	

swæria, sværia, sværiæ	swær	sor		m.dat.sg. sornum

(Reduplicating verbs)

fa	far	fic	fingu	m.nom.sg. fangen
ganga	gangær, gangar, gar			
høggia, høgga	høgger, høggar	hiog, hog		m.nom.sg. hoggen

(sa is conjugated weakly: *thagar granna hafua sat sæd sina* "as soon as the neighbours have sown their seed").

The ending in the pres.act.ind.3.pers.sg. is a svarabhakti vowel + r (see under biutha, cumma, gifua, taka, ganga), except when the stem ends in l, n, r or s, in which case the ending is zero, cf. bær, far, stial. The pres.sg. does *not* have i-mutation (the vowel in brytær, brytar is due to the development iu > ȳ after r), and the pret.subj., which is formed from the pret.act.ind.3.pers.*pl.*, does not normally have an i-mutated vowel (the only instance of a mutated vowel is brynni, where Codex Runicus has brunne).

Preterite-present verbs and modal verbs

inf.act.	pres.act.ind. 3.pers.sg.	pres.act.ind. 3.pers.pl.	pret.act.ind. 3.pers.sg.
	vil, wil	vilia, wilia	vildi, wildi
	scal, skal	sculu, schulu	sculdi, schuldi
	ma	mugu	
wita "know"	wet	vita	
aga "own"	a, á	ago, agho, ægo	atte

(The system of modal verbs is not as well developed as in modern Danish).

There is only one instance of the verb kunne: *æn biutha the æy botær. oc varther ænnar man drepin. tha bøtes han sum før ær mælt. oc kunni sig sialfuær yfuir. at the buthi æy bøter* "but if they do not offer (to pay) fines, and if any man is killed, then the wergild is paid for him as was said before, and they can reproach themselves that they did not offer (to pay) fines"; in OIcel kunna means "know, understand, know by heart" and also "be able", particularly of mental faculties. The word has thus a much more specialised meaning than in mod.Danish.

vil   has approximately the same meaning as in mod.Danish.

scal   corresponds to mod.Danish *skal* "shall" (of obligation), *bør* "ought", and *må* in the sense "must" (of necessity); it is thus not possible to distinguish between "obligation" and "necessity" by means of the ODan modal verbs.

ma   corresponds to both *må* in the sense "may" (of permission) and *kan* "can" (of possibility); it is thus not possible to distinguish between "permission" and "possibility" by means of the ODan modal verbs[12].

han a at means both "he shall" and "he may" and is thus, like the subjunctive, neutral with respect to the difference between "obligation" and "permission", and between "necessity" and "possibility". The same applies to *ær skyldugh at* "is obliged to" and "is entitled to").

As will have been seen from the paradigms above, there is universal commutation between pres. and pret.

The tenses are subject to rection. In B74 the following rule is particularly important: If the main clause is in the subjunctive, then it is always in the pres. if a related subordinate clause is in the pres., e.g.

> *oc dyl han dyli mæth tyltar eth* "and if he denies, let him deny with an oath of twelve".

In the laws the pres. tense is used relatively rarely of the present time; most frequently in certain oath-formulæ, the evidence of witnesses and sentences dealing with the law itself, e.g. *æn kunung vil at logum hafua* "but the king desires to have as law". In the ordinary rules of the law, however, the pres. represents limitless time: *fore watha sar. scal æy bøta kunungs ræt* "for an accidental wound, one shall not (at any time in the past, present or future) pay a fine to the king"; *bær thræl fræls man, bøte oc bonden thre marc* "whenever a thrall strikes a free-man, the owner shall also pay a fine of three marks".

The pret. is found almost exclusively in subordinate clauses and is used of an action which has taken place prior to the action or the situation which is referred to in the pres. in the main clause or another subordinate clause, e.g.

> *dyl hin ær graf grof. oc sac var yui gifuin, at han grof æy. sæli swa log fore. sum hins ær virthning ær fæ atte. oc scatha fic at thy fæ. ær thær do innan the graf* "if he who *dug* the hole, and was accused of it, denies that he *dug* it, then he shall produce proof on oath, the number of men swearing the oath to be dependent on the judgment of the man who *owned* the cattle and *incurred* loss in the form of the cattle which *died* there in that hole"; here the sentences that describe the law case are in the pres. (the subordinate clause *dyl hin* and the main clause *sæli swa log fore*); a subordinate clause whose action is contemporary with the case is in the pres. (*sum hins ær virthning*), and the remaining subordinate clauses, which describe situations or actions which precede the case, are in the pret. (*grof, atte, fic, do*).

Such a pret. can very often be translated most satisfactorily by a mod. English perfect with have, e.g.

> *late vth thæt han fic* "let him hand over what he has received"; *hafui til thæs twiggia manna withni. at han galt ællar løk andra lund* "so shall he have the testimony of two men that he has paid or arranged the matter in another way".

In the English sentence the perfect with have indicates not only something prior but also something contemporary, namely that a prior action is still having effect[13]. In B74 the perfect with have is employed less frequently than in mod. Danish and English. In B74, too, it indicates both something prior and something contemporary but the main stress lies here on the contemporary result of a prior action. E.g.

> *thagar granna hafua sat sæd sina. tha schulu the lægia lagstæfnu fore alla the i by bo samman* "as soon as the neighbours *have finished* sowing their seed, then they shall fix a date for all those who live together in the village";

witi mæth tyltar eth. oc twiggia manna vithni. at han tok han i æt mæth sæ. oc dyl han. dyli mæth tyltar eth. thæn ǽr han hafuir takit i æt mæth sic. scal bøta "let him prove by means of an oath of twelve and the evidence of two men that he *has (at some time) accepted* him into his family; and if he denies, he shall deny with an oath of twelve; the man who *(now) has* him as a member of his family shall pay (the fine). . . .".

2. The number category contains two members, the *singular* and the *plural.*

There is always *coalescence* of sg. and pl. in the *subj.* 3.pers. Here the ending in pres. and pret. *active* is *-i/e* in both sg. and pl., and in pres. and pret. *passive -i/e* + *s* in both sg. and pl. E.g.

> pres.act.subj.: *bøte, swæri, taki* sg. and pl.
> pres.pass.subj.: *næfnis* sg. and pl.
> pret.act.subj.: *han guldi* sg. "he paid"; *at the buthi æy bøter*
> pl. "that they did not offer (to pay) fines".
> pret.pass. subj.: no examples.

It is not only the *ending* of the subjunctive that is identical in sg. and pl. but also the *root.* In the pret. *ind.* of strong verbs there is a difference between the root of the sg. and the root of the pl. (e.g. *galt : guldu; bøth : buthu);* while the pret.subj. has the same root in sg. and pl. This is identical with the root in the pret.ind.*pl.* Unlike West Scandinavian, East Scandinavian does not normally have i--mutation in the pret. subj. of the strong verbs (cf. p. 182 n. 11).

If we assume that the pres.pass.ind.pl. of the ōn-verbs has the same formant as the inf.pass. (as is the case with the i̯an-, ian- and ēn--verbs), namely *-as,* then we must also record coalescence between sg. and pl. in the pres.pass.ind. of the ōn-verbs: *tapas* pres.sg.ind. and *tapas* inf.

Otherwise there is always commutation between sg. and pl.: pres.act.ind.:

> weak verbs: *gør : gøra, kærer : kæra, sigir : sigia,*
> strong verbs: *bitær : bita, bær : bæra, ær : æra, far : fa;* the forms of the pret.pres.verbs have been illustrated above p. 169

173

pres.pass.ind.:

(there are no examples from ōn-verbs); ian-verbs: sg. *kræfs,
schils, syns:* pl. *bærias* mæn i lans byum;
ian- and ēn-verbs: sg. *løses, bethes* (corresponding to OIcel
beiðisk), hittis, sigis : pl. *fullas* "are accomplished"; strong
verbs: sg. *gifs, taks, tacs, lucs* "is concluded": pl. **gifuas* (this
construction is based on the assumption that the pres.pl. has
the same ending as the inf.).

pret.act.ind.:

In the weak verbs there is always a contrast between sg. *-i/e*
and pl. *-u/o,* e.g. sg. *costathe, hafthi,* pl. *vithnatho, hafthu.*
In the strong verbs there is always a contrast between sg. *zero*
and pl. *-u/o,* and there is often also a difference between the
root-vowels of sg. and pl. and sometimes also between consonants, e.g. sg. *bar, fic,* pl. *baro, fingu.*

pret. pass. ind.:

There is presumably a difference between sg. *sundis* "was
denied" and pl. **sundus* but there are no instances of the pl.

The number category is both nominal and verbal. Nominal number
and the relationships within the category are discussed in the section on Declension which has not been included in the present
translation. As far as verbal number is concerned, the sg. can deputise
for the pl. *Usually* the verb is in the sg. when the subject is in the sg.,
and in the pl. when the subject is in the pl. This statement, however,
only gives a rough approximation to a correct description of the
relationship between the verbal numbers. Not a single medieval law
MS survives in which the sg. and the pl. of the verb appear under
mutually exclusive conditions: They all contain sentences in which
the verb is in the sg. even though the subject is in the pl., but never
sentences where the verb is in the pl. even though the subject is in
the sg. (except in instances where the subject has a collective signification). Examples of the subject in the pl. and the verb in the sg.
from B74 are:

tolf hors ær stod oc tolf nøt æra hiorth "twelve horses *is* a stud and twelve cattle *are* a herd";

swa ær oc log vm al annar giald "such *is* also the law (the word for "law" is always pl. in ScL) in respect to all other payments";

at atær standær af botum thre marc "that there *remains* three marks of the fines".

3. Personal conjugation. There are no instances of this in the section of the MS with which we are concerned: All the verbs are in the 3. pers. In the first section of the MS there occur 1.pers. *iac wil* "I shall" and 2.pers. *thu wilt* "thou wilt".

4. The mood category contains 2 members, namely *Indicative* and *Subjunctive* (there are no instances of the imperative).

There is coalescence between indicative and subjunctive in two cases:

1. In the pres.pass.sg. of ian- and ēn-verbs:
   ind. *bethes, sæctes, sigis,*
   subj. *bøtes, læggis, sigis.*
2. In the pret.sg. of weak verbs:
   ind. *costathe, giorthe,*
   subj. *førthe.*

Otherwise there is always commutation between ind. and subj.:
pres.act.sg.:
weak verbs: *callar : calli, dyl : dyli, sigir : sigi;*
strong verbs: *biuthær, biuthur : biuthi, brændær, brændar : brænni, ær : se*[14]*, far* "gets" *: fa, far* "goes" *: fare, fari, takar : taki, cumbær : cummi, wil : wili, ma : mugi, a : age.*

pres.act.pl.:
weak verbs: *dylia : dyli;*
strong verbs: *bæra : bæri, standa : stande, mugu : mugi.*

pres.pass.sg.:
weak verbs other than ian- and ēn-stems: *ilscas : *ilskis, lægs : læggis;*
strong verbs: *swærs : swæris.*

pres.pass.pl.
There are no instances (a contrast *-as : -is* or *-ias : -is* would be expected).

pret.act.sg.:
(weak verbs show coalescence), strong verbs: *var : vare, galt : guldi, for : fore.*

pret.act.pl.
weak verbs: (there are no instances but a contrast *-u/o : -i/e* would be expected),
strong verbs: ind. *baro, fingu :* subj. *buthi.*

pret.pass.:
There are no instances.

The moods are frequently determined by conjunctions:
A subordinate clause introduced by *vm* "if" is always in the ind. if it is in the pres. but can be either in ind. or subj. if it is in the pret.
A subordinate clause introduced by *vtan* (in ScChL : *num*) "unless", *tho at* "although", *swa at* "so that", *at* "that", can be in either the ind. or the subj.

For the employment of the subj. the following rules apply[15] :

Pres.subj. is employed first and foremost in *main clauses* in which the actual rules of law are formulated, e.g.

tha bøte twa øra "then he *shall* pay a fine of two øre";
graui vp ræf . . . oc nyti væl "he *may* dig the fox up and make good use of it". The subj. is thus used of both *obligation* and *permission.* If a distinction is to be drawn between obligation and permission, the modal verbs *scal* and *ma* are used in the indicative[16].
The same kind of pres.subj. is occasionally found in subordinate clauses which contain a report of a verdict, finding etc. e.g.

læggi thing mæn femt fore hin ær cost hafuir handa mællin.
at han wæri hema ofna brofial sinnj "let the thingmen appoint a respite of five days for him who has the goods in hand,

within which time he *shall be* at home on the plank leading to his house".

In conditional clauses introduced by *vtan* "unless" the pres.subj. seems to be employed when the content of the clause is of a hypothetical character, i.e. when it is represented as being doubtful whether the subordinate clause, if it had been in the pres.ind., would have agreed or conflicted with the remainder of the text[17]. e.g.

> *summi mæn sigia at thingmæn mugu æy dørna af thiufuj øra. ællar andra limmir. vtan kunungs vmbuzman late thæt døma af* "some men say that the thingmen must not sentence an ear or other limbs (to be cut) off a thief, unless the king's ombudsmand permits it to be sentenced (to be cut) off, (which might never happen, since the ombudsmand frequently betrays a deplorable humanity)";
> *dræpær man annar man. bøte halft af sino ægno. vtan ænnar frænde vili mæth gothvilia hanum nokat gifua til* "if a man kills another man, he shall pay as a fine the half of his own (property), unless one or other of his kinsman will voluntarily give him something towards it"; the sentence occurs in Appenr dix II, King Valdemar's decree on homicide, where the contribution of kinsmen to the wergild is made voluntary and represented as not being very likely to occur.

By means of *vtan* plus the indicative is expressed a condition which is *not* hypothetical, and *vtan* can often best be translated by "except when":

> *fiski gard ma man æy gøra frammer æn til mithstrøma. vtan han hafuir fangeth gardfæstu annar wag igen* "a man must not construct a fish weir further out than the middle of the stream, except when he has obtained the right to make the weir fast on the other side".

In a similar way as in conditional clauses with *vtan,* the subj. is used in concessional clauses introduced by *tho at* "although":

> *væri sic mæth tyltar eth. tho at gifui hanum sac til firitiugu marc* "he shall defend himself with an oath of twelve, even in

the (unlikely) case that he is accused of a crime for which the fine is 40 marks".

If the indicative is employed, the conditional clause is not hypothetical:

hafuir han nokat til ført i hins hœscap. œr han fœsti sic wither. tho at thœt œr œy mer œn eth las "if he has brought something into the household of the man with whom he has taken service, even though it *is* not more than one load".

After *swa at* "so that", which very often follows after a conditional clause in the pres.ind., the indicative and subjunctive seem to be used indiscriminately:

høggar man tolf las j annars mans hœgnathe scoge. œllar mera. swa at gøre widstord "if a man cuts twelve loads or more in another man's enclosed wood so that he *makes* (subj.) a great pile of wood";

warthœr man hoggen at eno hogge. swa at han far sar i alla fingra sina "if a man is struck with a single cut so that he *receives* (ind.) injuries to all his fingers".

Subordinate clauses introduced by *at* and containing indirect speech are generally in the indicative, both in cases where the quoted sentence is in conflict with the rest of the text, e.g.

dyl hin œr graf grof. oc sac var yui gifuin. at han grof œy "if he who dug the hole, and was accused of it, declares that *he did not dig*";

and in cases where it is uncertain whether or not it is in conflict with the context, e.g.

thœn œr andrum scal weta asswaru eth. scal bithia sœ swa gud hialpa. at han œr sandœr fore the sac œr han gifuœr hanum. oc han gør thœt œy fore afund. œllar fore il willia. vtan fore thœssaka[18]. *at han wet han sannan vara fore the sac œr han gifuœr hanum* "he who shall make an oath of accusation against another man shall so ask God to help him that he (the accused) *is* guilty in the case in which he accuses him, and that he (the accuser) *is* not *doing* it out of enmity or ill-will but for that reason that he *knows* him to be guilty in the case in which he accuses him". It is revealed by the context that the accused has the opportunity of proving by ordeal by iron the corresponding negated sentence: *at han ær æy sandær fore the sac,* and that this proof by ordeal was sometimes successful.

In a very few instances of this type the subj. is employed, e.g. *sigir bonden ællar brytin thagar schifta scal. at han age nokat utan fælage. oc annar therra sigir at the ago bathe i fælage samman. tha ær thæn therra næst logum at wita mæth tyltar ethe. ær bathom them vil wita til fælax* "if the farmer or the steward says, when they shall divide the estate, that he owns (subj.) something independently of what they have in joint ownership, and the other of them says that they both own (ind.) it jointly, then the one of them who will prove that it is in the joint ownership of both of them has the right to prove his claim by means of an oath of twelve". It is therefore likely that the first claim (the one in the subj.) will be disproved.

In these subordinate clauses the indicative and subjunctive are distributed in much the same way as the sg. and pl. of the verbs: the indicative can deputise for the subjunctive, but not vice versa.

The *pret.* subj. is sometimes employed in conditional clauses where the main clause is in the pres.ind., e.g.

far man mæth swina ward[19] *i annars mans hægnatha scog. tha ær thæt samma log sum før ær mælt. vm fore han i akra annars mans. oc j sæd hans* "if a man goes with a herd of pigs into another man's enclosed wood, then the same law applies, as has been named before, as if he *had gone* into another man's field and into his corn". Here the subordinate clause *vm fore han* would have been in conflict with the rest of the text if it had been in the pres.ind.; from a conditional clause in the pret.subj. belonging to a main clause in the pres.ind. it is actually possible to conclude that a corresponding negated sentence in the pres.-ind. would agree with the context: *han far æy i akra annars mans. oc æy j sæd hans.*

There is a single instance of the pret.ind. in a conditional clause which would conflict with the context if it were converted into the pres.ind. The iafnatha-oath, in which the man who has paid a wergild declares that he too would have been satisfied with fines, if it had been one of his kinsmen who had been killed, contains the following words:

> *tha vildi han slic sammu bøtær taka af them. vm the hafthu sva giorth vithær han. sum han giorthe vithær them.* "then he would (pret.ind./subj.) accept such fines of them, if they *had* (ind.) done to him as he had done (pret.ind./subj.) to them".

The indicative seems thus to be able to deputise for the subj. in the pret., too.

5. The voice category contains 2 members, *Active* and *Passive.*

Both the finite forms of the verb and the infinitive are conjugated in voice, and the same may also be true of the pres. part.: *liuande* "living" : *wrakandes* "being driven".

Active and passive are always kept distinct from each other. The passive is formed by adding *-s* to the active form when this either ends in a vowel or is of one syllable, e.g.

inf.act. *dylia* : inf.pass. *dylias,* pres.subj.act. *næfni* : pres.subj.-pass. *næfnis,*
pres.ind.act. *schil* : pres.ind.pass. *schils,* pret.act. *gaf* : pret.pass. *gafs.*

In the pres.ind.sg. of strong verbs and ian-verbs the passive is formed by substituting *s* for the svarabhakti vowel + *r* of the active form, e.g.

act. *gifuir* : pass. *gifs.*

In the pres.ind.sg. of ōn-, ēn- and ian-verbs the passive form is formed by substituting *s* for the *r* of the active form, e.g.

act. *tapar* : pass. *tapas;* act. *sigir* : pass. *sigis;* act. *hittir* : pass. *hittis.*

The voice category does not appear to be subject to rection.

The passive is employed first and foremost with *reflexive* and *reciprocal* meaning, i.e. equivalent to the verb in the active plus *sic* or *sæ.*

Instances of reflexive sense:

schilis bæthe vithær bonda oc vithær eng[20] *sina* "then she shall divorce herself both from the husband and from her property"; *bethęs man wæth* "if a man asks for a pledge".
Instances of reciprocal sense:

bærias mæn i lans byum ællar tuttas "if men in the villages fight each other or jostle each other".

On the other hand there are only a few instances of the so called normal passive sense, i.e. of cases where a verb in the passive linked with a nominative has approximately the same meaning as the same verb in the active linked with an accusative. An *apparently* certain example of these two constructions — pass. + nom. and act. + acc. — is the following:

tha ma thæt aldrig tapas. vtan é scal thæt atær gialda "then it [the loan] can never be lost but one shall always pay it back" (= "then one can never lose it, but it shall always be paid back)".

There is syncretism of nom. and acc. in the pronominal form *thæt*, however. The question is, then, whether or not this syncretism can be dissolved. The second clause probably contains the acc. because the acc. is found in a large number of similar clauses, e.g.
tha scal them scatha løst af ælta "then one shall drive them [the horses] away with impunity", where *them* can be the expression of the acc. but not of the nom.

(In a similar way the syncretism of nom./acc. ought to be dissolved in favour of the acc. in sentences such as: *tha ma han binda oc føra han til things* "then one must bind him and take him to the assembly", *tha scal øra af schæra* "then one shall cut off an ear"). On the other hand it is *not* possible to dissolve the syncretism nom./acc. in the *first* clause (*tha ma thæt aldrig tapas*), because both the nom. and the acc. are found in other similar sentences. Instances of the nom. are:

sithan læggis annur lagstæfnu "afterwards another date shall

be fixed"; *stæfna* is a fem. iōn-stem, in which there is coalescence of all the cases in the sg.: *annur*, however, can only be an
expression of the nom.; in the acc. it would be *andra*.
fore thy at summum stathum takas vndan twe lotær af rugsæth
"because at some places two plots sown with rye are excepted";
in *lotær* there is syncretism of nom. and acc. but *twe* can only
express the nom.; *takas* agrees with this nom. and is in the pl.
(the sg. would be *tacs*). The majority of the MSS, however,
have: ..*taks undan twa lotær*, where *taks* is in the sg. and
twa lotær in the acc.

An instance of the *acc.* is:

oc tha ofna thrithia thingi næfnis til gotha mæn oc ræta "and
then at the third assembly shall be nominated good and just
men"; *næfnis* is subj. with syncretism of sg. and pl.; in *mæn*
there is syncretism of nom. and acc.; *gotha* and *ræta*, however,
can only express *acc.*
There are probably two ways of describing this state of affairs:

1. In passive sentences acc. can deputise for nom., i.e.
   tacs vndan twa lotær   =   *takas vndan twe lotær;*
2. In sentences without nom. but with acc. the passive can
   deputise for the active, i.e.
   næfnis til gotha mæn oc ræta   =   * *næfni til gotha mæn
   oc ræta.*

The first possibility is unsatisfactory because it does not explain
the change of number in the verb.
The construction verb in the passive plus acc. (but without nom.)
would seem to be specifically Scanian. No corresponding examples
are found in M. Nygaard, Norrøn Syntax, or in Paul Öhlin, Studier
över de passiva konstruktionerna i fornsvenskan (Studies on the
passive constructions in Old Swedish); and it will hardly be possible
to find any instances from elsewhere in Denmark than Scania because
in sources from the other areas there are more instances of coalescence between nom. and acc. than are found in the best MSS of ScL.

182

NOTES

1   Omitting the treatment of the consonant system and the declension of nouns.
2   J. Brøndum-Nielsen, Sprogtekster til Universitetsbrug II 1, line 34.
3   In Brøndum-Nielsen's Sprogtekster I and II and in Gerd Wellejus and Nelly Uldaler, Gammeldansk læsebog (1968) 10-19, 22-38.
4   In Nordisk Kultur 28 (1943) 51 f. and Festskrift til Peter Skautrup (1956) 83 f.
5   For ę as a variant of e see Kroman in Festskrift til Skautrup (1956) 83.
6   Cf. Brøndum-Nielsen in ANF 34. 122 f.
7   In Prolegomena to a theory of language, trans. by Francis J. Whitfield (1953) 46.
8   For a general survey see Peter Skautrup, Det danske sprogs historie I (1944) 273.
9   *hanum var bæthe sundt* "both things was refused to him".
10   With epenthetic d between nn and the svarabhakti vowel + r, in distinction from brænnir, pres.act.ind.3.pers.sg. of the corresponding causative ian-verbs.
11   The pret.subj. is formed from the stem in the pret.ind.3.pers.pl., normally without i-mutation; the e shows that the a is "long".
12   For the modal verbs cf. Gunnar Bech, Grundzüge der semantischen Entwicklungsgeschichte der hochdeutschen Modalverba, 1951.
13   For the construction in mod. Danish cf. Paul Diderichsen, Elementær dansk Grammatik, 1st ed. (1946) 130 f. Tillæg 2.
14   *se* only in ScChL and in some other MSS of ScL; elsewhere the analogical forms *wari, wæri* and *æri*.
15   In what follows no account is taken of ScChL, in which the subj. is employed rather more frequently than in ScL; owing to the restricted length of ScChL it would hardly be possible to formulate reliable rules for this difference.
16   Cf. also Paul Diderichsen, APhS 15. 15 ff. – There are four instances of an inf. instead of pres.subj., e.g. *tha calli han til twa granna ællar thre. oc lata them høra* "then he shall summon two or three neighbours and let them hear", and one instance of subj. instead of inf. after *lata* in *læggi fore han iarn oc fiatur oc late han sialfan læggi ofna sic* "he shall lay before him iron and fetters and let him lay them upon himself".
17   Including the context in the widest possible sense.
18   The oldest surviving instance of free indirect speech in Danish.
19   Error for *wrad*.
20   Error for *egn*.

Postscript to the Grammar
of the language of the Zealand Laws

In the Grammar of ScL it was explained how the discovery of the concept of *participation* had made it almost unthinkable to attempt to describe a text with the aid of two different sets of rules, each valid for its own language: Most such attempts are based upon the — normally tacit — assumption that two members of a paradigm are always mutually exclusive. It was also asserted that it was necessary for such attempts to be based upon examinations of several contemporary but mutually differing texts. It was pointed out that the age of MS B74 of the Scanic Law makes it unique and hence that the condition necessary for distinguishing between two different linguistic strata in this text could not be fulfilled.

When the subject of study is the Zealand Laws, however, the situation is quite another. We have two different Laws from approximately the same period, one of which even survives in varying versions, and we have several approximately contemporary MSS of these Laws. We also have other unrelated texts which are approximately contemporary with the Laws, notably Latin charters containing Danish personal and place-names.

The Zealand law-texts have, therefore, been subjected to a good deal of attention in attempts to find information about more than one language; the present grammar, however, is the first to describe the texts with the aid of a single set of rules.

In the course of time claims have been made for the presence of three different pairs of languages in these texts:

1. Zealandic and Jutlandic in two different combinations:
the first assumes that originally Zealandic texts have been contaminated with Jutlandic forms by scribes from Jutland and the second assumes that Erik's Law is Zealandic but Valdemar's Law a mixture of Zealandic and Jutlandic. A summary of this research is given in Ti Afhandlinger (1960) pp. 166-70 and a criticism in the same work pp. 201-04.
2. Written language and spoken language: in the sense that the scribes have adapted the original texts to make them resemble their own spoken language. This view was in agreement with that commonly held about medieval texts in the first half of the present century but fits less well with modern thinking about regional written standards. This problem is touched on in Descriptions of the language in medieval texts above pp. 27-31.
3. Old language and new language: thus notably Viggo Såby in Aarbøger for nordisk Oldkyndighed (1872) pp. 197-228, Willi Spickermann in Das Verbum in den seelandischen Gesetzen (1912), and Anders Bjerrum in Ti Afhandlinger pp. 211-14.

Of these attempts the third appears most promising. We now know that the scribes from c.1300 sometimes archaised their texts (cf. the hypercorrect forms in -i in e.g. mycli, tapit; Anders Bjerrum, Grammatik over De sjællandske Love (1967) p. 11 footnote). We also have good evidence that the scribe of the exemplum of the surviving MSS archaised his text (cf. Grammatik over De sjællandske Love pp. 62ff.). These phenomena presuppose a tension between the old and the new language and it is easy enough to find evidence for such a tension on every page of the law texts. E.g.

Old word forms	New word forms
fær pres.sg.	*fār*
æc pers.pron.	*iæc*
fæc pret.sg.	*fic*
seghæ inf.	*sighæ*

getær pres.sg.	*gitær*
sun subst.sg.	*sun*

Old sounds	New sounds
that dem.pron.neut.sg.	*thæt*
haua pres.pl.	*hauæ*
watn subst.	*wadn, wan*
heem adv.	*hiem*
twiggiæ gen.	*twiggi, twiggæ*

Old inflexional forms, old word order	New inflexional forms, new word order
at sinum rætæ	*mæth sin lot*
iorh sinæ acc.	*sin eghin iordh*
mæth sinu dat.sg.neut.	*af sit eghit* acc.

To a certain extent it is possible to find evidence for some of the old sounds in the forms taken by personal and place-names in Zealand charters from the beginning of the 13th century and new ones in charters from the end of the century, cf. Kr. Hald, Dansk sprogstof i de sjællandske diplomer fra det 13. århundrede (Danish material in the 13th-century Zealand charters), Ti Afhandlinger pp. 149-62.

The following two scenes from Danish history are thus very likely to have taken place.

1. When he was a boy in about 1160, Saxo Grammaticus was in the habit of teasing his seven-year-old cousin by pulling her plaits. The reaction of the tormented girl would be to say:

æc sæghir that mothor minni.

This sentence has been constructed on the basis of the oldest linguistic forms in the Zealand Laws: *æc* is found in Valdemar's Law, cf. also Ti Afhandlinger pp. 202 f., 214; *sæghir* has been constructed on the basis of Valdemar's Law *seghæ* inf. (once) and the ending in e.g. *hauir; that* occurs once in Erik's Law; *mothor* has been constructed on the basis of *mothær*, with the ending replaced by the old form as evidenced in *nokot, houoth; minni* is constructed on the basis of the genitive *sinnæ* and the old dative ending -i; the word order with the possessive pronoun following the substantive is evidenced in e.g. *iorh sinæ* Valdemar's Law 358, 13.

2. When he was a boy in about 1280, Johannes Jutæ was in the habit of teasing his seven-year-old cousin by pulling her plaits. The reaction of the tormented girl would be to say:

iæc sighær thæt min mothær.

This sentence has been constructed on the basis of the youngest linguistic material in the Zealand Laws. For *iæc* instead of *æc* and *sighær* instead of *sæghir* see Ti Afhandlinger pp. 202 f., 213; *thæt* is the common form in the Zealand Laws; for *mothær* and *sighær* with *æ* see Grammatik over De sjællandske Love pp. 10 ff; for nom./acc. instead of dat. see the same work p. 33; the word order min mothær is the common one in the Zealand Laws.

I firmly *believe* that these stories are true as far as the language is concerned. To be honest, however, I must admit that I do not *know* that they are true. If anyone should ask whether it would be impossible for the first girl to have said e.g. *sighær, thæt* and *mothær*, the answer would have to be, "Oh no. Not exactly impossible". Why?

Because the linguistic argumentations in the two stories, just like so many other argumentations, are based on the following tacit assumption: When a given content in a given language is linked with one certain expression, then it cannot also be linked with another expression, e.g. When the pres.act.ind.3.pers.sg. of the verb $f\bar{a}$ in a given language is expressed by *faar,* then it cannot also be expressed by *fær* in the same language; in other words: A language cannot have genuine synonyms. *And this assumption is in open conflict with elementary facts.*

About the state of the language outside the text under scrutiny there is very little that we can know with certainty, much less indeed than many scholars have been inclined to believe. It is *not* possible for us to gather together the old elements in some law-texts and say: It is thus and only thus that the Zealand dialect was spoken in the 12th century. It is only possible to say: These linguistic possibilities must have been present in 12th-century Zealandic but there may also have been other possibilities.

Further: with the aid of comparative linguistics it is possible to construct with absolute certainty an original Old Danish fem. dat.sg. form *minni* and to ascertain that the form *sæghir* in the pres.act.ind.-3.pers.sg. is more original than *sighær*. These reconstructed forms, however, are only certain as long as they are considered as purely formal units, as abstractions. As soon as we *historicise* them and endow them with a *concrete* existence at a given time, we start to skate on thin ice. It is, for example, easy to see that my anecdote contains postulates about contemporaneity which are quite unjustified and in all probability unjustifiable.

It can be stimulating to speculate about linguistic situations of which we can know nothing with certainty but it is even more stimulating to study an available text about which something definite can be learnt, for example that from a diachronic point of view it contains a mixture of old and new features. It is most stimulating of all, however, to describe the text synchronically and assemble all the apparently conflicting features into one single set of rules.

Abbreviations

1. Sources and works of reference

ANF   Arkiv för nordisk filologi 1 ff. Christiania and Lund 1883 ff.
APhS   Acta philologica Scandinavica 1 ff. Copenhagen 1926 ff.
DF   Danske Folkemaal 1 ff. Copenhagen 1927 ff.
DgP   Danmarks Gamle Personnavne I-II, ed. Gunnar Knudsen, Marius Kristensen and Rikard Hornby, Copenhagen 1936-64.
DR   Danmarks runeindskrifter I-II, ed. Lis Jacobsen and Erik Moltke with Anders Bæksted and Karl Martin Nielsen, Copenhagen 1941-42.
DS   Danmarks Stednavne I ff. Copenhagen 1922 ff.
DSt   Danske Studier 1 ff. Copenhagen 1904 ff.
GG   Johannes Brøndum-Nielsen, Gammeldansk Grammatik I ff. Copenhagen 1928 ff.
SÅ   Sønderjydske Aarbøger. Åbenrå
ScChL   Scanic Church Law
ScL   Scanic Law
SK   Sprog og Kultur 1 ff. Århus 1932 ff.
SM   Sønderjydsk Maanedsskrift 1 ff. 1924 ff.
SRD   Scriptores rerum danicarum I-VIII, ed. Jacob Langebek et. al., Copenhagen 1772-1878.
Zeitschrift Zeitschrift der Gesellschaft für Schleswig-Holsteinische Geschichte.

2. Other abbreviations.

acc.   accusative
act.   active
c.   circa
cf.   confer
col.   column
Dan.   Danish
dat.   dative
ed.   edition or edited by
el(s).   element(s)
EMD   Early Middle Danish
f.   feminine
fem.   feminine

gen.	genitive
ind.	indicative
inf.	infinitive
LG	Low German
m.	masculine
masc.	masculine
MDan	Middle Danish
MLG	Middle Low German
Mod.,mod.	modern
MS(S)	manuscript(s)
n.	neuter
neut.	neuter
nom.	nominative
no(s).	number(s)
obl.	oblique
ODan	Old Danish
OIcel	Old Icelandic
part.	participle
pers.	person
pers.n.	personal name
pl.	plural
prep.	preposition
pres.	present
pret.	preterite
Scand	Scandinavian
sg.	singular
Stand.	Standard
subj.	subjunctive
subst.	substantive

Bibliography of Anders Bjerrum's
Linguistic Papers
by Lizzi Nykin

1927   [Contributions to the column 'Samleren'], SM III (1926-27), 142-44;
       IV (1927-28), 79-80, 158, 160; V (1928-29), 60, 63-64, 78-79, 112,
       174, 192; VI (1929-30), 15, 31, 174-75, 176, 190, 191; VII (1930-31),
       46, 48, 141-142; VIII (1931-32), 13-14. [Folklore from North Slesvig.]

1928   'Nogle vestslesvigske Beretninger om hensat Brand', SM V (1928-29),
       69-70.

       'En "Kløft" fra Vestslesvig. (Vodder Sogn)', DF II, 80-84.

1930   'Lidt sønderjysk Syntax', DF IV, 17-24.

1931   'Nogle Sprogprøver fra Fjolde', DF V, 113-127.

       [Contributions to:] Sønderjyske Stednavne. Udg. af Stednavneudvalget.
       I-V. (Danmarks Stednavne. III. 1944; IV. 1942; V. 1933; VI. 1936;
       VII. 1939).

1932   'Sydslesvigsk (Fjolde Sogn)'. In: Dialekttekster til Universitetsbrug.
       Ved Johs. Brøndum-Nielsen. II, 38-40.

1933   'Fra Fjolde Sogn', SM IX (1932-33), 113-118, 148-149, 187-189. —
       Reprinted in Poul Kürstein (ed.), Nørre og Sønder Gøs herred (1969).

       'De gamle Kalenderdage', SM IX (1932-33), 127-128, 143-144, 155,
       199-200; XI (1934-35), 31-32, 47-48, 72, 116-120.

       'Midtslesvigske Stednavne'. In: Sydslesvig. Udg. af Grænseforeningen
       ved Gunnar Knudsen og Knud Kretzschmer. I, 64-80.

       'Kulbrænding i Mellemslesvig', DF VII, 97-100.

1934   'Sydslesvigske Personnavne', DSt XXXI, 21-42. — The section pp.
       22-26 reprinted as 'Sydslesvigske gårdnavne i Nørre og Sønder Gøs
       herred' in Poul Kürstein (ed.), Nørre og Sønder Gøs herred (1969).

       Axel Olrik, Nordens Trylleviser. Udg. af Anders Bjerrum og Inger M.
       Boberg. xii, 209 pp.

1937   'K.J. Lyngby'. In: Fra Rask til Wimmer. Udg. af Selskab for nordisk
       Filologi, 83-112. [Paper read to Selskab for nordisk Filologi 6/4 1937.]

1938   'Gamle Tinne', DF XI, 1-8. — Reprinted in SM XV (1938-39), 193-200,
       and in Poul Kürstein (ed.), Nørre og Sønder Gøs herred (1969).

1939   'K.J. Lyngbys Breve om Sønderjylland 1856-1859', DSt XXXVI, 43-65.

       [Review of:] Carl Borgstrøm, 'Zur Phonologie der norwegischen Schrift-
       sprache', Norsk tidskrift for sprogvidenskap. IX (Oslo 1937), 250-273,
       and André Martinet, La phonologie du mot en Danois. (Bulletin de
       la Société de Linguistique de Paris. XXXVIII, 2. Paris 1938). In: Bulle-

192

tin du Cercle linguistique de Copenhague. IV (1939), 12-16; Selskab for nordisk Filologi. Aarsberetning for 1937-38 ([1939]), 3-5. [Abstract of paper read to Lingvistkredsen and Selskab for nordisk Filologi in Copenhagen 3/5 1938.]

1940   'Über die phonematische Wertung von Mundartaufzeichnungen', Bulletin du Cercle linguistique de Copenhague. V (1940), 29-51. [Paper read to Lingvistkredsen and Selskab for nordisk Filologi in Copenhagen 14/11 1939.] – Reprinted in Linguistic Papers (1973).

1941   'Atlas der dänischen Volkskultur', Folk-Liv. V, 113-123. [Paper read at Den nordiske Folkelivsforskningskongres, Århus 1940.]

1942   'De danske Folkemaal i Sønderjylland', Danmark. II (1941-42), 175-180.

K.J. Lyngby's Jyske Grammatik tillige med et Udvalg af hans Breve. Udg. af Anders Bjerrum. (Universitets-Jubilæets danske Samfunds Skrifter. CCCXXIX). 281 pp. [With a monograph by A.B.: 'K.J. Lyngby som Dialektforsker', pp. 3-49.]

1944   'Vort Sprogs gamle Sydgrænse', SÅ 1944, 1-20. [Paper read to Selskab for nordisk Filologi 8/12 1943; abstract in Selskab for nordisk Filologi. Aarsberetning for 1943·([1944]), 10-11. – The section pp. 1-8 reprinted in Poul Kürstein (ed.), Nørre og Sønder Gøs herred (1969).

'Folkesproget i Tønder gennem Tiderne'. *In:* Tønder gennem Tiderne. Red. af M. Mackeprang. (Skrifter udg. af Historisk Samfund for Sønderjylland. III), 440-464. – English version in Linguistic Papers (1973).

Fjoldemålets Lydsystem. 272 pp. [Doctoral dissertation, Univ. of Copenhagen. With a summary in English, pp. 257-272. Also published, without the English summary, as pp. 1-256 of APhS XVIII (1945-48). A summary by the author in 'Bibliography of Scandinavian Philology. XVIII', APhS XVIII (1945-48), 402-05.] – Pp. 6-8 reprinted as 'Fjolde sogn' in Poul Kürstein (ed.), Nørre og Sønder Gøs herred (1969).

[Contributions to:] Vejle Amts Stednavne. Udg. af Stednavneudvalget. (Danmarks Stednavne. VIII).

'Paul Diderichsen'. *In:* Dansk Biografisk Leksikon. Red. Povl Engelstoft. XXVII, 172-173.

1945   'Det danske Folkesprog i Sydslesvig', Berlingske Aftenavis. 25/7 1945.

'En østjysk Dialektbeskrivelse', SK XIV, 149-151. [Review of Ella Jensen, Houlbjergmålet (1944).]

1946   'Folkemaal og Rigssprog'. *In:* Den danske Bonde. Red. af M.P. Ejerslev. II, 189-214.

'Er Sydslesvig "dansk Folkegrund"?', Berlingske Aftenavis. 17/10 1946.

1948   [Contributions to:] Viborg Amts Stednavne. Udg. af Stednavneudvalget. (Danmarks Stednavne. IX).

193

1948   'Om sproglig Tvang i Grænselandets Skoler', Politiken. 13/11 1948.

1949   [Review of:] Erik Kroman, Musikalsk Akcent i Dansk (1947). *In:*
       ANF LXIII (Lund 1948), 223-231.

       'Fjolde — das Kirchspiel Viöl', Jahrbuch des Nordfriesischen Instituts.
       I (Åbenrå), 145-148.

       'Verbal Number in the Jutlandic Law'. *In:* Recherches structurales
       1949. Publiées a l'occasion du cinquantenaire de M. Louis Hjelmslev.
       (Travaux du Cercle linguistique de Copenhague. V. 1949 [photographic
       reprint 1970]), 156-176. — Reprinted in Linguistic Papers (1973).

       'En nationaldansk stridsmand', Gads danske Magasin. XLIII, 326-333.
       [Review of Gudmund Schütte, Udvalgte Epistler (1947).]

1950   [Review of:] Kr. Hald, Vore Stednavne (1950). *In:* Fortid og Nutid.
       XVIII (1949-52), 288-290.

       [Contributions to:] Bornholms Stednavne. Udg. af Stednavneudvalget.
       (Danmarks Stednavne. X. 1951).

1951   'Anglernes hjemstavn', SÅ 1951, 202-254. [With a bibliography, pp.
       245-254. — Paper read to Selskab for nordisk Filologi 7/10 1947;
       abstract 'Anglernes Herkomst' in Selskab for nordisk Filologi. Aars-
       beretning for 1947 ([1948]), 10-12.]

1952   'Anglernes hjemstavn. Replik', SÅ 1952, 238-241. [Reply to Gudmund
       Schütte's article 'Anglerne, det evige Stridsæmne', SÅ 1952, 204-237.]

       'De tryksvage vokaler i danske runeindskrifter fra tiden ca. 1000-ca.
       1250', APhS XXI, 53-65. — English version in Linguistic Papers (1973).

       [Contributions to:] Håndbog for danske Lokalhistorikere. Udg. af Dansk
       historisk Fællesforening (1952-56).

       'Utæn han ær opænbarlic gen guth', APhS XXII (1954), 11-32.
       [Summary in English, pp. 31-32. — Paper read to Selskab for nordisk
       Filologi 4/10 1051.]

1953   'Sproglig form hos Ferdinand de Saussure og Louis Hjelmslev', 'Ana-
       lyse af modalverber'. *In:* Semantiske problemer. Indledningsforedrag
       og diskusjonsreferater fra Krets 5, Nordisk Sommeruniversitet, 2.
       sesjon, Ustaoset 1952. Redaksjonskomité: J.R. Gjerløw, A. Bjerrum,
       H. Regnéll. (Oslo 1953 [mimeographed]), 21-25, 71-75. [Abstracts of
       papers read at the meeting of Nordisk Sommeruniversitet 1952; 'Ana-
       lyse af modalverber' also published in Nordisk Sommeruniversitet 1952.
       (Moderne Videnskab — Orientering og Debat. II. 1953), 172-174.]

       'Om de danske Dialekter i Sønderjylland', SÅ 1953, 101-124. — The
       section pp. 117-124 reprinted as 'Fjoldemålet' in Poul Kürstein (ed.),
       Nørre og Sønder Gøs herred (1969).

1954   Grammatik over Skånske Lov efter B 74. [Mimeographed.] 54 pp. —
       Reprinted 1966.

194

1954   Maribo Amts Stednavne. Udg. ved Anders Bjerrum og Christian Lisse. (Danmarks Stednavne. XI). xl, 250 pp. [The sections on Lolland, pp. 1-14 and 18-167, and parts of the introduction by A.B.]

'Høysgaards anden ortografiske prøve', SK XX (Århus 1958), 1-13. [Lecture given at the University of Copenhagen 13/11 1952.]

1955   'Information-Cronique. Denmark', [in collaboration with K.B. Jensen:] 'Bibliographia onomastica 1952. Denmark', Onoma IV (Louvain 1953), 79, 155. [Reports on the activities in the field of onomastic research.]

1956   'De danske sprogprøver hos C.F. Allen'. In: Festskrift til Peter Skautrup 21. januar 1956. (Århus), 297-309.

1960   [In collaboration with Lizzi Nykin:] 'Stednavneudvalgets virksomhed 1935-1960'. In: Ti Afhandlinger. Udg. i anledning af Stednavneudvalgets 50 års jubilæum. (Navnestudier. II), 1-9.

'Johannes Jutæ og Valdemars Jordebog'. In: Ti Afhandlinger. Udg. i anledning af Stednavneudvalgets 50 års jubilæum. (Navnestudier. II), 163-214. [Summary in English, pp. 298-299.] [Paper read to Selskab for nordisk Filologi 26/2 1959.]

1962   Studier over Blichers E Bindstouw. Udg. af Anders Bjerrum, Gordon Albøge og Kristine Heiede. (Studier fra Sprog- og Oldtidsforskning, CCIL). 180 pp. [Contributions by A.B., pp. 30-33, 39-53, 56-60, 76-84, 88-98, 110-133, 135-151.]

1963   'Den dansk-tyske sproggrænse i middelalderen', Namn och bygd. L (Uppsala 1962), 182-192. [Paper read at the IV Nordiska Namnforskarkongressen, Helsingfors 1962.] — Reprinted as 'Sprogskiftet i Mildsted og Svavsted sogne' in Poul Kürstein (ed.), Nørre og Sønder Gøs herred (1969); English version in Linguistic Papers (1973).

1964   'Adjektivernes accusativendelse -æn i Jyske Lov'. In: Danica. Studier i dansk sprog. Til Aage Hansen 3.9.1964. (Sprog og Kulturs Skriftrække. I. Århus), 1-5.

Stednavne i Århus og Skanderborg Amter. Udg. ved Anders Bjerrum. (Danmarks Stednavne. XII). 243 pp.

1965   'Sprogbeskrivelsen'. In: Det danske sprogs udforskning i det 20. århundrede. Udg. af Selskab for nordisk Filologi, 52-66. [Paper read to Selskab for nordisk Filologi 27/9 1962.] — English version in Linguistic Papers (1973).

'Paul Diderichsen'. In: Festskrift udg. af Københavns Universitet i anledning af universitetets årsfest november 1965, 129-136.

1966   Grammatik over Skånske Lov efter B 74. 64 pp. [Revised reprint of the 1954 edition.] — English version of pp. 7-19, 26-28 and 49-64 in Linguistic Papers (1973).

1967   Grammatik over De sjællandske Love efter AM 455 12°. Med tillæg
        om Jyske Lov efter Flensborghåndskriftet. 69 pp. — English version
        of pp. 66-69 in Linguistic Papers (1973).

1969   'Sproget i hyldingsbrevene fra 1387. Et bidrag til det danske skrift-
        sprogs historie'. *In:* Kopenhagener germanistische Studien. I, 256-274.

        Nørre og Sønder Gøs herred. Udg. af Poul Kürstein. (Sydslesvigske egne
        og byer. Flensborg). 252 pp. [Contributions by A.B.: pp. 44-50 [= Vort
        sprogs gamle sydgrænse (1944), 1-8], 51-58 [= Den dansk-tyske sprog-
        grænse i middelalderen (1962)], 181-183 [= Fjoldemålets Lydsystem
        (1944), 6-8], 184-189 [= Om de danske Dialekter i Sønderjylland
        (1953), 117-124], 196-200 [= Sydslesvigske Personnavne (1934), 22-
        26], 201-206 [= Gamle Tinne (1938)], 207-214 [= Fra Fjolde Sogn
        (1933).]

1971   'G[amme]lda[nsk] loghthæ og soghthæ'. *In:* Studier i dansk dialektolo-
        gi og sproghistorie tilegnede Poul Andersen på halvfjerdsårsdagen den
        8. juni 1971, 51-59.